The Dow Jones-Irwin Guide to

Fine Gems and Jewelry

The Dow Jones-Irwin Guide to

Fine Gems and Jewelry

DAVID MARCUM

DOW JONES-IRWIN
Homewood, Illinois 60430

ISBN 0-87094-687-0

Library of Congress Catalog Card No. 85–71432

Printed in the United States of America

1 2 3 4 5 6 7 8 9 0 K 3 2 1 0 9 8 7 6

To My Wife and Son
Michele & Peter

About the author . . .

David Marcum is President of the Marcum Report, Inc., a consulting firm that publishes a monthly newsletter covering the international market in gemstones. For over 10 years he has worked in various capacities in the gem business and is recognized as the gem industry's outspoken consumer advocate. Mr. Marcum is a frequent public speaker on issues in gemstones and jewelry and has had numerous articles published on the topic. He is also co-editor of *Sources and Forecasts,* a monthly financial newsletter.

Preface

A gemstone is one of the most incredible creations of the universe. For most people, gems represent prestige, wealth, and power. Gemstones have literally saved lives in times of political and economic peril, and they have come to symbolize the deepest love between a man and a woman. Gems mystify, and they are admired and coveted. To me, however, they are all of the above and more.

A gemstone's origin is locked in the secrets of the formation of the cosmos. That gemstones exist is a wonder in itself, particularly in our solar system. Our sun is incapable of creating, through nuclear fusion, elements that are heavier than carbon. Yet, in many stones there exist elements such as chromium, manganese, vanadium, and iron. These metals, which give emerald its rich green color, the ruby its dazzling red, and sapphire its serene blue, were not created in the sun's nuclear fusion cauldron. Rather, they were captured during the formation of our solar system, bits of galactic debris, the dead remnants of exploded stars and collapsed planetary systems.

The chances of our embryonic solar system scooping these rare elements out of the vacuum of space were remote. Even more remote were the chances that these coloring agents would meld with the appropriate chemicals on our planet, in just the right conditions, and remain intact through millions of years so that people could find and fashion them. This is the true wonderment of gems: Those who train their eyes and minds see a story billions of years old in each crystal.

Gemstones are ironic commodities. They are sublime in their origin and creation; yet, of all the things humans value, they are probably the most intrinsically useless. They can't be eaten, and they won't keep out the cold of winter. At one time gems were thought to be medicinal and able to ward off evil spirits. Twentieth-century technology has abolished those old wives tales.

Essentially, there are only a few reasons why people purchase gemstones, the most important of which stems from human vanity—the obsession with surrounding and adorning oneself with objects of beauty. Gemstones represent success and a discretionary income of magnitude. They are a statement to the world that the owner appreciates the finer, aesthetic things of life. Some see the unfolding of the cosmos in the stone on their finger. All are eager to touch, see, and own a magnificent piece of the universe.

Beauty and vanity aside, there are other, less ethereal, reasons to own gemstones. As many have found through the centuries, gemstones can save a hard-earned fortune, make a profit when more traditional investments fail, and buy time and distance from a place where the fabric of civilization is busily unraveling. Gems, with the precious metals, are the original storehouses of value, a way to hold purchasing power. They are a form of insurance against a paper currency that has run amok on a printing press, as well as the ultimate lifesaver during political and economic chaos—a passport to freedom weighing as little as 1/142 of an ounce.

Regardless of why a gem is purchased, the purpose of this book is to ease the pain, anxiety, and confusion that is so commonly felt by the layperson who is contemplating that purchase. The book is not a gemological treatise; it is a practical guide. Whether you are buying jewelry as a gift, buying a first-class stone with the intention of resale, or building a collection for personal enjoyment, this book will be a valuable reference that you can use over and over again. And if nothing else, it is my hope that this book will forever put gems into proper perspective so that rather than being intimidating, they will be more enjoyed and treasured.

David Marcum

Acknowledgments

The following people and companies have contributed to the creation of this book. Their help is greatly appreciated.

The author gives special thanks to: Dallas Davenport (The Davenport Organisation, North Hampton, New Hampshire) for his careful reading, thoughtful insights, and constructive criticisms of the manuscript; Robert H. Meier (Meier & Associates, DeKalb, Illinois) for his 15 years of unwavering friendship, moral support, and encouragement; and Caspar "Cap" Beesley (American Gemological Laboratories, New York, New York) who generously gave his time and contributed many of the color plates.

Other important contributors include: Robert Marcum Bielenberg, Hamilton, Montana; James Breski, James Breski & Company, Chicago, Illinois; Christie's Auction House, New York, New York; Ajith S. DeSilva, Sarita's Limited, St. Louis, Missouri; Robert Genis, National Gemstone Corporation, Tucson, Arizona; Richard Harig, Harig Financial Services, Chicago, Illinois; Dan & Ed Lueking, California Gemological Laboratories, Costa Mesa, California; Steven Lindsay, Lindsay + Wasser, Inc., Toronto, Canada; Gem Trade Laboratory, Gemological Institute of America, Santa Monica, California; Dennis Schmelzenbach, Investments International, Bethany, Oklahoma; Sotheby's Auction House, New York, New York; James Swenton & William Bates, Zimmelman & Sons Mfg., Inc., Los Angeles, California; Kurt & Jacques Voorhees, Polygon, Dillon, Colorado; Adele Woods & Myron Chon, Jade House, Chicago, Illinois; and to the author's parents, Paul and Virginia, who always taught that an honest character was the true measure of a person.

Introduction

For most of history, ownership of gemstones rested in the hands of the privileged few. Because of the rarity, beauty, and often attributed magical and mystical powers gems possessed, they soon became symbols of wealth, power, and prestige. The lore of precious stones is loaded with anecdotes about the rarest diamonds and colored stones. It is believed that a Chinese emperor traded a city for one piece of carved jade. The Darya-i-Nur diamond, weighing 186 carats, once belonged to the first Mogul emperor of India and now resides in the crown jewels of Iran where it is part of a collection that backs the country's currency. The Hope diamond is supposedly cursed, and its history is allegedly fraught with diabolical happenings to its owners.

The democratization of the Western World, the rise of capitalism, and the development of international trade have all contributed to the dazzling increase in the standard of living for millions of people in the 20th century. More people have the discretionary income to purchase and enjoy precious stones than at any time in history. Although the prices of world-class stones are still beyond the reach of most, ownership of smaller, top-quality gems is no longer the impossible dream it was only 100 years ago.

Human beings have an almost a priori "sense" of appreciation for these treasures of nature. By any method of measurement, the finest examples are breathtaking to behold. There are, however, only four reasons why gemstones are purchased. The first reason is virtually universal; the other three are often secondary considerations. They are:

1. The pleasure of ownership and self-adornment.
2. A hedge against political instability.
3. A capital gains trading vehicle.
4. A hedge against the inflation of paper currencies.

Self Adornment Jewelry is one of the most pleasing of all gifts. The fact that discretionary income is placed in such an intrinsically valueless commodity just for the beauty it imparts is immensely flattering. The wearing of a superbly crafted piece connotes that the wearer has good taste, an eye for beauty and value, and, in most social circles, the image of success. It is one of civilization's shorthand ways of saying, "I have arrived." Yachts, mansions, and stock portfolios cannot be taken to a social gathering. In fact, to brag about these items is considered in bad taste; the wearing of jewelry is not.

Political Hedging In countries where there is economic and political stability, the last three reasons for buying gems are often a minor consideration. In some countries, however, they are integral to the first. Gems concentrate huge amounts of money into a very small place, they do not set off airport detectors, and they have an international resale market. They are untraceable, an important attribute in a war-torn or police-state nation. History has shown that rare stones are the single best hedge against political chaos and war.

The use of precious stones as hedges against unstable governments or the threat of war is not confined to some yellow-paged history book. Experts agree that thousands of Europeans have such stones stashed in their basements. Their continent has been trampled by armies so many times that nobody with means takes a chance. The safety deposit boxes of Swiss banks are filled with hundreds of millions of dollars in diamonds, rubies, sapphires, and emeralds whose owners are scattered throughout the globe. The wealthy of Southeast Asia invariably have a cache of Burma rubies and Kashmir sapphires tucked away for political emergencies.

One of the most graphic illustrations of gemstones used as a political hedge can be found in South Africa. Most do not realize that South Africa has very strict currency and exchange controls. Any citizen taking money out of that country without permission is open to an immediate jail sentence. A person cannot leave South Africa and take all of his or her wealth. Only a minor percentage may be taken; all other assets are "blocked" or kept in the country. The loopholes are few for those who wish to diversify their risk. Gemstones are the single, major way that South Africans get their money overseas. Smuggled out by citizens during legitimate business and holiday travel, the stones are then sold, and the money placed in anonymous numbered accounts.

Capital Gains From the end of World War II until the 1970s, prices for diamonds and colored stones rose gradually. Rough diamond prices were, and still are, pegged to the strength or weakness of the U.S. dollar. Colored stones also followed the dollar, but without the guiding hand of a world quasi-monopoly such as DeBeers. After the closing of the U.S. gold window and the floatation of major currencies, inflationary cycles caused gyrating supply and demand for fine gems in different parts of the world. Between the roller coaster of inflation, paranoia concerning Third World debt, and speculation about the future of the world's major economies, great opportunities have developed for laypersons to make capital gains by buying and selling rare gems.

A few gems have developed pricing patterns that result in excellent capital gains over time. These stones increase in, or maintain their value during recessions and escalate wildly in inflationary periods. Their avid purchase by both members of the traditional gem trade and the public is creating resounding shortages and the opportunity to make huge capital gains.

Obtaining capital gains through buying and selling is a specialty that many cannot or even may not want to engage in. The main point is this: Rare diamonds and precious gems always have a market. Even though local gem demand may be down, somewhere in the world there is a buyer. The fact that certain types of stones have cyclical demand patterns, and certain countries have preferences for specific stones, makes it possible for sophisticated investors and collecters to profit by purchasing a stone in one part of the world and selling it in another. For example, it may be possible to purchase a jade carving or stone in the United States and sell it in Hong Kong where the price of jade is higher. The Asian love for jade creates an almost automatic arbitrage situation.

Inflation Hedge The fourth reason why people buy stones hits closer to home in the Western world, especially the United States. Protecting wealth from the cyclical, yet ongoing inflation of major currencies is a real concern since automatic inflation is built into every monetary system in the free world. The average citizen generally puts money into medium- to long-term investments, and gems fit this category. It does not matter if inflation moves up and then falls. Even in its tumble, small amounts of buying power are still being eaten up by the continual, albeit slower, growth of the money supply. In periods of high inflation, such as occurred in the United States in the late 1970s, traditional investments were surefire losers. Even the traditionally safe U.S. T-bill gave a negative return.

Hedging inflation was the primary reason that people moved away from the purchase of gemstones for sole use as adornment, particularly in the United States, Europe, and Australia in the late 1970s. Although the popular media has given this form of gem "investment" as much positive press as it gives negligent landlords, many individuals made tremendous profits from the mid 1970s to early 1980 in diamonds, and from the late 1970s to late 1981 in colored stones. Those who made fortunes are not going to send bulletins to *The Wall Street Journal*, while those who bought at the height of the pricing cycle or purchased substandard stones because they didn't do their homework are going to scream bloody murder. It is the losers we hear about, not the winners. Despite the bad press, when inflation rebounds in the next few years and traditional investments yield negative returns, the public will be running after the more promising and rare gems again. People's instinct to survive financially is very strong.

Establish a Dual Purpose for Your Gem Purchases

Inexpensive gems and jewelry, by their very nature, can only be used for the purpose of adornment. Their lack of rarity does not permit them to escalate greatly in price, and they are common enough so that the amount they realize on resale will be but a small fraction of their purchase price. These items usually cost under $1,000. Although the remainder of this book will *greatly* help consumers who wish to obtain jewelry in this price range, the primary focus will be on *fine* gems and jewelry. Virtually every stone in this category can serve a convenient dual purpose for the buyer.

The first reason for purchase should be one of personal enjoyment. To simply buy stones and cast them into a vault is to cheat the buyer out of *the* fundamental pleasure of ownership. By far the most important reason why some stones have a higher value than others is that they are more beautiful. It has been shown repeatedly that those who buy gems *solely* for future profit lose money. The love of stones is what makes one a shrewd and confident buyer, not the greed that is typical in stock and commodity trading. This first purpose is the most important. Without it, the gem can be likened to a magnificent Monet painting that is being hidden in the basement of somebody who hates art and is rich enough not to let the world enjoy it.

Establishing a second purpose when selecting an expensive item is very important. Whether that purpose is to hedge against adverse political situations, to make money through capital gains, or to preserve the buying power of money against inflation, there is a stone whose color and appearance will bring aesthetic pleasure to the owner. The rarest gems, however, are also forms of money. They are not the most efficient forms, for they are not homogeneous and divisible like the precious metals, but they are one of the classic alternatives to currency.

The nature of recent price movements for the finest gemstones also dictates that a second purpose be found. Prior to the 1970s, prices generally rose a little each year, no matter which stone was selected. In the last 10 years, however, we have seen enormous gyrations, both up and down, for diamonds and colored stones alike. Understanding these gyrations will help you to obtain the best values; and the fact of these fluctuations makes it imperative that you have a portfolio plan in mind.

The term *gemstone portfolio*, unlike *stock portfolio*, is alien to most people. A gemstone portfolio may be comprised of almost anything: only one diamond or a group of loose diamonds and colored stones; high quality, contemporary jewelry; signed, antique pieces; or any combination of the above. The two factors that influence what form the portfolio will take are personal preference and what purpose, beyond adornment, the pieces will serve. Stones that will match the portfolio's purpose are defined by their usual price reactions to different economic stimuli.

Commonly traded stones tend to act within six different economic pricing modes. Virtually every stone has characteristics of more than one mode, but usually conforms more to one mode than another. The categories are:

1. Inflation hedge.
2. Capital gains vehicle.
3. Conservation of buying power/store of value.
4. Combination inflation hedge/store of value.
5. No hedging or capital gains ability.
6. Highly speculative and difficult to grade.

Inflation Hedge Gems that fall into the inflation hedge category are those whose prices are greatly affected by the combined movement of interest rates and inflation. The economic structure of the market for these stones is such that large amounts of credit are used in the global distribution pipeline. The classic stone in this category is diamond. Other stones that may fall into this category include Thailand ruby, Sri Lankan sapphire, African emerald, some tourmalines, and pink and imperial topaz.

Capital Gains Vehicles Historically, there is a group of stones whose price behavior is relatively impervious to high interest rate conditions. They tend to go up in price or level off when interest rates peak. Typically, these stones are out of the "mainstream," but they always exhibit the beauty that people desire. The supply is just enough to partially satiate a global demand, but is limited for either geological or political reasons. Among these stones are tsavorite (green garnet), red and pink spinel, tanzanite, and some of the fancy colored sapphires such as pink, padparadscha (orange-salmon-pink), and golden.

The capital gains category is the most difficult in which to find bargains. Recessions do not make these stones' prices collapse like some other stones. While bid-ask spreads are often narrow, prices are very firm. The latter, however, is an advantage to individuals who wish to resell. While shopping for diamonds is relatively easy, these stones present a logistical difficulty. Traditional jewelers are relatively uninformed in this area, and gem-quality stones are so rare that only a few dealers or consultants handle them on a regular basis.

Store of Value For those who do not wish to "play" the inflation cycles or become active in buying and selling, but want to maintain the buying power of existing capital, the "conservation of buying power/store of value" stones may be appealing. Their pricing history demonstrates a unique ability to just keep pace with inflation over extended periods of time. The classic in the area is Colombian emerald. Other stones in this category include: natural, fancy-colored diamonds (although their pricing cycle acts more like an inflation hedge when inflation jumps over 10 percent); gem star rubies and sapphires; and to a lesser extent, alexandrite. Alexandrite is primarily a collector stone and can be difficult to resell; its price history and concentration of value have put it in this category.

Combination Inflation Hedge/Store of Value This is perhaps the most interesting of these categories and one for which only two gems qualify: superb quality, Burma origin ruby and Kashmir origin blue sapphire. They are the stones purchased and given by millionaires and royalty—the so-called cornflower blue and pigeon blood colors. Each stone is a masterpiece—one-of-a-kind. No price history can be given for them as a group; however, experts know that during recessions their prices do not drop. They are, like fine emerald, a reliable store of value. During inflation their prices explode upward.

No Hedging or Capital Gains Ability Certain gems, which are used extensively in jewelry, have no potential for any purpose beyond adornment. Some of these include all forms of quartz including amethyst, smokey, and citrine; blue topaz; most green tourmaline (with the exception of the chrome variety); peridot (with the exception of gem-quality Burma origin material); green sapphires; nonphenomenal chrysoberyl; white sapphire; turquoise; decorative stones such as malachite, lapis lazuli, soldalite, tiger eye, onyx, and agate; amber; all synthetic stones and anything of commercial quality. All of these combined form a large percentage of the jewelry commonly sold in stores. They are relatively abundant and inexpensive, but can add a fascinating dimension to a color coordinated wardrobe.

Highly Speculative and Difficult to Grade This category is fascinating and some argument may be made that a small percentage of these stones can provide the dual purpose desired. These stones, however, are either hard to grade on a standardized basis, are very subjectively valued in the eyes of consumers, and/or do not have a large enough trading market to make ease of resale available to the average person. They include all mineral specimens; exceedingly rare collector stones (such as taafeite) that are not in great enough supply to create an international trading market; and popular stones such as opal, jade, and pearls. It is true that black opal may run thousands of dollars per carat. Jade can be similarly priced, and strands of pearls costing well over $100,000 are not unknown. The problem is that each is a unique and highly specialized market with little standardized grading. This makes these stones highly speculative in the resale area. Pearls and jade are, perhaps, the most difficult of all expensive gems to grade and price.

In each of these categories, there are stones of different colors and appearances. For the customer who wishes to establish a dual purpose for stone purchases, the question must be asked, "What do I want my gems to do for me beyond the pleasure I receive when I wear them"? Finally, it must be remembered that regardless of an individual's purpose in buying stones and jewelry, the grading methodology and criteria for what constitutes excellent value for the money are the same. Many are under the impression that "investment" stones are graded differently than jewelry stones. This is not the case. A gem-quality ruby is a gem-quality ruby for whatever reason it is purchased!

Contents

1 Basic Gemology and Market Insights

To begin a journey of a thousand miles, one must take the first step.
Ancient Oriental Proverb

A consumer, in order to be protected against overpaying and fraud, must know the meanings of the basic terms of gemology and something of the nature of the global gem business. Of all the things people buy, they know less about jewelry in relation to the money they spend than any other item. For example, when people decide to buy a car, they ask friends about their car's performance, read consumer guides, spend hours with salespeople, and kick many tires. They seriously consider color, gas mileage, ease of repair, availability of parts, insurance costs, and a host of other details.

When purchasing a $5,000-dollar piece of jewelry, however, they often know so little about what they are buying, it is unbelievable. Much of the gem industry has tacitly encouraged this ignorance. They have purposely created a mystery around gems so that customers will feel unable to comprehend what they are buying. Actually, getting a grasp of the critical concepts is not difficult, and understanding the basics is imperative if you are to obtain any fine stone or piece of jewelry at a reasonable price.

Gemology is the science and study of gems. Without a doubt, in the eyes of the public it is the most underrated of all scientific studies. Laypeople are constantly in awe of physicians and nuclear physicists. Yet, to become an accomplished gemologist takes years of intensive study and experience. There are only a few thousand gemologists in the world and most work for gem importers, wholesale dealers, or are independent appraisers. The majority of firms that sell to the public do *not* have gemologists on their staffs. Therefore, the amount of accurate, technical information a customer can receive is limited. Unfortunately, the more expensive the piece, the greater the possibility of overpaying and/or receiving synthetics or "doctored" stones. To help bridge this information gap, you must gird yourself with as much information as possible.

Although gemology is extremely complex and the inner workings of the industry may seem shrouded in fog, there are a number of simple concepts that will open new vistas of understanding to the public. Before a consumer can understand what is being said by a salesperson, these concepts must be understood: The journey starts with the first step.

A Short, but Important Overview

What is a gem? Webster defines gem as a "cut and polished precious or semi-precious stone; jewel." The Gemological Institute of America (GIA) defines it as "those specimens of minerals and organic materials used for personal adornment that possess beauty, rarity and durability." The GIA elaborates, "The subject of gemstones is divided into two classifications: diamonds and colored stones. The term Colored Stones is used in the jewelry industry and refers in its broadest sense to all gem minerals plus organic gem materials, but does not include diamonds. . . . Diamond has never been considered in the same category as colored stones for several reasons: (1) in its finer qualities it is usually nearly colorless, whereas the finer qualities in the major varieties of the other gem minerals are colored; (2) the physical and optical properties are sufficiently different from other gems to make its beauty and subsequent use totally distinctive; (3) unlike good quality colored stones, diamonds have been consistently available in both quantity and quality to permit standardization in general marketing procedures and pricing."

There are two factors that are important concerning this elongated definition. The first is that colored gems, particularly those of the finest quality, are extremely rare. For each handful of top-quality Burma ruby, Kashmir sapphire, large gem red spinel, or top-quality tsavorite (green garnet), a whole driveway could be surfaced with fine quality diamonds.

Second, the trade differentiation between colored stones and diamonds goes beyond the GIA definition. Because of the dearth of quality colored stones, there is no worldwide marketing organization for them. Diamonds, on the other hand, have a world market monopoly through DeBeers Consolidated Mines, a South African firm that effectively controls distribution and the base price for a large percentage of rough (uncut) diamonds. The closest thing to DeBeers in the colored stone business are the tightly allied Chinese and Thai dealers in Bangkok. They loosely control the base price for ruby and sapphire. On an even smaller scale, the Colombian emerald dealers have a clique that most other global dealers look to for pricing. But these two "organizations" are miniscule compared to DeBeers. Despite DeBeers' success in the United States, some cultures value colored stones above diamonds. Both emerald and ruby can be more expensive per carat than the best diamond, a fact that few people know or appreciate.

DeBeers wields a mighty image. Through advertising, it has "diamondized" the layperson. By "diamondized," I mean that the layperson has a tendency to judge all gems by diamond-grading criteria. Doing this demeans the beauty and unique appeal of many other stones. Although colored stones, by their very nature, do not sparkle like diamonds, they can exhibit a dazzling optical effect. To be an astute consumer, you must drop this exclusive orientation to diamonds.

However, DeBeers does deserve credit. Their determination to make diamond the most popular stone through relentless advertising campaigns has worked like a charm. Not to degrade the beauty and value of diamonds, one of the major reasons that diamonds have monopolized counters in jewelry stores is that the standardization of grading has made them easy to mass market. Selling colored stones to the layperson is a chore for uneducated jewelers and cuts their profit margins.

Brief Notes on the Distribution Pipeline

How do stones get to the retail jewelry store or any other firm that sells to the public? People who sell to the public may employ a myriad of methods to obtain stones and jewelry. It is important to realize that these methods differ considerably between the diamond and the colored stone market.

Obtaining stones for inventory within the diamond market is accomplished through a well-established pipeline. After the DeBeers cartel sells rough to what is known as "sight buyers," the stones go to cutters. Figure 1 indicates the path a typical diamond takes from source to consumer. From cutters, they may be (*a*) sold to diamond wholesalers, who in turn sell to retailers; (*b*) sold to manufacturers, who in turn sell to retailers, (*c*) sold to other cutters, who in turn sell to retailers or wholesalers; or (*d*) sold to the public directly if the cutter so desires.

It is an unwritten code of ethics in the diamond industry that those who supply retailers do not sell to the public. This code, however, hasn't the strength of the paper it's written on. In any case, if, after reviewing Figure 1, you think that diamonds go through many hands, you are absolutely right. The point to keep in mind is that if a person does not buy directly from a cutter *or* from someone who buys from a cutter, chances are, he or she will be contributing to the livelihood of *several middlemen*.

Even if you are able to buy as directly as possible, you are *not* ensured a low price. The only reason a firm will undercut the prevailing retail price for a specific quality of diamond is to be competitive, *not* to do the customer a favor. Virtually *any company* in the industry can offer low prices, depending on their connections, cash needs, profit expectations, and overhead. Thus, knowing prices and shopping carefully will pay huge dividends. The only other ways of obtaining diamonds at a cost lower than the prevailing average market price are through auctions, estates, listing services, or private individuals.

Ultimately, it is very difficult for any consumer to purchase a diamond significantly below the current average market value. Therefore, rather than trying to do so, you should aim at getting good value for your money. The standardization of diamond grading has produced, quite logically, a standardization in prices. These prices are published by several companies including private circulation newsletters. Since these newsletters are available for a nominal fee, the discerning buyer can easily obtain information. Well-informed consumers can figure out approximately what percentage markup the firm is using by studying these price lists.

Distribution in the colored stone market can be straightforward or more convoluted than in the diamond market. This can work to the benefit or detriment of the consumer. Most colored stones are mined, cut, polished, and wholesaled at or near the mining sites. There are many reasons for this, not the least important being that it is difficult to tell prior to cutting what quality

Figure 1

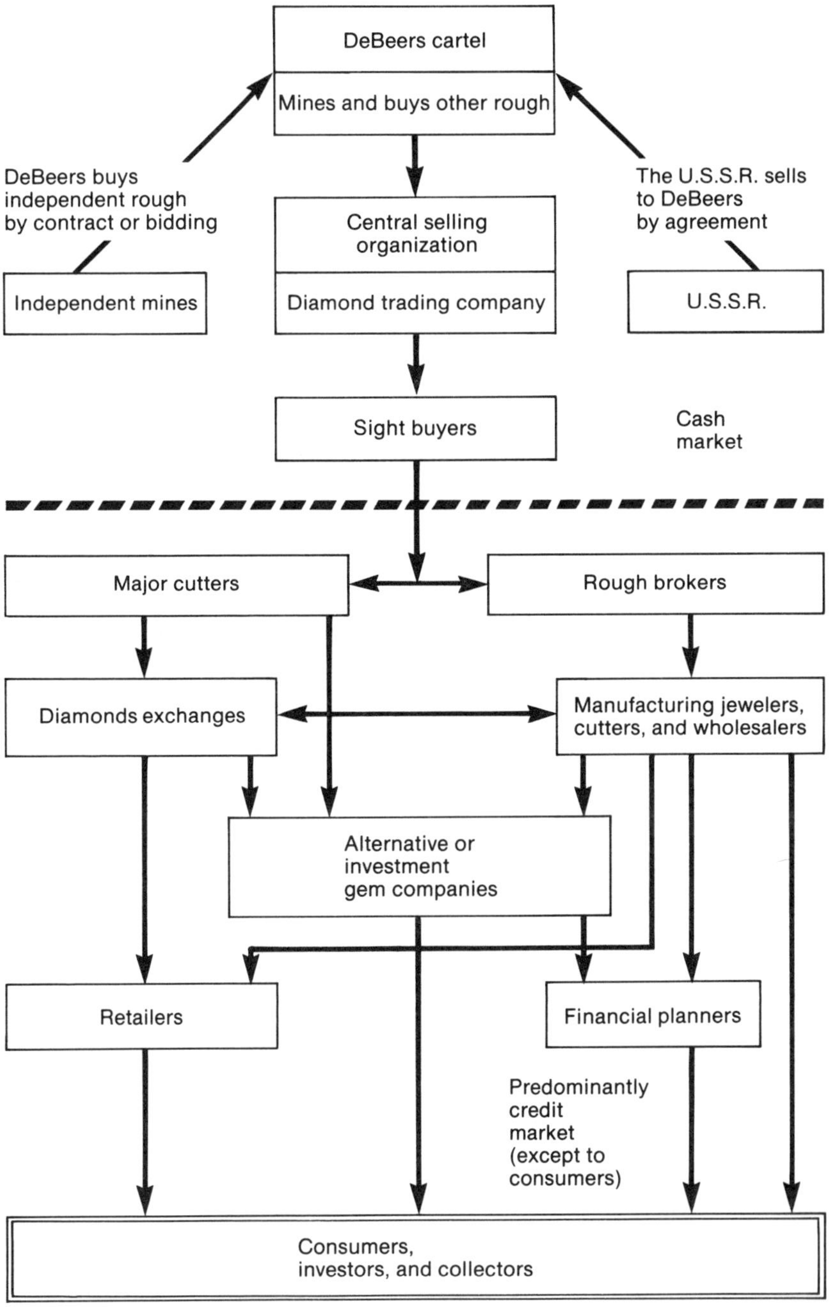
DeBeers cartel
Mines and buys other rough
DeBeers buys independent rough by contract or bidding
The U.S.S.R. sells to DeBeers by agreement
Central selling organization
Diamond trading company
Independent mines
U.S.S.R.
Sight buyers
Cash market
Major cutters
Rough brokers
Diamonds exchanges
Manufacturing jewelers, cutters, and wholesalers
Alternative or investment gem companies
Retailers
Financial planners
Predominantly credit market (except to consumers)
Consumers, investors, and collectors

stone a piece of rough will cut. Beware of the urge to buy at the source. The pitfalls are immense. Just two are that (1) many sources are at or near the equator, therefore, the intense sunlight makes stones appear more brilliantly colored than they really are; and (2) if you are not a regular buyer at the source of supply, you become a tourist, or a "one-time pigeon" as they say in the Orient. Your chances of buying misrepresented, unethically treated, or synthetic stones are high. The prices for colored stones are not as easily categorized as the prices for diamond; thus, prices to the public vary considerably. In reality, few retail jewelers travel overseas to purchase their colored stones. There are exceptions, but most obtain these stones through local importers or wholesale middlemen.

The key to buying colored stones rests in understanding a few concepts concerning the distribution system. Figure 2 shows the typical route of a colored stone from mine to jeweler. Compared to the relative rigidity of prices in the diamond pipeline, the colored stone distribution system permits far wider price differences to the consumer for the same type of stone. Firms that sell to the public can buy direct from the source. They can also buy from a manufacturer, who buys from a wholesaler, who buys from an importer, who buys from the source! For the consumer who is unaware of average price ranges for specific qualities of colored stones, overpaying may be the result.

Careful shopping is essential if you are to get the best value. In the case of very rare, extremely high-quality colored stones (e.g., gem tsavorite), a layperson can *sometimes* buy at the same price, or better, than a traditional jeweler. How can this happen? First, let's assume the layperson buys the gem from a firm that purchases directly in East Africa. The layperson buys at a markup of 30 percent over the company's cost, which is the average markup for a legitimate "alternative" or "investment" company in fine, colored stones. A jeweler who does not often have clientele for such a stone, but gets the same request, will call his colored stone supplier. Because the stone is so rare, the supplier probably will not have it, at which point he will call somebody who will call somebody else. By the time the retailer obtains the stone on memorandum (temporary loan), he is paying as much, or more, than the customer who bought the stone from the investment company. Another factor that should not be discounted is that many jewelers cannot accurately grade and value colored stones. This

Figure 2
Typical Paths of Colored Stones from Mine to Jeweler

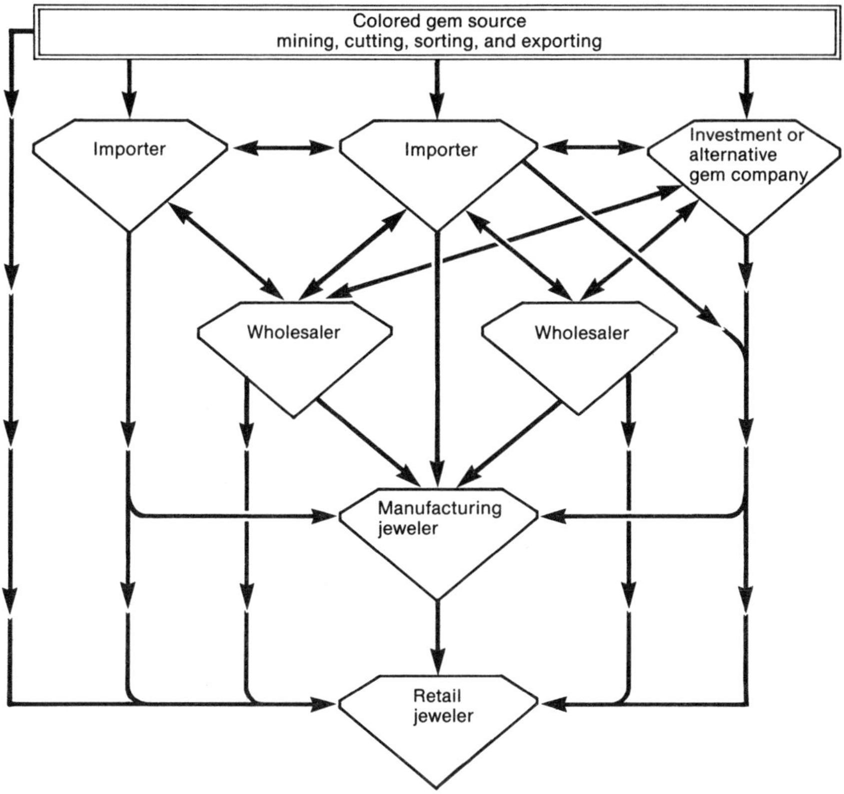

lack of knowledge sometimes allows consumers to buy below market.

Technical Gemology

The information above is an overview, a slight scratching of the surface that attempts to create the proper perspective for the consumer. Similarly, the gemological concepts defined in this section are *only* a beginning but will point you in the right direction.

The science of gemology has progressed in leaps and bounds over the last 20 years. New technologies have brought it out of the dark ages of reliance on hardness, scratch, and unaided observational tests. In the modern laboratory, all of the tests that are performed on gemstones to determine identity and quality are nondestructive. They have to be because the value of rare stones creates a massive liability problem for both appraisers and laboratories. Although today's gemological laboratories often look like the inside of an intensive care ward, much of the equipment in them is there to analyze and determine only a few physical and optical facts concerning a particular gemstone. The facts that gemologists want to determine are discussed below.

Family and Species Gemstones are classified in a manner that is similar to the classification system used for the plant and animal kingdom. Gems whose chemical compositions are the same or similar fall into what is known as a family. The particular color or type of stone to which reference is made is the species of that family. For example, corundum is a family of stones of which ruby and blue sapphire are species.

Crystal Systems Most gems have a crystalline structure that falls into one of six categories: cubic, tetragonal, hexagonal, orthorhombic, triclinic, and monoclinic. The perfect forms of these crystals appear in Figure 3. Crystallography is an immensely complicated scientific discipline. You can get a Ph.D. in the subject.

Fortunately, the consumer only needs to know a few fundamental facts. In laboratory identification and evaluation, the specialist does not look for the type of crystal system the item in question possesses because the identification of family designates that system. For example, all garnet is cubic and all jade is monoclinic. From a consumer's viewpoint, the six crystal systems are primarily an academic concept. Becoming familiar with them, however, will help you understand why some stones commonly appear in a particular shape or cut. For example, the beryl family crystallizes exclusively in the hexagonal system. It is easy to visualize how two emerald (rectangular) cuts can be made by cutting the crystal down the middle, parallel to the long axis. For beryl, the emerald cut is standard and most desired.

A common shape of diamond rough is an octahedron. Figure 4 shows an octahedron crystal; these have eight sides. When the octahedron is sawed in half, two, four-sided pyramids are created. Each can be formed into a round, brilliant cut, with the flat bottom of the pyramid becoming the top of the diamond and

Figure 3
Models of the Six Crystal Systems

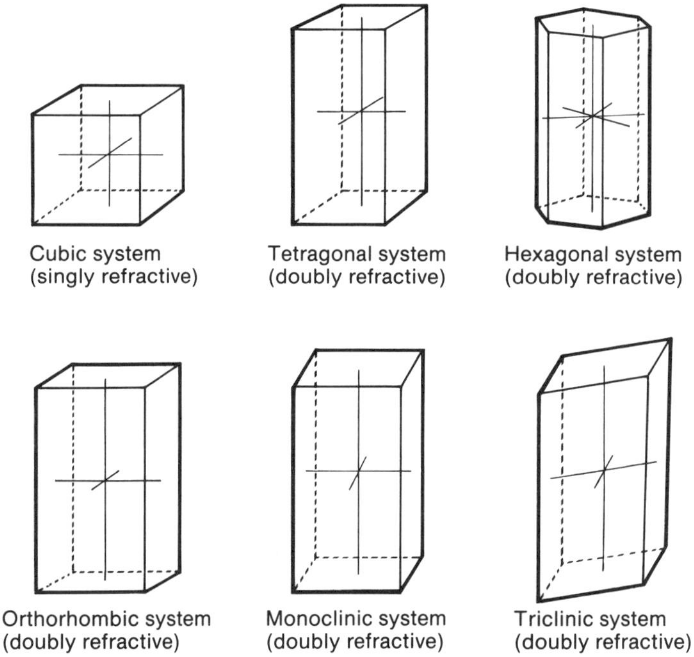

Figure 4
Octahedron Diamond Crystal
The Octahedron is a non-perfect form of the cubic system. It is, however, commonly found in nature. When sawed in half, the two pyramids can be cut into round, brilliant cuts.

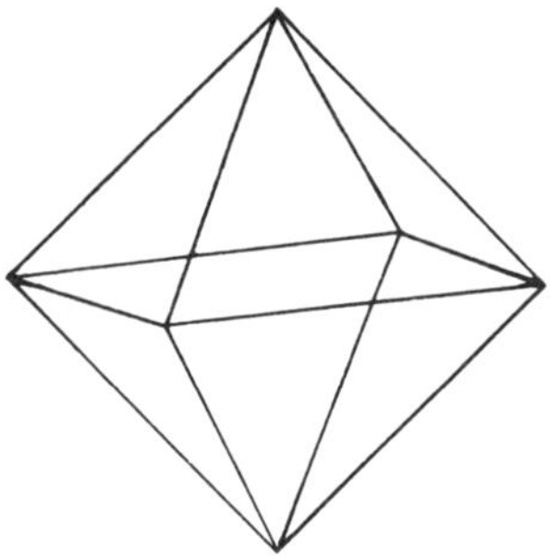

the point of the pyramid becoming the bottom. The majority of cut diamonds are rounds, and like beryl, the most common form of cut in diamond (the round cut) is the most expensive. This generality is not quite as sweeping for diamond as for beryl, however. Fashion changes or short supplies of specific types of rough will occasionally push fancy cuts into a higher price-per-carat range than that of rounds.

Crystal systems can also display a phenomenon that is often important in the identification of a gem. All but the cubic system create what is termed *double refraction*. Double refraction, although a complicated concept, simply refers to the stone breaking or splitting visible light into two beams and moving those beams, through the crystal, in different directions at different speeds. This optical phenomenon can be determined by a gemological instrument called a polariscope. The result of this phenomenon is what is known as pleochroism (multiple colors). Many stones with double refraction, such as sapphire, ruby, and emerald, create dichroism (two colors). If you hold a stone that is doubly refractive and look down one optic axis, the color will be slightly different than looking down another optic axis. For example, a blue sapphire may look greenish blue from one direction, and violetish blue from another. The stronger the difference in color, the stronger the dichroism. The cubic system is singularly refractive, and the stone's color appears the same regardless of the direction from which it is viewed. Double refraction, an interesting and fun concept for laypeople, is often vital to gemologists in identification.

Refractive Index Refractive index refers to the degree to which a gem bends light as it enters the stone. The easiest way to visualize refractive index is to put a straw into a glass of water. The straw appears bent. This optical effect is caused by the refraction of light in the water. In gemology, the measurement of refractive index by an instrument called a refractometer is probably the most important single test for determining the family to which a stone belongs.

Every family bends light in a way that is consistent and generally different from that of other families. Sometimes the range of one stone's refractive index overlaps with that of other stones. When this occurs, additional tests will be needed to identify the gem. It is particularly important to remember that the higher the refractive index, the more a gem will "sparkle"—if properly cut. Also, the lower the refractive index, the deeper the stone must be to bring out the maximum "sparkle" effect. If a stone is cut with too shallow a depth, the light will not reflect correctly and come back to the viewer's eye. It will, instead, leak out of the bottom of the stone and create a "window" or blank area when the stone is viewed from above. Windows are not tolerated in fine and rare stones.

Specific Gravity This very simple concept is often the final test in identifying a gem. It refers to the number of times a stone is heavier than the weight of its own volume of water. Ivory, a light organic gem, has a specific gravity of only 1.85. Ruby and sapphire have a specific gravity of 4.00. Specific gravity is actually an expression of density. Observant consumers have probably noticed that a carat opal often looks bigger than a carat ruby. That is because their specific gravities are different. Opal is less dense and, therefore, takes up more space to weigh one carat. The heaviest commonly used gem for jewelry is hematite. It appears primarily as a cameo or intaglio in men's rings and women's bead necklaces, and has a specific gravity of 5.20.

Hardness Hardness is defined as the ability of a gem to resist scratching. Usually, the Moh's scale of hardness is used in gemology. In this scale, the ratings run from talcum (1) to diamond (10). The main point to remember concerning the Moh's scale is that the difference in hardness between the numbers is not uniform. Although diamond is ranked as 10 and ruby is ranked as 9, diamond is estimated to be many times harder than ruby. Hardness tests are not often used in gemological testing. At best, they are unreliable and can cause serious damage to the stone.

Hardness does indicate much about a stone's long-term ability to resist wear. Diamond cannot be scratched easily. However, since diamonds will scratch each other, it is not a wise idea to "throw" diamond jewelry together in a jewelry box. Also, slow abrasion may wear down facet junctions (lines where facets come together) over a period of many decades of continual wear. Most commonly used stones are at least as hard as low-carbon steel. Many people believe opal is soft, and, indeed, it is softer than many gems. The reason it so easily breaks, however, has more to do with toughness and the amount of inclusions in the stone. A very fine, solid, opal crystal can actually be worn without fear. Most people buy very inexpensive opal and receive stones with many inclusions and flaws. Moreover, there may not be much thickness to the inexpensive stones. The same misconception holds true with emerald. Many people erroneously believe that emerald is a soft stone. In reality, it has a hardness of 8—very high. By contrast, a pair of good quality scissors has a hardness of 6 to 6.5.

Cleavage A concern for customers is cleavage. Cleavage is a weakness in the crystal's atomic structure that gives a stone a tendency to split easily in a specific direction. A properly placed blow can make any stone with cleavage split in two. Diamonds have perfect cleavage, but their toughness and hardness help prevent what would otherwise be a dangerous situation. Nonetheless, if a diamond is hit hard enough, it can cleave. Stones that should be worn carefully because of cleavage are topaz, tanzanite, moon and sun stone, and kunzite.

Toughness Many people believe that hardness directly influences a stone's ability to withstand breakage. To an extent that is true, but toughness plays a more important role. For example, jadeite and nephrite, the two common forms of jade, have a hardness of between 6.5 and 7.5, medium hard. Their toughness, however, is ranked as exceptional, and breaking jade is very difficult. Diamond, despite having perfect cleavage, is extremely tough. Topaz has a highly ranked hardness of 8, but has perfect cleavage and is not considered particularly durable. In determining a stone's overall durability, hardness, cleavage, and toughness should be taken into consideration.

Another factor of interest is the stone's degree of transparency. In general, transparent stones are more expensive than translucent stones, and translucent stones are more expensive than opaque stones. Opaque stones such as malachite, tiger eye, and lapis lazuli are primarily decorative and inexpensive. There are some exceptions to this rule including jade and opal.

These observations on the gem market and fundamental gemological concepts may seem difficult to grasp at first, but take time to sort them out. If anything seems unclear, go back and read it again before starting the next chapter.

2 The Families of Rarity

This chapter is designed to do two things for the reader: (*a*) discuss facts and buying tips pertaining to commonly traded gems; and (*b*) serve as a portable reference while shopping.

The information presented here is basic. There are many fine points concerning gems that must be obtained through experience, but having access to the following data will start you on the proper road to developing a sharp aesthetic sense. The stones discussed in this chapter are those that are commonly sold and traded. Rare collector and mineral specimens will not be discussed; their market, pricing, and evaluation parameters are a whole different ball game and the public's interest is limited. For more information on these, please refer to the recommended reading list.

Each family of stones will be discussed and analyzed according to the following three broad categories:

1. The basic gemological (optical and physical) properties. Please refer to Chapter 1 for definitions.
2. Geographic sources, current price ranges, and price histories of individual species, as well as interesting observations and concepts.
3. Protective measures, inside tips, and caveats for the consumer.

Note Most gemstones are treated to improve color and/or clarity. These issues will be discussed in Chapter 8.

BERYL

$Be_3Al_2(SIO_3)_6$

Beryllium Aluminum Silicate

Common Species	
White, Green, Emerald	Refractive index: 1.577–1.583
Pink (morganite)	Specific gravity: 2.72
Yellow (heliodor)	Hardness: 7.5–8.0
Red, Aquamarine	Crystal system: Hexagonal
Golden	Transparent to opaque
	No cleavage
	Toughness: Good

Sources

The mineral beryl is found around the world. Much of the material is not cuttable. Gem beryl is often formed in pegmatite dikes, hollow areas that branch off the sides of volcanos or similar formations. The crystals continue to grow, virtually unrestricted, so long as the physical elements and temperature necessary to form the crystal are present. As a result, rough crystals weighing several pounds can be formed. Emerald is an exception as it seldom occurs in large sizes. A casual examination of available, gem-quality aquas reveals many that are over 20, 30, and 40 carats. Emerald, by contrast, is very difficult to find in good quality over 2 or 3 carats; 5- to 10-carat gems are rare treasures.

The finest emerald is found in Colombia, Africa, and Brazil. Colombian emerald is the most prized of the group. Two famous emerald mines, Chivor and Muzo, produce a myriad of qualities, from the lowest commercial to the finest gems found anywhere in the world. In the gem trade, the terms *Muzo* and *Chivor* are often used not so much to designate the mine of origin, but the quality of the color. Muzo emeralds are considered to be a warm green and often take on the luminous color of lime Jell-O, with the major secondary color being yellow. Chivor stones are cool green like the rolling hills of Kentucky, with a major secondary color of blue. Both types may come from either mine.

The Colombian mines have been worked since the days of the Incas. The average quality of stones produced is very high, but the quantity is not large. Commercial and some better-quality emeralds, those used in middle- to slightly higher-priced jewelry, currently come from Africa. There are two distinct types of emerald: One comes from the Sandawana Valley in southern Zimbabwe (Rhodesia) and the other comes from Zambia.

Sandawana emeralds were the first to be found. Indian dealers were buying them in the 1950s. James Breski, a highly respected colored stone specialist, describes them. "Sandawana emeralds are a velvety, medium to rich green with less brilliance than stones from some other sources. Many of the finest specimens with better clarity still belong to the original Indian buyers and have everything one could want in an emerald concerning color, clarity, and life. Zambian material is a paler, often watery bluish green, but exhibits a higher degree of clarity. They often lack the intense green that is commonly expected in emerald and frequently have almost the appearance of green tourmaline."

Origin cannot always be established for cut and polished emeralds. Some stones, however, exhibit such positive characteristics, like the high clarity of Zambian material or the inclusions peculiar to Colombian, that the origin can be safely assumed.

Emeralds also come from India, the Soviet Union, and South Africa. The north Transvaal deposits of South Africa are believed to be an extension of the Sandawana deposits. Today, emeralds are also being found in the jungled interior of Brazil. They are very fine quality, but cut and polished sizes rarely exceed a carat. Emeralds also occur in North Carolina: The deposit, which has been known for years, was never considered commercially viable. But rock hounds have worked the deposit and found several very fine stones. Recently, a private, limited partnership was formed to commercially mine and market these emeralds.

Aquamarine is the next most popular beryl. Most aqua rough is a delicate greenish blue. It is heat treated to remove the green, and the process is permanent. For many years most aquamarine originated from Minas Gerais, Brazil. Fine specimens also come from Madagascar, which is known for its richly colored, purple-red morganite. Like emerald, aquamarine is found in a number of localities, although the two mentioned above are currently the most commercially viable.

The majority of golden, yellow, pink, green, and white beryl also comes from Brazil, although these stones are also found in numerous other places. Red beryl comes from Utah and is often sold as mineral specimens rather than cut stones.

Price Ranges and Price Histories

Like so many crystalline gem materials, in its pure chemical form, beryl is clear: white beryl. It is not expensive and is seldom used in jewelry. Collector samples cost just a few dollars per carat. By contrast, emerald is one of the most expensive of all gems. The only difference between emerald and white beryl is that a green color is created in emerald by the minute presence of the metal chromium within the stone's atomic structure. Beryl's other colors are also created by small amounts of metals called chromophores. The most common chromophores are chromium, vanadium, manganese, magnesium, and iron. Various combinations and permutations of these, added in miniscule percentages, create many hues.

Emerald is the most expensive of all commonly sold beryls. Aquamarine and morganite are next. Green, golden, and yellow follow. Highly intense, reddish purple morganites and lemon-yellow beryls are extremely rare. They are not nearly as expensive as emerald because their numbers are so small, there is no large demand for them: They are collector stones. Gem emerald,

Figure 5
Price History Curve of 1-Carat, Emerald Cut Colombian Emerald (fine gem quality, no grey or brown)*
Approximate AGL Grading: 3.5 Color; 65–75 Tone; MI;
Good Proportion and Finish 4–5; Average Brilliancy 60% + .

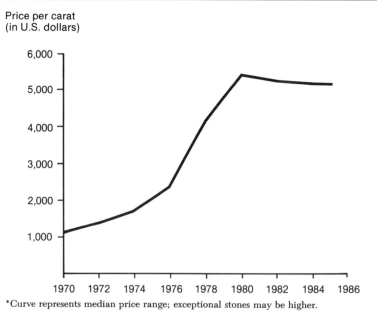

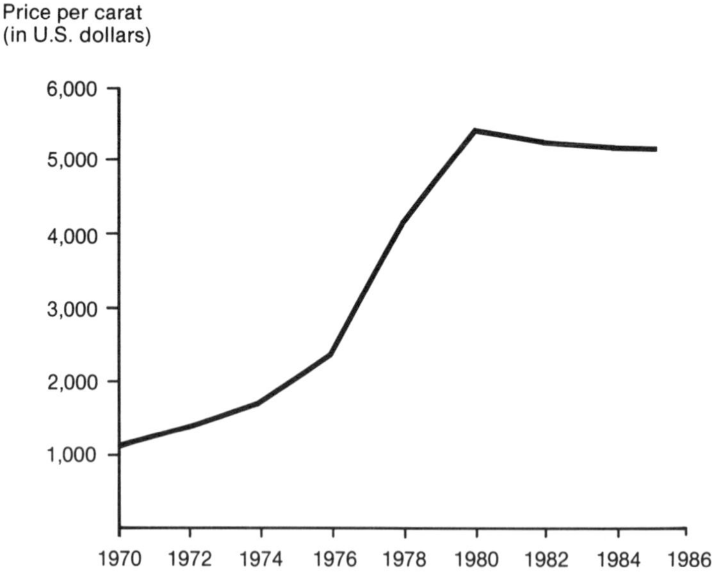

*Curve represents median price range; exceptional stones may be higher.

which is many times rarer than the best diamonds, exists in sufficient quantity to create an international trading market. This latter factor is critical for any precious gem to reach very high price-per-carat ranges.

Figures 5 and 6 show the price histories of 1-carat gem emerald and 10-carat aquamarine. Emerald is one of the best ways to store wealth and prevent the value of that wealth from being destroyed by inflation. The historical price curve for emerald is quite stable with no great downward trend. Aquamarine is not a volatile stone and has shown a gradual appreciation over the years. In the last two or three years, aquamarine has been relatively stable in price. Downside pressure on aqua is strong currently, and the cost of this stone may come down in the next few years. The public has discovered inexpensive blue topaz and has been using it as a substitution. The finest "electric blue" topaz costs below $100 per

Figure 6
Price History Curve of 10-Carat, Emerald Cut Aquamarine (fine gem quality, no grey)*
Approximate AGL Grading: 4.0 Color; 65–75 Tone; FI; Proportion and Finish 4–5; Average Brilliancy 60% + .

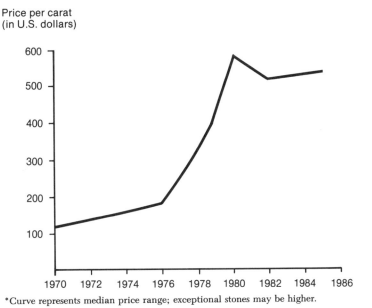

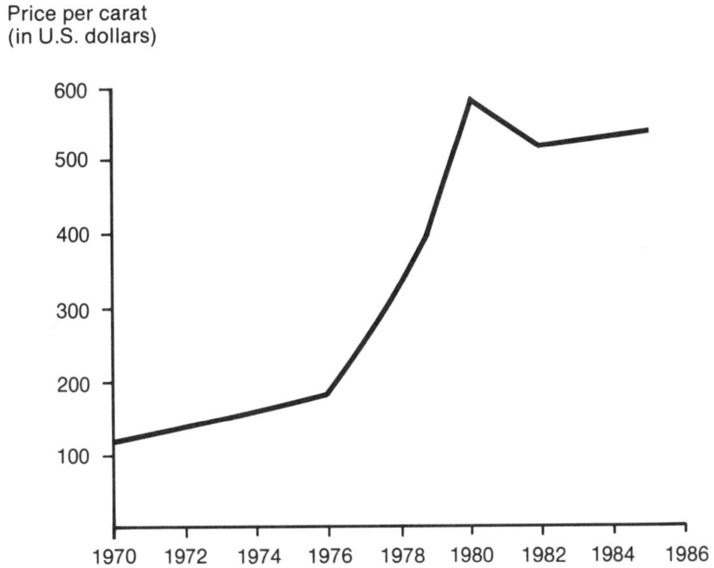

*Curve represents median price range; exceptional stones may be higher.

carat, while the same size and quality of aqua can cost $500 to $700 or more per carat.

Consumer Tips

A 1984 poll of jewelers found that emerald was the most popular expensive colored stone. Perhaps, as the ancient Romans believed, the serenity of the green evokes tranquility during troubled times. Emeralds come in a wide price range, but even the "commercial" variety are quite dear. A price of $1,000 to $4,000 per carat is not unusual for a good, one-carat emerald. In larger gems (five carats and more) the finer stones will often start at $10,000 per carat. Magnificent 10- to 30-carat, world class Colombian goods will *wholesale* for a minimum of $10,000 to $15,000 per carat, and easily move well over the $20,000-per-carat mark.

In the gem trade, the difference between emerald and green beryl is a matter of semantics. Emerald is defined as a "medium to intense" green. The borderline is not clear, but there are definitely pale, greyish green stones that by no stretch of the imagination can be called emerald.

Be careful of jewelers pawning off green beryl or opaque emerald as "fine emerald." It is true that of all colored gemstones, emerald will exhibit the largest quantity of inclusions—even in stones that command stellar prices. This is natural and desirable. The lovely, velvety texture that emerald displays is partially caused by this multitude of inclusions. For those people who have been "diamondized" beyond repair, head for the Zambian material; the color will not be as intense, but a better clarity and sparkle will be available.

Some consumers are overly fearful of buying emerald because of the existence of synthetics. Manufacturers are extremely ethical in their sale of this material, and any gemologist can easily differentiate between natural and synthetic stones with a few basic tests. The "problem" of synthetics being switched for natural stones simply does not exist among ethical and reputable people who sell to the public.

When purchasing aquamarine, there are two key factors. Color is very important. If you are looking for a top-quality gem, be advised that there is a significant difference in price between an intense "sky" blue and an intense "greyish blue." Some aquas have a strong greyish tint and may be represented as the finest gem quality: They are not. Aqua also tends to crystallize cleanly. Obtaining a flawless or very close to flawless stone is not impossible. Stay away from included stones. An inclusion that is obvious to the naked eye is highly undesirable.

For other beryl, the more intense and pure the color the better. Pale stones are common. It is hard to obtain a saturated color in any of these species. All of these varieties can be obtained in clean crystals. The best yellows, goldens, and pinks usually run no more than $100 to $200 per carat.

CHRYSOBERYL

Be Al_2O_4

Beryllium Aluminate

Common Species	
Brown, Green	Refractive index: 1.746–1.755
Yellow, Cat's Eye	Specific gravity: 3.73
Alexandrite	Hardness: 8.5
	Crystal system: Orthorhombic
	Transparent to translucent
	No cleavage
	Toughness: Excellent

Introduction

The term *chrysoberyl* is largely unknown to the public, yet two of the more popular and expensive gemstones come from this family. They are alexandrite and cat's eye. Brown, green, and yellow varieties of crystalline material are not commonly used in jewelry. If they were used, the main advantage would be that they form in large, clean sizes and would make wonderful jewelry at relatively little cost. Despite this, these stones are primarily bought by collectors.

Some dealers have touted green, yellow, and brown chrysoberyl as investments, but the public's awareness of the stone is so minimal, it would take an intellectual revolution for them to be usable for this purpose. Over 95 percent of all jewelers do not stock them, and most don't know anything about them. Prices for brown, green, and yellow are usually under $100 per carat, with better qualities costing slightly more.

Alexandrite and cat's eye, on the other hand, are well known. Alexandrite changes color from bluish green to brownish red respectively when moved from ultraviolet to incandescent light. The stone's value is based about 80 percent on the quality of the color change. The purer the colors and the sharper the color change, the more expensive the stone. Fine gems in 3- to 10-carat sizes often cost more than $10,000 per carat. Consumers frequently find them more fascinating than beautiful, but for those who know what they are, glances of envy toward the owner are very common.

Cat's eyes are frequently used in men's rings because of their subtle beauty and toughness. Wholesale, they may exceed $2,000 to $3,000 per carat. Golden body colors are preferred to greenish golden or pure green body colors. The finest goldens are called "milk and honey." The eye of these stones should be thin, bright, white, or bluish, and the stones should be translucent. The quality of the phenomenon, termed *chatoyancy*, is the major determinant of value. Price graphs are not available for alexandrite or cat's eye; each stone is unique and priced according to its merits.

Sources

Current mining of gem-quality chrysoberyl is primarily confined to Sri Lanka and Brazil. Originally, alexandrite came from the Ural mountains, but most believe those deposits are exhausted. Alexandrite from Sri Lanka and Brazil often do not undergo as dramatic a color change as the old Russian stones. Connoisseurs, in the hopes of finding an old Russian stone, will often look for alexandrite in estates rather than on the contemporary market. The greatest delight of collectors is the cat's eye alexandrite. While only a few are known, they are priced at approximately the same level as good alexandrite. They display not only the color change, but also a cat's eye. In superb qualities, they are one of the most sought after stones by museums, collectors, and investors. Most gem cat's eye comes from Sri Lanka. Even in the rich gem gravels of that country, however, they are quite rare.

Consumer Tips

Green, yellow, and brown chrysoberyl are easily obtainable but don't expect the jeweler to have them in stock. He can, however, get them easily.

Alexandrite is only carried by fine jewelers and investment dealers. The average jewelry store will never have one in stock. To obtain a fine, large stone with a striking color change may take several months. Therefore, unless you are a serious buyer, don't bother the jeweler just to see one. He will probably pull his hair out and run up several hundred dollars worth of phone bills just locating the stone. Besides, a five-carat, gem-quality stone will cost at least $50,000. The jeweler will undoubtedly verify a customer's buying ability before trying to find such a stone.

Most alexandrites exhibit a partial color change. When the stone is moved from incandescent (reddish color showing) to ultraviolet (greenish color showing), or vice versa, a residual of the other color will remain in the stone. The less residual color remaining, the finer the stone. Some jewelers will explain the color change as red to green. Actually, the colors are never that pure. They usually run from a brownish reddish raspberry to a greyish bluish green. Some stones may show a change in only one area. This is less desirable. Clarity is a minor issue in alexandrite as long as the stone is not so included as to be opaque. Cut is also a minor issue as long as the stone is not so shallow that it has no sparkle.

Synthetic alexandrite is available. It is often distinguished from the real thing by the presence of microscopic platinum particles that run throughout the stone. The platinum comes from the crucible in which the stone was made. There is also a synthetic sapphire that exhibits color change. These stones are commonly sold as Mexican alexandrite. They can be purchased wholesale for around $5 per carat, but they are sold to the unsuspecting for $40 to $100 per carat. Those who sell this merchandise usually claim it is natural alexandrite: It is not.

Chrysoberyl cat's eyes should not be confused with tiger's eye; they neither look nor cost the same. Tiger's eye is made of quartz and is a pseudomorphic form of asbestos. The quartz replaces the asbestos fibers in a geological process, and the thin, needlelike fibers of quartz create the chatoyancy. The eye of a tiger's eye is very crude compared to that of a cat's eye. In chrysoberyl, the eye seems to "float" above the top of the stone. When placed between two direct light sources at 45 degrees to the rim of the stone, the eye will split in two and open and close as the stone is rotated. A tiger's eye will not do this.

CORUNDUM

Al_2O_3

Aluminum Oxide

Common Species

Ruby, Sapphire (blue, pink, orange, purple, golden, green, padparadscha, yellow, white)

Refractive index: 1.762–1.770
Specific gravity: 4.00
Hardness: 9
Crystal structure: Hexagonal
Transparent to opaque
Parting cleavage
Toughness: Excellent

Introduction

Chemically pure corundum is clear and is called white sapphire. White sapphire has more uses in jewelry than white beryl. Before the invention of diamond substitutes such as cubic zirconium and yttrium aluminum garnet (YAG), white sapphire was used in jewelry to imitate diamond.

When corundum is red it is called ruby; when it is any other color it is called sapphire. Sapphire can appear in virtually any color gradation. Most prized are padparadscha (pink-orange), blue, pink, and golden, respectively. Yellow is relatively inexpensive and is gaining in popularity in the United States. It comes in large, clean crystals. Cut yellow sapphires from Sri Lanka may be found in the 100- to 200-carat range—large enough for a marvelous paperweight!

Ruby is universally acknowledged as the king of gems. In sizes over 10 carats and in its finest qualities, no gem can exceed its price per carat, particularly the Burma variety. An interesting historical point can be made about ruby. Before the mid-1960s much of the ruby sold in America originated in Burma. Experts considered Thailand ruby, now the mainstay of the world's ruby business, a laughable stone that looked more like a red garnet. They were used to the lighter, brighter stones from Burma. And the discerning layperson had always associated ruby with the Burma type stone. Since production in Burma has been on a serious decline for the last 20 years, and because the communist government has made the Burmese stone difficult to export, Thai ruby has gained acceptance and increased in price tremendously. In fact, the generally darker Thai stone is now considered the norm. An average consumer will currently describe ruby as a "very dark red" and probably will not recognize the very bright Burma material as the finer and more expensive gem!

Thai rubies are more valued when they are lighter and the red in them mimics the Burma type stone. For those interested in obtaining a gem ruby, the common notion that "dark red is superlative" must be eliminated.

The same is true for blue sapphire. Much currently available material is of Sri Lankan or Australian origin. Australian sapphire is usually inky blue. Today, the overly dark Sri Lankan material is preferred by retail jewelers; they can sell a dark, intense blue for less money than a bright, intense blue. Burma and Kashmir blue sapphires, in their finest forms, are not overly dark, but by current consumer standards, these lighter-toned sapphires would probably not be recognized as particularly fine specimens. The common belief that sapphire, if not blue, is only "semiprecious" must be reconsidered. Currently, excellent padparadschas cost at least $2,000 to $4,000 per carat, and fine pinks command prices in the same range. Ten-carat padparadschas may run over $10,000 per carat!

Origins and Formation

Corundum is found all over the world. Nongem corundum is used as an abrasive, but gem-quality corundum is very rare. Moreover, corundum's usual mode of geological formation seldom allows large rough crystals to be formed.

Gem corundum is often formed by a process called contact metamorphism. In this process, a magma (molten rock) intrudes into an area of, for example, solid limestone. This was how the vast Thailand ruby deposits were created. The magma cooks the limestone and the aluminum oxide melts. Chromophores, if present, are incorporated into the forming and cooling crystal. By the very nature of the process, the chances of enough raw materials being present in any one position to make a large crystal are slight. Some sapphire, however, is formed in pegmatite dikes. The blue and multicolored sapphires from Montana are perfect examples of this.

Gem corundum is found in a number of localities. The major source for sapphire is Sri Lanka. Thailand produces sapphire and is particularly noted for its fine goldens; Burma blue and pink sapphire are among the best in the world. Australia produces a decent yellow-golden sapphire, but their blues are often overly dark. Kashmir blue sapphire, from northern India, is considered the finest in the world. The Umba river valley in Africa usually produces small, pastel-colored sapphires. Montana has two sapphire deposits. Fancy colors come from the west end of Montana, near Hamilton, while the blues come from the famous Yogo mine near Lewiston.

The majority of ruby comes from Thailand, although some Burma ruby is smuggled into Bangkok for sale. Sri Lanka produces a less intensely colored ruby, often thought of as pink sapphire in the United States. Some commercial material is mined in Kenya. India also produces ruby, but it is often not of faceting quality. Many of the cabochons and poor-quality stars used in jewelry are from that area.

Gem corundum, in virtually any color, is rarer than fine diamonds. Even the more common yellows are geologically rarer. The superlative gems, such as premier Kashmir or Burma sapphire, and ruby and gem padparadscha, are so scarce that only a handful may be available at any time. Kashmir sapphire was only mined for a couple of decades near the turn of the century. Accounts of mining are fascinating. It was reported that Kashmirs were found in little pockets in the sides of mountains. The material that surrounded the sapphires was soft, like kaolin clay, and could be scooped out of the indentation in the solid rock. One miner likened the process to digging for potatoes!

The mountainous region that produces these stones, however, is inaccessible except by foot and mule, and the brutal Himalayan winters twist and change the appearance of the terrain. A pocket of sapphire found during one short season of exploration will surely disappear into the changing formations by the next season.

The Burmese deposits occur in the area around Mogok, northeast of Mandalay. Mogok rests at an elevation of 4,000 feet above sea level and frequently has over 100 inches of rain per year. It produces the most impressive array of gemstones anywhere in the world and is known to have been worked since 1200 A.D. The finest ruby, exquisite sapphire of all colors, chrysoberyl, topaz, jadeite, and spinel are just some of the stones that come from this area. Currently, production is low and, since the Burmese government is not hospitable, fine gems are smuggled across the Thailand border. The punishment if caught is death. It is well known that the most efficient gem smugglers are also those who traffic heroin.

Sri Lanka produces most of the blue and much of the fancy colored sapphire seen in jewelry stores. Some Sri Lankan material is magnificent, but commercial quality is the norm. The government of Sri Lanka realizes that gemstones bring it much-needed foreign currency, and the State Gem Corporation has helped the industry develop tremendously.

Price Ranges and Price Histories

On the left, below, is a survey that shows the comparative geological rarity (in descending order) for selected colors of corundum; it includes all qualities. On the right is the descending order of expense per carat for the finest possible quality in each color.

Geological Rarity	Cost P/C In Finest Quality
1. Padparadscha.	1. Ruby.
2. Pink sapphire.	2. Blue sapphire.
3. Orange sapphire.	3. Padparadscha.
4. Purple sapphire.	4. Pink sapphire.
5. Golden sapphire.	5. Orange sapphire.
6. Ruby.	6. Golden sapphire.
7. Blue sapphire.	7. Purple sapphire.
8. Yellow sapphire.	8. Yellow sapphire.
9. Green sapphire.	9. Green sapphire.
10. White sapphire.	10. White sapphire.

Many think that diamond is the most expensive gemstone. Although natural blues and pinks are high, the best white diamonds pale in comparison to the cost of some fine corundum. The various colors of corundum, in the finest qualities, for multiple carat sizes can exceed the following prices:

Ruby	Over $50,000 per carat
Blue sapphire	Over $20,000 per carat
Padparadscha	Over $10,000 per carat
Pink sapphire	Over $4,000 per carat
Orange sapphire	Over $3,000 per carat
Golden sapphire	Over $1,000 per carat

Purple sapphire	Over $500 per carat
Yellow sapphire	Over $300 per carat
Green sapphire	Over $100 per carat

Figures 7, 8, 9, 10, and 11 show the price histories for gem-quality, one-carat Thailand ruby, and 2-carat, gem-quality blue sapphire, pink sapphire, golden sapphire, and yellow sapphire, respectively.

Figure 7
Price History Curve of 1-Carat Cushion or Oval Cut Thailand Ruby (fine gem quality)*
Approximate AGL Grading: 3.5 Color; 70–80 Tone; LI_2; Proportion and Finish 4–5; Average Brilliancy 70%–80% +.

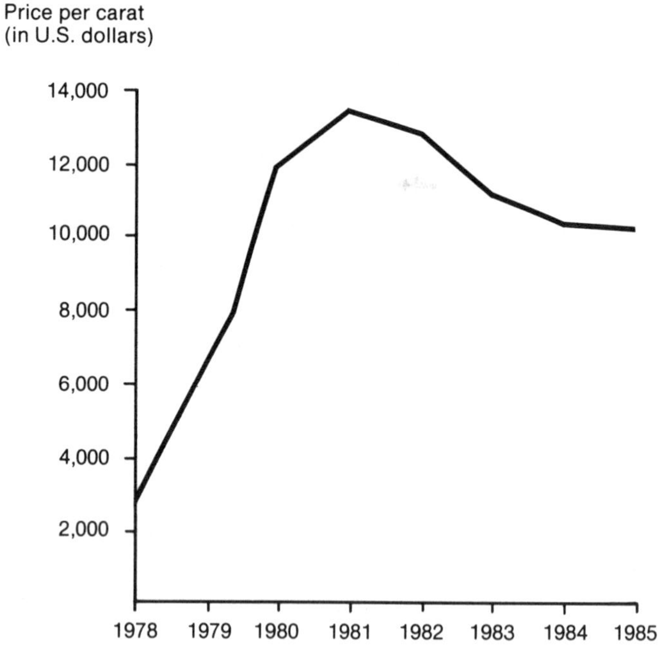

*Curve represents median price range; exceptional stones may be higher; slightly darker tones will be lower.

Figure 8
Price History Curve of 2-Carat, Cushion or Oval Cut Sri Lankan Sapphire (fine gem quality)*
Approximate AGL Grading: 3.5 Color; 70–80 Tone; FI–LI_2; Proportion and Finish 4–5; Average Brilliancy 70%–80% +.

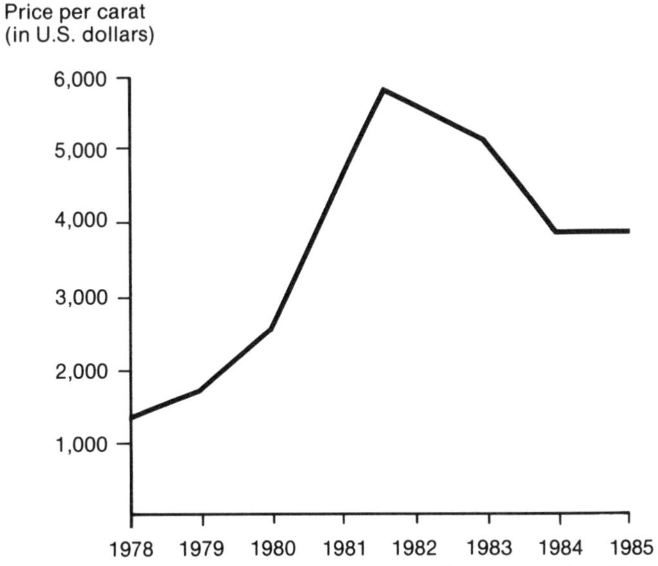

*Curve represents median price range; exceptional stones may be higher; slightly darker tones will be lower.

Consumer Tips

It is imperative that you adhere to the following points when buying. These will help ensure that you obtain the best stone however much you intend to spend.

1. Make sure the stone is natural and not synthetic. Corundum has been synthesized in the laboratory for decades. For stones under $1,000, this is hardly a problem, but for expensive stones, it can be. Recent advances in hydrothermally grown crystals have resulted in synthetics that are difficult to distinguish from natural stones. The most suspect is ruby. Synthetics such as Kashan and Ramaura, brand names for synthetic ruby, are very close to the natural. Although these companies are ethical about their representation, the ignorant or unscrupulous are not prevented from selling these stones as naturals.

Figure 9
Price History Curve of 2-Carat, Cushion or Oval Cut Pink Sapphire (Burma) (fine gem quality)*
Approximate AGL Grading: 4.0 Color; 65–75 Tone; LI_1–LI_2; Proportion and Finish 4–5; Average Brilliancy 70%–80% +.

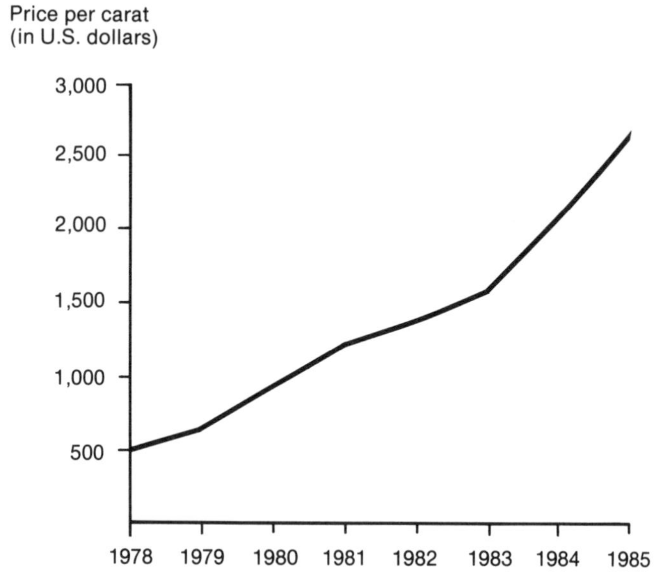

*Curve represents median price range; exceptional stones may be higher; stones with brown will be lower.

When buying any corundum above $5,000, demand an independent laboratory verification of natural origin, if not a full, quality analysis.

2. Of the stones that are within your specified price range, choose one with the most intense primary color and one that is not too dark. Brilliancy is important; the better cuts will exhibit a nice sparkle. The more shallow the stone, the less expensive—no matter what the color. Most rough corundum crystals are flattish and many cut stones are quite shallow. Go for the deeper stone as long as it is not so deep that it looks like a golf tee.
3. In the gem trade, a pinkish or orangish red ruby is more valued than a purplish red. Violetish blue sapphire is preferred over greenish blue. Padparadscha must have a color that can be defined as an intense, pink-orange-salmon—something like

Figure 10
Price History Curve of 2-Carat, Cushion or Oval Cut Golden Sapphire (fine gem quality, "bourbon whiskey" color)*
Approximate AGL Grading: 4.0 Color; 70–80 Tone; LI_1–LI_2; Proportion and Finish 4–5; Average Brilliancy 70%–80%.

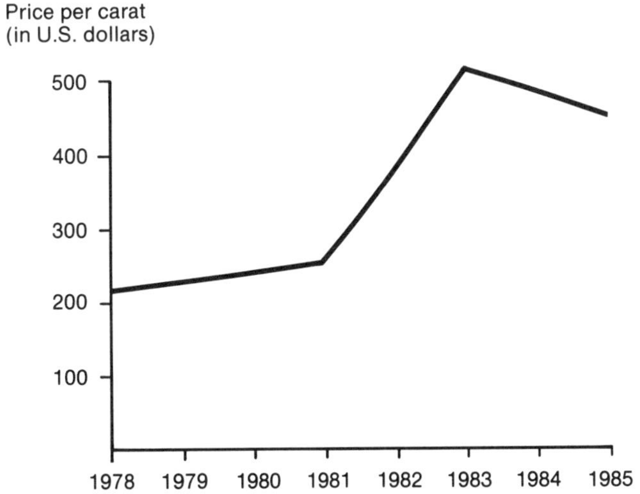

*Curve represents median price range; exceptional stones may be higher; five or more carat stones will be higher.

a Florida sunset. Superb orange sapphire should evoke an urge to squeeze the juice out of it. Avoid those with a brownish cast. Pale, pastel pinks, which are less expensive, should not be brownish. Fine pinks can only be described as "neon": They seem to glow like the pink in a 1960s blacklight poster. Lemon-colored yellows are preferred to those with a brownish cast, and goldens are best when they mimic the color of bourbon whiskey. Green sapphire is usually a muddy green; very little material is close to a pure green. The better green varieties are often in collections and seldom in jewelry. Recently, some unscrupulous companies have been touting green as an outstanding investment. Forget it!

4. Burma rubies are more valued than Thai rubies—not only for their color, but also for their fluorescence. They "glow" in ultraviolet light and tend to stay bright red in all lighting. Thai stones tend to go dark in low-intensity light.
5. Assume that corundum has been heat treated. Most have, al-

Figure 11
Price History Curve of 2-Carat, Cushion or Oval Cut Yellow Sapphire (fine gem quality)*
Approximate AGL Grading: 4.0 Color; 65–70 Tone; FI–LI; Proportion and Finish 4–5; Average Brilliancy 80%–90%.

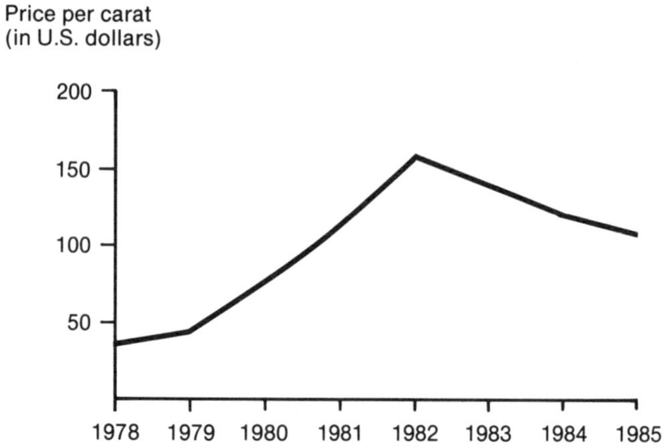

*Curve represents median price range; exceptional stones may be higher; no brown; twenty or more carat stones will be higher.

though those that can be proven natural in color may carry a premium price, particularly in top colors. Heat treatment is not an issue to worry about.

In top-quality corundum obtain a written, money-back guarantee that the stone has not been treated by surface diffusion, color coating, or dying. All are detectable.

A Final Note Commercial or better corundum makes for durable and exciting jewelry. Accent diamonds provide a perfect background to “pop” the color. No matter what your favorite color, corundum can provide the answer to your desire.

DIAMOND

C

Carbon

Common Species
White–Yellow

Also occurs in
Blue, Pink, Grey,
Brown, Purple,
Orange, Black,
Green, and many combinations of the above

Refractive index: 2.417
Specific gravity: 3.52
Hardness: 10
Crystal system: Cubic
Transparent
Perfect cleavage
Toughness: Excellent

Introduction

Diamonds are the stuff of dreams, murder mysteries, poems, and songs. They are the most popular of the "precious" gems. Their popularity, to a great extent, is the product of the kind of marketing that the Fortune 500 companies only hallucinate about in their most euphoric moments. It can be safely assumed that if the DeBeers cartel had not virtually monopolized the rough market and had not had such brilliant advertising, diamonds could easily have been just another gemstone. Unless you really study the history of this ambitious and mysterious company, and understand the full impact of the way people have been socialized to believe that diamonds are—at the least—a necessary, one-time purchase, you might consider their popularity as axiomatic as Newtonian physics. Although gem-quality diamonds are rare, they are more common than any other gem-quality colored stone: They only seem rarer because of the mystique DeBeers has created.

These comments are not intended as criticism of either diamonds or DeBeers. They are simply meant to give you a little perspective. Most people are so used to the positive image created by advertising that they cannot see behind the stage props.

In fact, diamonds were not popular until the 18th century, (although they had been known for centuries). Before the 18th century, diamonds were essentially the playthings of Asian potentates. Part of the reason for their insignificant role as jewelry was that nobody had discovered how to cut them—and an uncut diamond is not that beautiful! Until the 19th century, the only major diamond source was the Golconda mines in India. The long trek to Europe used by diamond traders did not help in obtaining sufficient quantities to create a trading market in the Western countries.

Two events really helped to popularize diamonds. First, during the early part of the 17th century, Cardinal Mazarin helped develop what is now known as the rose cut, a 16-facet diamond. This so improved the appearance of diamonds, they moved from being used solely as a neutral background to enhance a colored gem to being set alone and in groups. With the multiplicity of chandeliers in 18th-century royal courts, this jewelry flashed with light as dancers made their way across ballrooms. By the middle of the 19th century, diamonds were the rage with the wealthy.

The second event that boosted the popularity of diamonds was the massive finds in South Africa at the end of the 19th century. These mines provided more stones, thereby enabling the rising merchant class of Europe and America to enjoy their beauty. Continuing strides in refining the diamond's cut also helped.

Many take the tradition of the diamond engagement ring for granted and believe that it has been a part of civilization since ancient times. (Somebody once asked the author how large the diamond engagement ring was that Anthony gave to Cleopatra!) Little is known by the public about how much money DeBeers has put into creating this tradition. It has been going on for decades in America, but only within the last 20 years has DeBeers made a significant impact on creating positive attitudes toward the diamond engagement ring in places such as Japan and West Germany.

Sources

While some poor-quality gems have virtually no value, *all* diamond has value—either for industrial cutting and abrasive applications or as gemstones. Diamonds are found on almost every continent, yet it takes literally tons of ore, called "blueground," to produce one carat of diamond rough. A piece of rough that can actually be cut to produce a full carat stone is very rare, and of these stones, a diamond that will produce a D color (the whitest possible stone) in a flawless clarity is literally one in millions. In any given year, only a few hundred to a few thousand carats of this quality come from the ground. The majority will cut stones below one carat. When compared to the 20 million plus carats of diamonds mined every year, this finest quality stone seems like one lonely star in the milky way.

As was mentioned previously, the earliest major diamond source was India. But Indian mines have essentially been played out. Currently, the majority of cuttable diamonds come from Africa where many countries produce them. Some of these have mostly industrial-quality material, while others have a good proportion of gem-quality material. Famous sources include South Africa, Zaire, Namibia, and Sierra Leone. Some of the finest natural, fancy, colored diamonds come from Sierra Leone. The premier diamond mine in South Africa produces a good spectrum of rare colors.

Other sources include Brazil, the USSR, and, recently, Australia. Brazilian diamonds can be of good quality but are usually small. Rough from the USSR is often clean, commercial white. The USSR, however, tends to produce round brilliants in quarter- to half-carat sizes. Australia's deposits, although vast, are industrial and contain small brownish cuttable crystals. A few decent stones have been found, but the run-of-the-mine will surely end up in oil drills or will be cut for low-quality jewelry. The United States has a diamond mine in Arkansas, now commercially abandoned, that offers the opportunity for individuals to mine. Guayana produces some fine, natural, fancy colors.

Diamonds are igneous stones that are formed within a volcano. The only types of volcanos that produce diamond are those low in silica and rich in olivine. There are few of these types of geological formations. As a rule, the deeper one mines into a volcanic pipe, the less the yield. Although diamond pipes are a common source on the African continent, many other areas, including Sierra Leone, Namibia, and the Golconda mines of India are alluvial; that is, the diamonds are available in rocky beds or, in the case of Namibia, along the beach. Erosion has carried these stones away from their volcanic source. Alluvial deposits sometimes contain large, fancy colored diamonds.

Price Ranges and Price Histories

Diamond abrasives used in industrial or drilling processes are often priced between $1 and $3 per carat. The finest fancy colors can cost in the five and six figures per carat. The range of possible diamond prices is immense. Even in half carats, prices to the public can be a few hundred dollars to over $3,000. The price of a diamond, with the exception of cut proportions, depends on its rarity in nature. Large stones are rarer and therefore more expensive. Stones with less yellow and few inclusions—also rare—are more expensive. Natural, fancy colors are the rarest of all and can command stellar prices. Figures 12 and 13 show the price histories for a high-quality, commercial, half-carat and one-carat round diamond. Round, brilliant cuts provide the benchmark price for diamonds. Fancy cuts such as pear, marquise, emerald, oval, and heart may be more or less expensive depending of fashion trends, size and quality, or availability of rough.

Sometimes, specific sizes of fancy shapes are more expensive than rounds, while the same cut in a different size may cost less. In 1983, marquise cuts under one carat were often as or more expensive than rounds. At the same time, three- and four-carat, high-color, high-clarity marquises could be purchased for 30 percent less than rounds. In the 1950s and 60s, emerald cuts were the rage. Now they account for only a small percentage of engagement ring sales and are less expensive than rounds. Since the early 1980s, ovals have become more popular. Hearts are always less expensive.

Figure 12
Price History Curve of ½-Carat, Commercial Round Diamonds (H–I color; SI clarity range)*

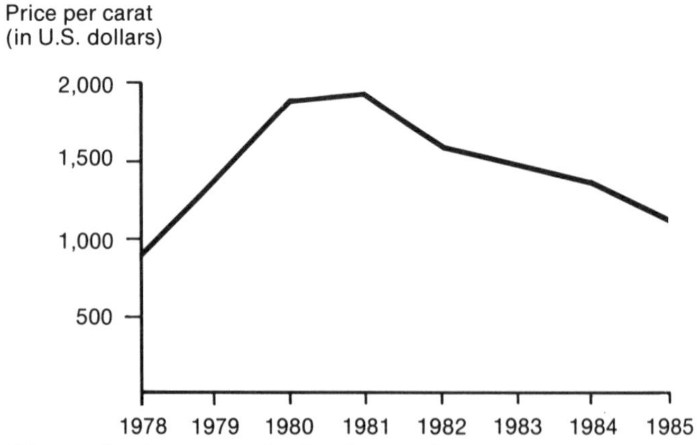

*This graph indicates a trend rather than specific prices.

Figure 13
Price History Curve of 1-Carat, Commercial Round Diamonds (H–I color; SI clarity range)*

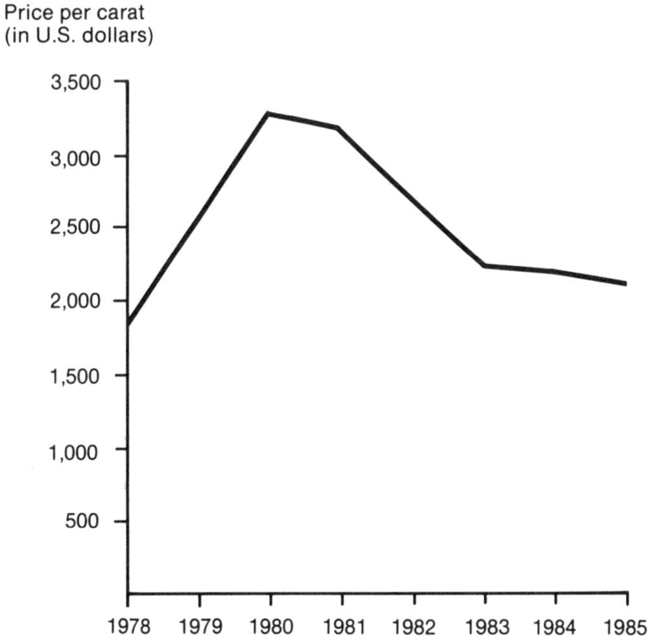

*This graph indicates a trend rather than specific prices.

One of the most interesting developments of the early 1980s was the shortage of commercial-quality fancy shapes (marquise, pear, emerald cut, and so on) in sizes above two carats. While DeBeers reduced sales of large rough to help firm the market after its collapse in 1980, it was found that many two-plus carat fancy shapes had been recut into rounds during the investment boom. That left an even greater shortage than predicted. As a result, large, commercial, fancy shapes were one of the first types of diamonds to firm in price during the recovery. By 1984, locating a three- or four-carat emerald, pear, or marquise had become very difficult.

Consumer Tips

Quality jewelers sell diamonds based on universally accepted grading scales such as the G.I.A. or the American Gem Society (which are almost interchangeable). Many jewelers provide laboratory documents to both protect and assure their clients. The standardization and common acceptance of the G.I.A. grading system is a great benefit to diamond buyers. It allows consumers to comparative shop for price and quality. For any single diamond above $1,000, there is absolutely no excuse for the jeweler not to offer either (*a*) accurate grading using G.I.A. terminology, or (*b*) an actual grading report from the G.I.A. After considerable experience in the retail trade, I can confidently say that there are only two reasons why jewelers will not offer G.I.A. terminology and grading accuracy on major diamonds. The first is that they cannot grade diamonds. The second is that their diamonds are overpriced and they do not want their customers to be able to comparison shop. There is no reason for stores to use their own grading scales. Such scales are misleading and they confuse the public. These firms should always be held in suspicion.

Jewelers use another trick that is more subtle than just classifying diamonds as "AAA" or "Our Premium Quality." These firms have their own grading scale, but they will present it along with the G.I.A.'s to give the appearance of credibility. After close examination, consumers find that the store's color and clarity grades are lumped together to encompass two or even three grades on the G.I.A. scale. One well-known national chain of carriage-trade jewelry stores lumps F and G colors (see Chapter 3 on diamond grading) together. In a survey of the lumped grade that was conducted by the author, it was found that 8 out of 10 stones were Gs; however, the stores were regularly obtaining F prices for these Gs. In a half-carat stone, the difference in price may be only a small percentage, but if multiplied by the number of sales in more than 200 stores, the dollars really add up. Hence, avoid firms that do not use universally accepted grading systems.

Americans have developed an unfortunate bias against natural, fancy colored diamonds. Europeans and Asians are more aware and appreciative of blue, pink, canary, green, and other colors. Pinks, blues, and greens are always astronomical in price; most people cannot afford them. For those in the highest economic and social circles, however, these stones bring more compliments and attention than the white varieties. Other fancy colors are not so expensive such as light fancy yellow and a multitude of browns from cinnamon to coffee to light beige. Greys and blacks are often affordable. Pinks with a light brownish cast are a fraction of the cost of pure pinks and give almost the same look for less money. Oranges are not commonly offered in the United States but they are popular in Africa and South America. A good orange is no more expensive than a decent canary yellow.

The largest and best diamonds are often sold at a lower markup by reputable, "investment" gem companies. Stones under one carat will probably be priced similarly to those of a retail jeweler. The author's research indicates that natural, fancy colored diamonds and large, D and E color, flawless, or internally flawless diamonds are usually less expensive when purchased from these alternative firms than when purchased from the typical retail jeweler—unless that jeweler has a branch specializing in these stones and can therefore offer them at a much lower markup than commercial jewelry. In this case, the two types of firms are competitive.

Fancy colored diamonds can be created by irradiation. These stones are not a problem for the consumer because they can be easily identified. No reputable firm would ever misrepresent them because of ease of detection. They are priced in the lowest yellow color range regardless of their clarity. A small amount is added to the price per carat for the bombardment process. To the trained eye, irradiated diamonds often appear more metallic than the natural colors.

If consumers cannot remember prices, they should not be afraid of taking an accurate diamond price list to a gem dealer. A jeweler should not just accurately represent the carat weight, color, and clarity of a diamond—particularly in half carat plus sizes. The cut proportions are also very important to the value of the stone. In any given size and quality, the difference between a superbly cut and polished diamond and one that is poorly executed may mean a difference in price of 10 percent to 30 percent. Disreputable firms are notorious for selling good color and clarity with a very poor cut and charging a price that would only apply to the better cut. Sales pitches such as "it is a good cut, a beautiful cut," or "it was personally selected by Joe Blow, the owner," are meaningless. The actual cut proportions can be broken down into numerical data. Any diamond that is radically outside of acceptable parameters should be rejected (see Chapter 3 for details on proper cut proportion parameters). Remember, consumer demands for good cut proportions are not a matter of snobbery. A well-made stone is a more beautiful stone.

GARNET

$R_3M_2(SiO_4)_3$

R = Calcium, Magnesium, Ferrous Iron, or Manganese

M = Aluminum, Ferric Iron, or Chromium

Common Species:
- Pyrope, Rhodolite
- Almandite, Andradite
- Grossularite, Spessartite

Refractive index: 1.72–1.875
Specific gravity: 3.47–4.15
Hardness: 6.5–7.5
Crystal system: Cubic
Transparent to opaque
No cleavage
Toughness: Good

Introduction

Most people believe garnet is a red stone. In fact, garnet is a large family of stones related by a similar but not identical chemical composition. The range of possible color is vast, including green to purple, brown to red, and many variations. Garnet can be worn daily.

The mineral garnet occurs commonly in either metamorphic or igneous formations. It is found as microscopic crystals that continue for acres, as well as in areas affected by contact metamorphism. Garnet often grows in solid rock. Garnet is present in many gem deposits in all parts of the world including the diamond mines of Africa and the sapphire deposits of western Montana.

Price Ranges and Price Histories

Only two varieties of garnet are expensive: tsavorite, a green garnet from East Africa, and demantoid, also green, the best of which comes from the Ural mountains.

Fine demantoid is seldom seen today. Nearly 100 percent of all that comes on the market is from estate pieces. Demantoid infrequently occurs in parts of the world other than Russia, but its qualities are not anywhere near the best Russian material. Sizes under one carat are the norm, and any stone of good quality that is over two carats is automatically considered collector or museum quality. A price history of this stone cannot be represented because so few are traded. Greyish green stones under one carat may cost only a few hundred dollars. Stones over two carats in a bright, pure green can run several thousand dollars per carat. Yellow is the major secondary color in the fine greens. Demantoid is easily identified through its physical characteristics and singly refractive nature. Almost every stone contains "horsetail" inclusions. No other stone has quite the same inclusion structure.

Tsavorite is one of the great success stories in gem history. First exported from Kenya and Tanzania in the mid-1970s, it was almost ignored by the gem trade. Today, its supply, while enough to create an international trading market, is much less than its demand. Over the last 10 years, its price has literally exploded. In its finest qualities, tsavorite's color approaches that of the best Colombian emerald and its crystals are cleaner. Geologically, it is rarer than emerald. Figure 14 shows the price history of a one-carat, gem-quality tsavorite.

Any stone over two carats is considered quite rare, particularly in better qualities. Tsavorite can have a yellowish or bluish green

Figure 14
Price History Curve of 1-Carat, Cushion, Oval, or Emerald Cut Tsavorite (fine gem quality)*
Approximate AGL Grading: 3.5 Color; 70–80 Tone; LI; Proportion and Finish 4–5; Average Brilliancy 70%–80%.

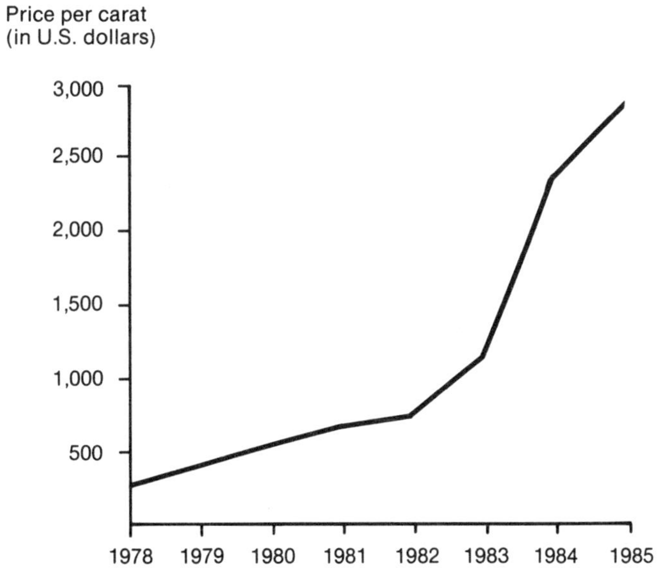

*Curve represents median price range; exceptional stones may be higher.

color, just like emerald. Here again, the trade does not have any particular preference, so long as the green is highly intense. It has been claimed by many that if tsavorite had been discovered before emerald, it would now be the major green gemstone.

The price of tsavorite started accelerating in the late 1970s at which time superb gem stones, although not abundant, were obtainable. Since 1982, the only material to come on the market, either in rough or cut form, has been either light yellow green or so dark in tone that it has the color of evergreen. Unless or until more pockets of rough are found, the finest material appears to have been already absorbed by the market. In the current market it is almost impossible to locate a gem-quality stone over two carats. The only, occasional source in this size is gem-quality stones that are being resold by the original buyers.

Other garnet is inexpensive. Pyrope, also known as Bohemian garnet, is a dark, "blood red" stone that is used as an accent in fine fashion pieces. It is particularly well known for its use in 19th-century, low-priced jewelry. The stones are often so dark as to appear black under low-intensity lighting, but in bright light the crystals are highly transparent and quite beautiful. Pyrope is frequently carried by jewelers and costs just a few dollars per carat. Pawn shops often display old pyrope pieces.

Almandite is also frequently found in jewelry stores. It is a dark red with an orangish or purplish tint. Small, birthstone rings and inexpensive fashion rings often contain this variety. Prices are $20 to $50 per carat.

Rhodolite garnet is a fabulous purple to purple-red stone. Obtainable in large sizes (five carats plus), a well-cut stone positively dances with lucious beauty. The very finest rhodolites may run as high as $150 to $200-per-carat in intense purple-pink-reds. These stones have a slightly lighter tone than is commonly associated with garnet.

Spessartite garnet is the rarest of the reddish variety. In their finest forms they are a pure orange, although more often they will be an orangish red. Pure oranges are very rare and will sell easily to a collector. Most are in the $75 to $200-per-carat range.

Consumer Tips

There are a few caveats that you should keep in mind concerning garnet. First, there is a form of massive, green grossularite garnet that comes from the Transvaal, South Africa. It is often carved or cut en cabochon (nonfaceted, flat bottomed, smooth round top) and is sold under the name "African jade." This material is inexpensive and is not related to the jade family. Jade of the typical green color of this grossularite is much more expensive.

Garnet is seldom misrepresented. Tsavorite has properly been sold as an investment, but only when it is in its finest quality. Commercial tsavorite has a strong jewelry market but is hard to resell for investment purposes. Demantoid is not an investor stone per se; it is a collector stone. Remember, the true collector is not necessarily an investor, and demantoid may be very difficult to resell without the right connections. Although collector and investment markets may cross, they are separate entities.

One of the newest varieties of garnet to come on the market is called "malaya" garnet. It, like tsavorite, comes from East Africa, and is a lovely cinnamon-golden-reddish color. Commercial quality stones are about $20 to $60 per carat while premium gems in large, well-proportioned sizes may reach $200 to $300 per carat. Some disreputable investment firms have tried to push Malaya, which in Masai means "out of the family," as investments. Some of the worst cases of fraud have been perpetrated using this stone, with people being charged $400 to $800 per carat for $20 material. Malaya garnet is not an investment stone, although it makes beautiful jewelry.

JADE

Jade is a Generic Term for Two Stones: Jadeite and Nephrite

Jadeite: $NaAl(SiO_3)_2$

Nephrite: $CaMg_5(OH)_2(Si_4O_{11})_2$

Common Species	Refractive Index:	1.66–1.68 Jadeite
Green, Grey, White		1.606–1.632 Nephrite
Black, Lavender	Specific gravity:	3.34 Jadeite
Reddish, Brown		2.95 Nephrite
Less Common Species	Hardness:	6.5–7 Jadeite
Red, Blue, Purple		6–6.5 Nephrite
Orange, Apricot	Crystal system:	Both monoclinic
		Translucent to opaque
	Hidden cleavage	
	Toughness: Superb	

Introduction

After primitive humans first tied a jade stone to the end of a stick and whacked an animal over the head, the look on their faces was probably akin to that of the same people seeing a solar eclipse: pure amazement. Jade is one of the toughest minerals on earth. Ask any lapidary how many diamond saws must be destroyed just to cut through a boulder. Yet, some of the most exquisite artistic accomplishments have been achieved using this material, with many pieces taking *years* to complete via constant, hand-powered abrasion with a leather thong containing grease and corundum crystals. Even with modern, high-powered, diamond-cutting tools, forming a stone or a carving takes hours, days, or weeks of work.

Unfortunately, only a tiny portion of the population has experienced jade beyond the drab olive green nephrite that is seen in most jewelry stores. The jewelry industry's ignorance about this stone is abysmal. Not one in a hundred dealers can discern an expensive piece from a commercial one, and the typical layperson can look at the most incredible piece of imperial green jadeite without having any idea what price it carries. Jade is most appreciated by Asians. When they see a gem-quality piece, their pupils enlarge and they gasp. The finest green jadeite stones can carry price tags in the tens of thousands of dollars. Exquisite carvings, awash with artistically placed areas of intense color, can cost hundreds of thousands of dollars!

One of the most common myths associated with jade is that it comes from China. Recently, some jade has been discovered in China's western region, but for thousands of years the Chinese imported jade from the Himalayas and later from Burma. Essentially, there is no such thing as "Chinese jade," and any jeweler who claims their jade is from China is either uninformed or pulling somebody's leg.

Perhaps one of the most fascinating aspects of jade is that carved pieces can be selected as gifts to wish the recipient a particular pleasure or attribute. The use of symbolism in Oriental culture is rich and complex. One of the favorite diversions of the nobility was to commission a carving made of specific symbols that carried a special message. The lotus is the symbol of integrity, a chrysanthemum represents wealth, and the bat is the symbol of happiness. Incidentally, the bat symbol is based on a pun in

Matching pair of fine quality Colombian emeralds. These gems have extremely high clarity compared to most emeralds.

Photo courtesy American Gemological Laboratories, New York

Milk and honey, superb chrysoberyl cat's eye. Two light sources have caused the eye to "open." The stone weighs 23 carats and has wonderful translucency. *1.34 carat, square cut Burma ruby. Although the clarity is a borderline MI_2-HI_1, the highly saturated red makes this stone a real prize.* *10 carat oval Thailand ruby. This stone has fine color, but note the dark tone. In low intensity lighting, the red may all but disappear. Compare to colorplate at lower left.*

Photo courtesy American Gemological Laboratories, New York

Photo courtesy American Gemological Laboratories, New York

Photo courtesy American Gemological Laboratories, New York

■ *Imperial green jadeite cabachon. Notice the intensity of the emerald green color and the outstanding translucency.* ■ *Extremely fine, 7 carat Australian opal. The stone has virtually no blank spots, just intense color play.* ■ *80 carat, oval, irradiated brownish/orange topaz.* ■ *Highly popular, inexpensive, treated blue topaz.*

Photo courtesy American Gemological Laboratories, New York

Photo courtesy American Gemological Laboratories, New York

Photo courtesy American Gemological Laboratories, New York

Photo courtesy American Gemological Laboratories, New York

■ *Mint green, 8 carat tourmaline from the state of Maine. This stone is a marvelous example of tourmaline from this locale.* ■ *An outstanding, gem quality tanzanite weighing 50 carats.* ■ *An exciting, deep blue zircon. This color does not exist in nature; the stone has been heat treated. The color change is permanent.*

Photo courtesy American Gemological Laboratories, New York

Photo courtesy American Gemological Laboratories, New York

Photo courtesy American Gemological Laboratories, New York

■ *Magnificent, 15 carat, cushion cut Kashmir sapphire set in a diamond accented ring. The bright blue flashes emanating from the stone are the best kind of blue in a sapphire.* ■ *Intense, treated orange sapphire. Stones of this color are rare.* ■ *Is it an intense purplish/red ruby, or reddish/purple sapphire? Whatever you decide, this stone is stunning!* ■ *Remarkable array of multicolor sapphire rough from Skalkaho Sapphire Ranch near Hamilton, Montana. Note the beautiful pinks and oranges.*

Photo courtesy/American Gemological Laboratories, New York

Photo courtesy American Gemological Laboratories, New York

Photo courtesy American Gemological Laboratories, New York

Photo courtesy of Robert Marcum Bielenberg

■ *The Taylor-Burton diamond. An exceptional pear shape weighing 69 carats.* ■ *A 3 carat, cushion shaped tsavorite (grossularite garnet) from East Africa. Tsavorite in this size is quite rare.* ■ *Finely rendered, antique jadeite vase (probably 19th century). It is surrounded by intense, apple green jadeite jewelry. A vase of this quality is worthy of the best collection.*

Photo courtesy American Gemological Laboratories, New York

Photo courtesy American Gemological Laboratories, New York

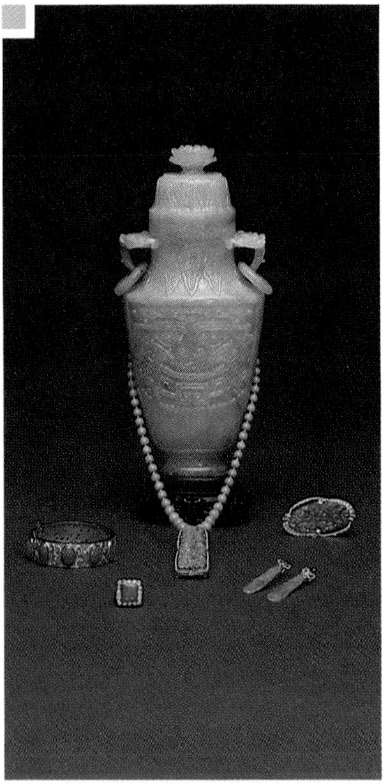

Photo courtesy Jade House, Chicago

■ *A pure, 24K gold Etruscan belt. The craftsmanship is remarkable as each figure was formed by tapping and pushing on the back of the belt. The process is known as repoussé.* ■ *Delicate antique necklace laced with high quality Colombian emeralds.* ■ *A fantasy in gold and blue sapphires. The contemporary, 18K gold peacock necklace is made in Sri Lanka. The gold is hand finished in various textures and granulation.*

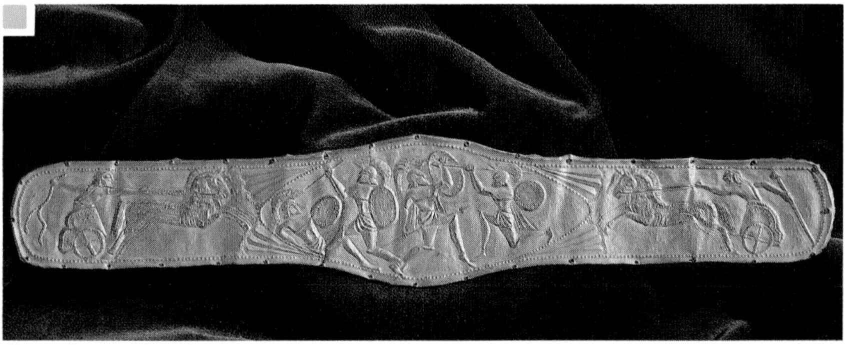

Photo collection of the author

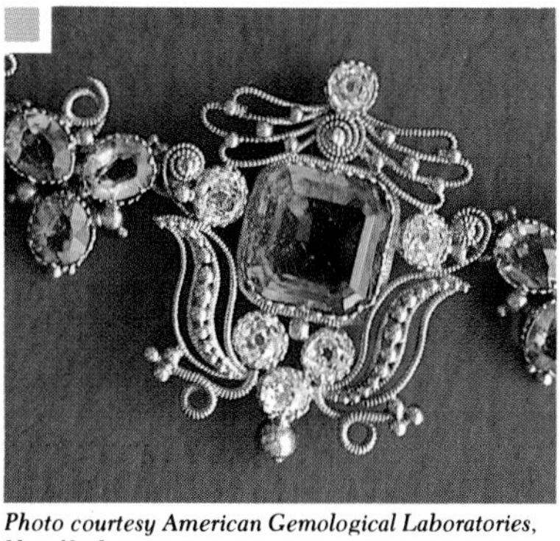

Photo courtesy American Gemological Laboratories, New York

Photo courtesy Sarita's Limited, St. Louis, Missouri

A hand-painted design for an emerald and diamond, wire mount ring. Often, exquisite jewelry is born of such a rendering.

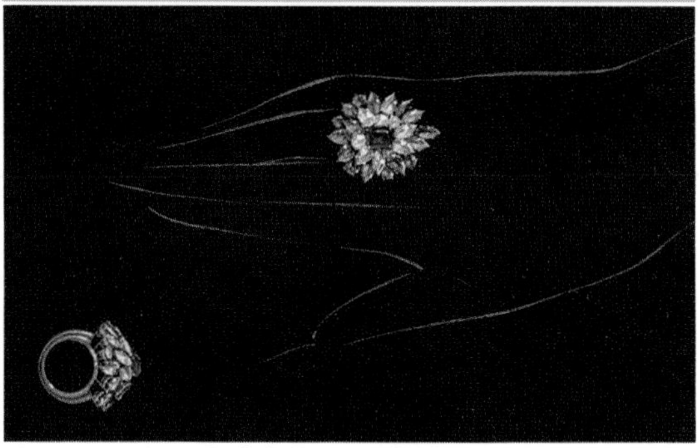

Photo courtesy James Breski & Company, Chicago

the Chinese language; both the word for bat and happiness are the same, but each is said with a different inflection of the voice!

Sources

The premier source for fine jade is Burma. Burma jadeite was not discovered until the late 1700s. It was imported into China by the great and artistic emperor Chien Lung. It is very hard to date jade carvings because Chinese culture encourages veneration and thus copying of past motifs and designs. Jadeite carvings, however, are known not to have existed before the late 1700s. All jade items predating that period were made of nephrite, most of which came from now unknown deposits in the Himalayan mountains.

Before the Burma finds, imperial jade was the purest snow white. Only the emperor could wear this color. The intense green of jadeite eventually supplanted the white, although the white continued as a favorite of royalty. Burma jadeite also occurs in apple green, white, lavender, purple, reddish brown, black, and the rare bright red, apricot, and blue. Jadeite also occurs in combinations of colors, one of the most sought after being pure white laced with emerald green, called by the Chinese "moss entangled in melting snow."

Jadeite is found in Guatemala and Siberia. Most of the olive green nephrite seen in jewelry stores either comes from British Colombia, Canada, or Wyoming. Other important sources include Siberia and Alaska.

Consumer Tips

Color in jadeite and nephrite is graded in reverse. Jadeite is more valuable as the color intensifies; nephrite gains value when it becomes paler. Intense green and lavender are the most expensive commonly seen jadeite, while pure white or "mutton fat," a yellowish white, are the most expensive in nephrite. Both have higher values when the translucency is high. Most gemologists believe that jade is always translucent to opaque; however, very rare forms of transparent jadeite exist and are known by the Chinese as "water jade."

There are two important factors in carvings: the quality of artistic expression and polish, and the use of natural color to bring out the design. Well-made carvings are smooth as silk throughout, even in the grooves and pierce work. Modern carvings often lack this smoothness. The master carvers of jade believe that the carving is already in the stone; it is their job to release it. This attitude is much like Michelangelo's toward blocks of marble. One of the finest examples of this principle that I have ever seen was a piece no larger than the palm of a hand. It represented, in the purest white jadeite, a three-dimensional lotus leaf. Atop this leaf was a brilliant, emerald green grasshopper, also in three dimensions. The intense green stopped at the exact spot where the grasshopper's feet touched the leaf. It was breathtaking.

Jadeite will take a higher polish than nephrite. Many describe highly polished nephrite as appearing slightly "waxy." Despite this, both forms have a similar appearance. The major caveat with jade is that approximately 30 stones can look like it. A common form of fraud is the selling of serpentine, often called "new jade," as jade. In its best forms, serpentine looks like carved vaseline and is about 1/10 to 1/5 the price of good nephrite. Mexican and African jade are not jade but aventurine and grossularite garnet, respectively. So few jewelers know about or carry jade that a collector or consumer has to search it out. Prices in the United States are often lower than prices in the Orient (contrary to most peoples' belief). The two most famous and reputable jade merchants in the United States are Jade House in Chicago and Mannheim Galleries in New Orleans.

OPAL

$SiO_2–nH_2O$

Silica with Water, Usually 3%–10%

Common Species
- White body color
- Grey body color
- Black body color
- Various combinations of play of color or single body color

Refactive index: 1.42–1.47
Specific gravity: Normal 2.15
Hardness: 5.5–6.5
Crystal system: Amorphous
Transparent to opaque
No cleavage
Toughness: Poor to good

Introduction

The first available opal for jewelry came from Hungary; it was not of high quality. The opal finds in Australia opened up European and American eyes to the beauty this gem could exhibit. The play of color is caused by a microscopic diffraction grating that breaks light into spectral colors. Opal is one of the most commonly sold gems in the United States and its value is directly related to the amount and intensity of its play of color. Its devotees number in the tens of thousands; its detractors believe it is bad luck and will break easily.

Opal will break easily in three situations: (*a*) if it is exposed to extremes of heat and cold, which can shatter the stone due to its high water content; (*b*) if it is abusively treated or not maintained properly; and (*c*) if a poor quality piece is hit just right, in which case inclusions (often sand-shot, sand running through the stone) will split apart and cause cracking. Unfortunately, many people do not buy quality opal and therefore suffer this latter misfortune. With a hardness of 5.5 to 6.5, it is almost as hard as steel. Well-formed crystals are durable and often have excellent color play. Some people insist on paying only a few dollars for an opal ring and expect it to make the climb up Mount Everest.

Those who believe opal is unlucky have never asked how the myth originated. It is common knowledge in the gem trade that the rumor was started by a group of disreputable dealers who were trying to corner the market on Lightening Ridge opal in the 19th century. By demeaning opal, they attempted to stop European buyers from competing with them. The myth never fooled the buyers, but some people picked it up and kept it alive through folklore. End of myth!

Opals can exhibit every spectral color. As an investment they are questionable because there is no standardized way to grade them. Fine-quality opal has gone up in price considerably in the last 10 years, but more common opal is subject to a pricing cycle as the stone goes in and out of fashion.

Sources

Opal without any play of color is found abundantly all over the world but has no value. Australia provides the majority of opal seen in jewelry stores: The finest comes from that continent. Australian opal is found under sandy overburdens in desert areas and is softer than the recently discovered Brazilian vein opal. Brazilian opal is much harder, with some stones approaching a hardness of seven, and has no sand-shot, which is common in the

Australian variety. Less expensive Brazilian stones make ideal replacement stones because of their strength.

The most famous Australian find is Lightening Ridge. It produces a deep, black, body color material that has intense color play. Andamooka and Coober Pedy (other Australian mining areas) produce fine white and grey body colors with poor to excellent color play. Brazilian material comes in white to grey body colors. Due to the formation of this material in the veins of solid rock, the color play sometimes looks like small rainbows or striations in the stone. This phenomenon is hardly ever encountered in Australian stones.

Consumer Tips

Successful opal buying involves knowledge of four important areas.

1. Body color is highly significant. The most expensive body color is coal black. Next is grey, from dark to light, and then comes white.
2. The play of color is important no matter what the body color. The most valuable color is red, which is quite rare and very desirable. Next is orange. At the bottom are green, blue, and purple which are more common. The more red and orange, the more expensive the stone. Many consumers like to obtain a stone with a balanced spectral blend, not because it is more expensive but because it goes with everything in their wardrobe. Single-color opals such as Mexican fire opals (a solid orange or red with no play of color) can be attractive, are sometimes faceted, and are not expensive.
3. Opals that display a geometrical pattern are often more valuable. The famous "harlequin" design mimics that of the well-known clown's costume. Pinfire and "flash" opals are desirable. Pinfires have a play of color that manifests itself as tiny points of different colors. Flash opals are quite amazing; few laypeople have seen them. As the stone is moved, a giant, intense flash of color appears and rushes across it, only to disappear again.
4. Opals that are well proportioned and have sufficient thickness to give strength are more valuable than very thin stones. In superb black stones with harlequin, flash, and pinfire patterns, proportion is less important.

Opal that is manufactured synthetically is always represented as such by the fine jeweler. Synthetic opal, to the trained eye, looks a "little too good to be true" and the colors appear different from natural opal. Some opal is fine in quality, but so thin that it is sandwiched between black onyx and a clear quartz or synthetic top. These stones are called doublets and can be very beautiful. They are less expensive than a natural, full-sized stone of the same quality, but should not be looked upon with disdain. Often, they provide an expensive look for just a few dollars. Because of their protective quartz layer, they have excellent durability.

Finally, never put oil or petroleum products on opals. Opals should be stored in distilled water to keep their water content in balance.

PEARLS

$CaCO_3$ + H_2O + Organic Matter
Calcium Carbonate

Common Varieties
- Natural and Cultured
- Spherical or any other shape
- White, Pink, Cream
- Black, Gold, Yellow
- Purple, Blue, Green

Refractive index: 1.53–1.69
Specific gravity: 2.66–2.74
Hardness: 2.5–4
Crystal system: Aggregate
Translucent to opaque
No cleavage
Toughness: Poor to good

Introduction

In the early 1970s, many small pearl wholesalers either declared bankruptcy or moved into selling other stones. Those that hung on have done well in the early 1980s; pearls are once again the fashion rage. The soft fashion look, coupled with the use of vibrant color and the "high fashion" trend set by the Reagan administration have created a demand for pearls not seen since the 1920s. Customers have found over the years that good pearls have become very expensive. Dealers have responded to less princely endowed buyers with inexpensive, free-form, fresh-water jewelry and dyed pearls. These "informal" pearls are being purchased by young and old alike.

Gem-quality pearls come from many species of mollusks. There are several different types of pearl available to the consumer including natural, cultured, and fresh water. Before the early 20th century, all valuable pearls were natural; that is, they were found in salt-water mollusks and were formed by a natural process. Since pearls are created by a nacre coating of an irritant that imbeds itself between the shell and mantle (a membrane that separates the body from the shell), it was found that man could impregnate the mollusks with irritants and the pearls could be harvested. One of the important founders of this process was a Japanese, K. Mikimoto. Since natural pearls are rare, cultured pearls have become the mainstay of the business. Cultured pearls are real pearls, not synthetics; people simply assist nature in their creation. For decades, fresh-water pearls had no value, but the high prices of fine cultured and natural have recently made them very popular.

Sources

Most of the fine natural pearls come from the Persian Gulf area. They are often called "oriental pearls" in the trade. Other natural pearls are harvested off the coast of Sri Lanka, Tahiti, Venezuela, and Australia. The vast majority of cultured pearls come from Japan, and popular, fresh-water pearls are harvested from Lake Biwa in Japan and the United States.

Prices

A pair of small pearl earrings can be purchased for $20 to $30, while some strands of cultured and natural pearls can cost hundreds of thousands of dollars. The price range in pearl is as great as that of diamond. Each pearl is unique and one of the main labor costs is the tedious and time consuming matching that is done by pearl jewelry manufacturers. Of all pearl shapes, round is the most expensive; baroque (oddly shaped) are usually less expensive. The seeds used in cultured pearl automatically form a round or close to round shape. Natural pearls are seldom round because the irritants that start them are seldom round. In identical quality, round, natural pearls are tremendously expensive compared to round, cultured pearls because of the rarity factor. Visually, there is no difference between the two. Naturally colored pearls are many times more expensive than those that are dyed. Some of the most expensive pearls are natural golden or black rounds that are more than 15 millimeters in diameter. These may cost tens of thousands of dollars each!

Consumer Tips

There are six areas to consider when buying pearls. Each has a significant impact on the price. Lower-priced pearls will lack quality in some or all of these areas, but prices to the public for the same grade vary considerably. Pearls are very difficult to grade—even for professionals; therefore, some jewelers will take advantage of this "blind item." In whatever price range, a comparison of the following factors will allow you to get the best for your money.

Body Color Many people want pink; however, their price often pushes buyers to the less expensive whites and creams. South Americans often like creams or expensive yellows. Whatever the pearl's body color, it should be even throughout; pearls with uneven colors are not as valuable.

Shape Perfect rounds are the most expensive. Strands are graded and valued from high to low in this order: all round, almost all round, off-round, semibaroque, and baroque.

Matching Strands of pearls that are well matched for body color are more valuable than those that are not. Inexpensive strands will contain lower-quality body colors with very loosely color-matched pearls. In the finest strands, each pearl is virtually identical in body color.

Luster Pearls with thick nacres and even surfaces will have a higher luster than those without. Both of the above attributes, which create higher luster are desirable. Luster is rated (in descending order) from bright through high to medium to dull.

Nacre Thickness The longer a pearl is in the making, the thicker the nacre will be. Thick nacres create high luster and give the best pearls their appealing "glow." Thin-nacred pearls are inexpensive and dull.

Blemishes Pearls without blemishes are more expensive. Most have, at the least, very small blemishes. Perfectly smooth pearls are probably imitations—until proven otherwise. Bad blemishes include ridges, pits, bumps, and scratches that can be easily seen with the naked eye. These significantly lower the value of the pearl.

There are many pearl imitations including cheap plastic spheres with opalescent paint. Some imitations are more expensive and look very much like fine pearls. There is no chance of these being sold as real by reputable jewelers. Pearls require extra care. (Please refer to Appendix A.)

SPINEL

$MgA_{12}O_4$

Double Oxide of Magnesium and Aluminum

Common Species
- Red, Orange, Pink
- Purple, Green
- Blue, White, Brown
- May appear in almost any color

Refractive index: 1.718
Specific gravity: 3.73
Hardness: 8
Crystal system: Cubic
Transparent to opaque
No cleavage
Toughness: Good to excellent

Introduction

Most laypeople are not familiar with natural spinel, and if they are, they often associate it with a cheap synthetic stone. This situation is not their fault. Many jewelers wear blinders and see only diamond, ruby, sapphire, and emerald: They like to sell names, not stones. This is unfortunate because spinel is one of the most visually exciting of all gems. It is as hard as aquamarine, it sparkles beautifully when well cut, and it displays colors that are as rich as any that can be imagined. The red variety is rarer than ruby, yet in its finest qualities it is often one fifth the price of an equally fine ruby. Fine pinks and oranges compete favorably with the best Burma pink sapphires and flame-colored topaz.

Two of the most famous "rubies," the Black Prince and Timur—both in the crown jewels of England—are actually fine Burma spinels. Despite its obvious beauty, spinel has received a small nod of approval from the gem community and consumers alike only in the last few years. For a stone that has been mined for 2,000 years, it has certainly been treated as an orphan—and with no good reason.

Sources

Currently, most spinel comes from Burma and Sri Lanka. Sri Lankan stones are primarily commercial in quality, although occasional gems surface. While Burma produces a multitude of qualities, the best spinel comes from this country. It has been estimated that top-quality red spinel in one-carat plus sizes is approximately 200 times rarer than the best ruby.

Price Ranges and Price Histories

Obtaining commercial-quality blues, pinks, and brownish oranges is not difficult and they are inexpensive. Prices for pleasant stones are in the $100- to $300-per-carat range in two-carat sizes. Commercial reds that are brownish or purplish red with darker tones are slightly more expensive, particularly those over two carats. The acquisition of bright, pure oranges, so-called "day-glow" pinks, and intense reds is difficult in the extreme. Even with the relatively small increase in demand over the last few years, prices for these stones have skyrocketed. Figures 15, 16, and 17 show price histories for two-carat, gem-quality red, pink, and orange spinel.

Most gem colors come in subcarat sizes. Anything over two carats in this quality is very scarce. If ordering a three- to four-carat gem red, you may have to wait for months before it appears. Prices are inflexible. As an investment, the finest material has proven to be a marvelous capital gains vehicle. At this level of quality, resale is easy compared to many other stones, although those that are slightly less than premium may have some difficulty being absorbed by the market. The quality level cutoff point for what are considered investment quality and commercial quality is very sharp. The fact that gem spinel has continued to rise in price despite the recession of the early 1980s gives it an edge over other stones. Given its geological rarity, the price has excellent upside potential, albeit the stone will never be as popular as ruby.

Figure 15
Price History Curve of 2-Carat, Cushion or Oval Cut Red Spinel (fine gem quality)*
Approximate AGL Grading: 4.0 Color; 70–80 Tone; LI_2; Proportion and Finish 4–5; Average Brilliancy 70%–80%.

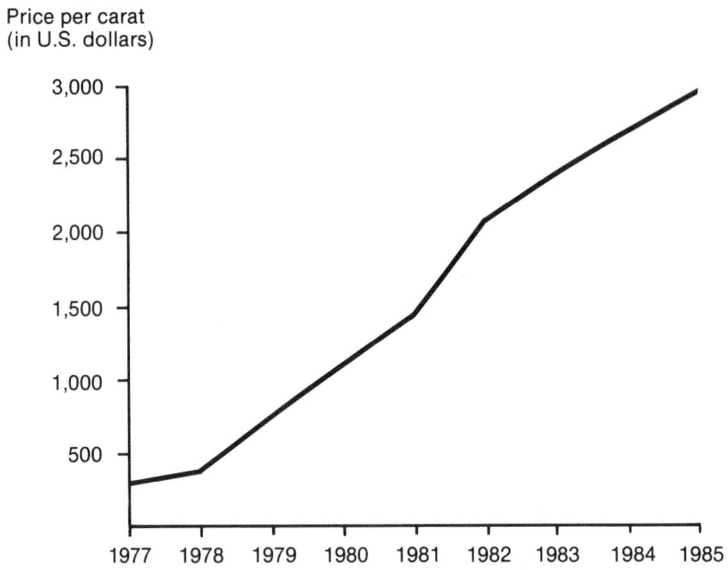

*Curve represents median price range; exceptional stones will be higher; brownish reds will be lower.

Consumer Tips

There are three caveats when purchasing any fine spinel:

1. Spinel rough is often flat. Stones may have good color and tone, but they are so shallow that when they are cut a large window will exist. Their appearance can be improved through proper mounting but not their quality. Properly cut stones with excellent brilliancy are very dear.
2. In a fine red, avoid an overly dark or a strong brownish tint. The slightest brown can reduce the value dramatically. Spinel, in particular, can contain much brown and grey—which deadens its color. The finest red mimics gem rubies; gem pinks resemble Burma pink sapphires.
3. Because of their high specific gravity, one-carat spinels often look small. Two carats is the normal trading size for pinks,

Figure 16
Price History Curve of 2-Carat, Cushion or Oval Cut Pink Spinel (fine gem quality)*
Approximate AGL Grading: 4.0 Color; 70–80 Tone; LI_2; Proportion and Finish 4–5; Average Brilliancy 70%–80%.

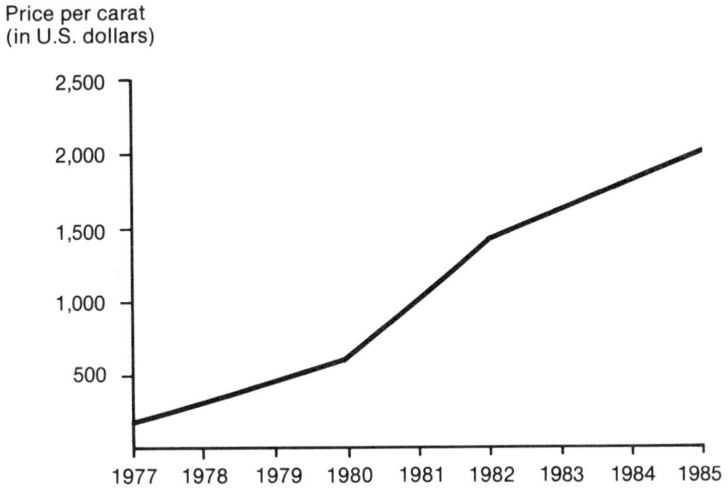

*Curve represents median price range; exceptional stones will be higher; no brown.

oranges, and blues, although the higher the color, the less weight is a consideration. Superb reds are acceptable in one-carat sizes but for the serious collector and investor, a two-carat or larger stone will command a premium price and buying audience at a later date.

A Final Note Synthetic spinel has been produced since the early part of the 20th century. It comes in many colors and is used in inexpensive costume and birthstone jewelry. It is flawless and cut with the precision of fine diamonds. Natural spinel is cut in mixed ovals and cushions and often has some asymmetry. Likewise, natural stones often have inclusions. To the trained eye, there is a world of difference between the two.

Figure 17
Price History Curve of 2-Carat, Cushion or Oval Cut Orange Spinel (fine gem quality)*
Approximate AGL Grading: 4.0 Color; 70–80 Tone; LI_2; Proportion and Finish 4–5; Average Brilliancy 70%–80%.

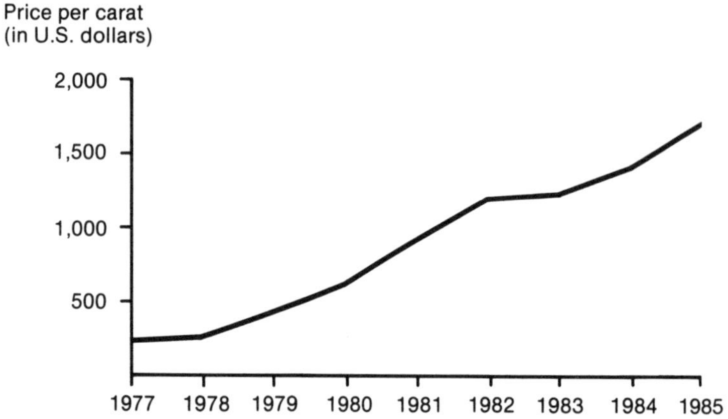

*Curve represents median price range; exceptional stones will be higher; brownish orange will be lower.

TOPAZ

$Al(F, OH)_2SiO_4$

Fluorosilicate of Aluminum

Common Species	
Yellow, Brown, Blue	Refractive index: 1.619–1.627
White, Pink, Red	Specific gravity: 2.72
Violet, Orange	Hardness: 8
	Crystal system: Hexagonal
	Transparent to opaque
	Perfect cleavage
	Toughness: Fair to good

Introduction

The velvety sparkle and rich colors of topaz are unique. Topaz enjoys a steady following with customers. Because of its perfect cleavage, stones must be worn with some care.

Collectors enjoy topaz because of its incredible diversity of color. Topaz suites, which look like miniature rainbows of subtly shifting color, are a delight and, as a collection, can carry a hefty price. As an investment, this stone, for all its desirable characteristics, has been a dismal failure. There are two reasons for this:

1. Red, pink and violet are very rare, but commercial qualities in the yellow, orange, and brown tints are obtainable in large quantities. During the early 1980s, while most other miners slowed production, the Brazilians continued at breakneck speed. The market was flooded and prices collapsed. Only in 1984 was there sufficient absorption of this material to firm prices. The Brazilian miners were caught in a monetary trap. The cruziero was inflating so badly that the only reliable way of maintaining monetary value was to sell stones for hard currency, particularly U.S. dollars. This need created a never-ending supply and accompanying downward price spiral, causing prices for the best topaz to collapse along with the commercial goods.
2. It became apparent in the early 1980s that pink, red, and violet stones were not only being heat treated but were also being irradiated. In some cases the color remained stable; in others strong colors paled after a few days in sunlight. Permanent treatments of gemstones are common and accepted, but those resulting in instability of color are not. This situation also caused prices to tumble. Since that time, it has become common trade practice to buy topaz on a contingency basis. Half of a gem is covered with masking tape and the stone is then placed in the sun. If, after a specified time, it does not fade, the purchase is consummated. You can request the same process when buying an expensive stone.

Sources

Topaz occurs widely, but gem quality comes from only a few places. Minas Gerais, Brazil, is the main source for gem and cutting quality. Blue, white, and green stones come from Sri Lanka. Other sources include the Pala region of California, Burma, Africa, Madagascar, and Australia. Fine blues were once associated with the Ural mountains.

The search for topaz in Brazil is most interesting. Not only are crystals found in pegmatite cavities, but water action has eroded many stones into the area's rivers. As with the streams below the Colombian emerald deposits, hundreds of peasants work these rivers in hopes of finding some material. The mining of the pegmatite cavities is tedious. Blasting is avoided to protect against breakage of large, expensive crystals, so much hand labor is used. It is a hot, dirty, and often disappointing job.

Price Ranges and Price Histories

Yellow or yellowish brown topaz is very common. Jewelry of this material may cost less than $200. Blue topaz is exceedingly popular and has almost replaced aquamarine because of both its beauty and its inexpensive price per carat. The finest blues often retail in the $40- to $100-per-carat range. Much of this material can be purchased directly from Brazilian dealers for $10 to $15 per carat, but the public will balk at buying such a beautiful stone at $20 to $30 per carat. Interestingly, the higher markups have made blue topaz more desirable to most consumers. Those who have tried to offer the stone at a 100 percent markup, however, are often unsuccessful because the public doubts that it is the same material. All intense blue topaz has been heat treated and probably irradiated. Clear or white topaz has little jewelry use.

Imperial topaz is the term used by most dealers to describe an intense brownish-orangish red stone. Topaz of this quality is often the best that consumers will see in a jewelry store. Prices range from $300 to $1,000 per carat. The rarest colors are the pure reds, intense pinks, and violets. Wholesale prices of these stones range from $800 to $1,500 per carat.

Topaz price histories can only be tracked generally. Their qualities can be accurately described on a laboratory certificate, but they have not been traded with such documents in volume. Therefore, Figure 18 shows a median trend history for five-carat, imperial topaz. This graph in particular represents *trends* rather than specific prices.

Consumer Tips

Topaz is available in high clarities. A stone can easily be free of inclusions or almost free of them. Highly included material is not acceptable. Commercial quality yellow-browns are often sold in large parcels at the wholesale level. The color and clarity are uniform for each parcel; however, there is often a difference in

Figure 18
Price History Curve of 5-Carat, Oval Cut Imperial Topaz (fine gem quality)*
Red/Orange/Pink Color; 70–80 Tone; LI_2.

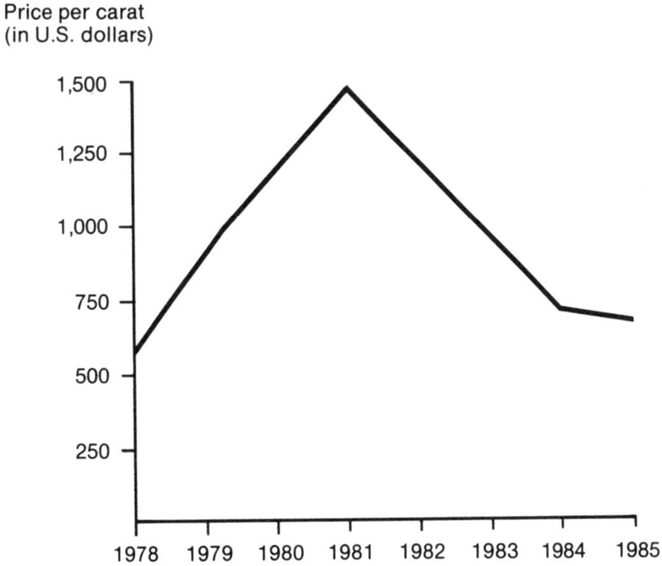

*Curve represents median price range; exceptional stones will be higher.

cut quality. Fine cuts can be had in less expensive stones, but you do have to look for them.

Large topaz is often well cut. The pegmatite formation of crystals allows for superb dimensions. Seeing many stones will give you a better grasp of what constitutes gem color. Recently, a beautiful violetish pink topaz was found in Pakistan. This material is often not treated. While it lacks the intensity of Brazilian material, its price is much lower, $300 to $500 per carat.

TOURMALINE

A Highly Complex Boron-Aluminum Silicate

Common Species
Green, Blue, Pink
Red and most other colors

Refractive index: 1.624–1.644
Specific gravity: 3.06
Hardness: 7–7.5
Crystal system: Hexagonal
Transparent to opaque
No cleavage
Toughness: Good

Introduction

Ten years ago, most customers would not have known what tourmaline was or have been able to appreciate its beauty. Tourmaline is derived from the Sri Lankan word *Turmali* meaning "mixed precious stones." Ruskin once described the stone: "It is more like an alchemist's formula than a respectable mineral." Despite his disparaging remarks concerning its chemical composition, this stone has grown in popularity by leaps and bounds, particularly in the green varieties.

The true lover of tourmaline, however, is not so much taken with the greens as the vibrant blues and reds. They are known as indicolite and rubellite, respectively. Also greatly admired is a specific green called chrome tourmaline.

Tourmaline is one of the best stones for jewelry. It is hard, has good toughness, no cleavage, and comes in clean, well-cut crystals. Its color variations allow customers to indulge their fantasies. The best varieties are under $1,000 per carat, but most tourmaline is under $200 per carat.

Sources

Again the fountain of gems—Brazil—is a key provider of tourmaline. Sri Lanka is an important source, as well as California. Other sources include the state of Maine, Burma, Madagascar, and Siberia.

Tourmaline is formed under many conditions but the most important, which produces gem-cutting material, is the pegmatite dike. In these formations, large crystals occur some of which are bi- or multicolored.

Price Ranges and Price Histories

As a mineral, tourmaline is not particularly rare. Cuttable material is scarce, particularly in intense spectral colors. Brown and black (schorl) material are common in cuttable quality but have no commercial market. There has been a recent increase in the collecting of tourmaline mineral specimens by the public at large. Some specimens are incredibly beautiful and make fascinating desk or shelf decorations.

Common green tourmaline costs between $50 and $150 per

carat in two-carat plus sizes. Chrome tourmaline, which is very hard to find, often runs into the $200- and $300-per-carat range for exceptional stones. Indicolite is in the $100- to $200-per-carat range in better qualities, although superb museum specimens have been known to cost several hundred dollars per carat. Rubellite is the most expensive: When bright red to reddish purple and having few inclusions, $400 to $700 per carat is not unheard of in 10-carat plus sizes. Pink tourmaline is priced much like the common greens.

Green and blue tourmaline occur in very clean crystals. Red and pink seldom do. They typically have inclusions that appear as little needles running through the stone. Because of this, knowledgeable consumers look for specimens whose parallel needle inclusions run perpendicular to the top of the stone, thus giving the visual appearance of much cleaner material.

In November 1981, there was a fabulous find of gem-quality rubellite in Ouro Fino, Brazil. As a group, these were the best crystals ever discovered. There were only 5,100 carats in the deposit. Eighty-five percent cut into stones below two carats, and only an aggregate of 250 carats were over 10 carats each. Rick Harig, a Chicago dealer and one of only a few people originally involved with this find, says the pocket of delectable crystals is totally played out and only a few remaining stones are available: Most are in collections.

Consumer Tips

Because of the nature of tourmaline's crystallization, stones with beautiful cut proportions can be obtained. Shallow stones are simply unacceptable. Other than the rubellite and pink varieties, accepting highly included stones is a mistake. As an investment, stones other than museum quality indicolite and Ouro Fino rubellite are highly questionable. Chrome tourmaline is an interesting speculation.

When buying common green tourmaline, do not accept too dark a stone. Lighter, brighter material is available for the same or a slightly higher price. Searching will be well worth your patience in terms of both appearance and beauty. Indicolite is often so dark, the blue is almost impossible to see. The price will jump quickly on a stone that does not possess this problem. The finest stones have a blue comparable to gem aquamarine. Be careful of jewelers representing commercial-quality, bluish green tourmaline as indicolite. Bluish green stones are very inexpensive, often below $50 per carat.

No rubellite is a pure red, but the higher the red content the better. Pink tourmaline is more expensive in intense colors than in pale hues.

ZOISITE

$Ca_2Al_3Si_3O_{13}$

Calcium Aluminum Silicate

Common Species	
Tanzanite (blue)	Refractive index: 1.691–1.704
	Specific gravity: 3.45
	Hardness: 6–7
	Crystal system: Orthorhombic
	Transparent to translucent
	Perfect cleavage
	Toughness: Fair

Introduction

A gem-quality tanzanite is one of the visual wonders of the world. Its color is reminiscent of the incredibly intense sky of Van Gogh's *Starry Night.* So beautiful is this stone, it is hard to remember that virtually every piece that comes out of the ground is a drab brownish color. All tanzanite is heat treated and the process is permanent.

First introduced to the world by Tiffany & Company in the 1960s, top-quality stones have risen from about $60 per carat to over $2,000 per carat in a little over 20 years. Its color is unique—not blue like sapphire and not purple like amethyst, but a velvety combination of both.

Tanzanite's only fault is its relative softness and perfect cleavage. Stones over 10 carats are often mounted in necklaces rather than rings. In the fashion world, tanzanite has been as hot as its price rise.

Sources

Tanzanite, as one might guess, comes from Tanzania. There is no other source in the world. The area from which it originates is small. The supply is limited, yet there appears to be enough to satisfy part of the world's appetite. Supplies of this material follow a strange and unpredictable cycle. For months, finding a superb, large stone may be extremely difficult. Then, suddenly, the market will be flooded. This feast and famine situation is primarily caused by the Tanzanian government, which behaves capriciously about those to whom they issue export licenses.

Price Ranges and Price History

Given that there is only one source for tanzanite, to say that it is rare is a gross understatement—particularly when it is being mined in a country whose political climate doesn't encourage free enterprise. Figure 19 shows the price history of 10-carat, gem-

Figure 19
Price History Curve of 10-Carat, Cushion, Oval, or Emerald Cut Tanzanite (fine gem quality)*
Blue/Purple Color (no Grey); 80–85 Tone; LI_1–LI_2.

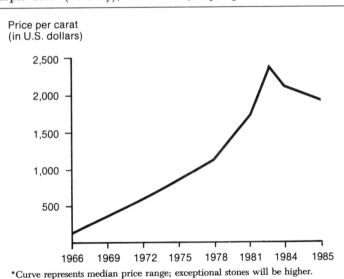

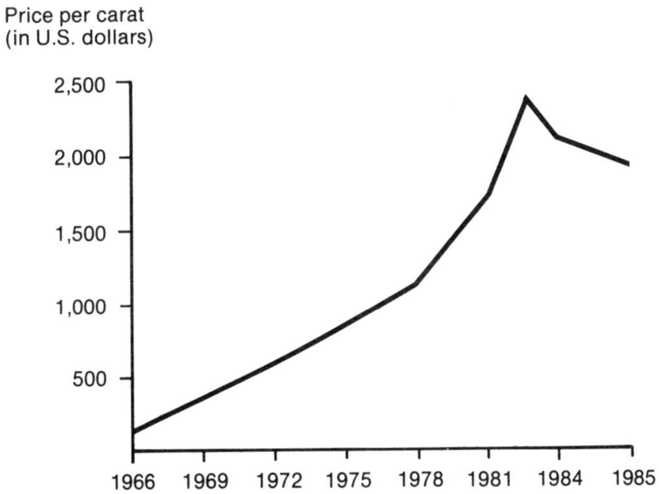

*Curve represents median price range; exceptional stones will be higher.

quality tanzanite. Commercial-quality stones in the two-to-five-carat range run much less: $100 to $500 per carat.

Consumer Tips

In fine tanzanite, it is important to buy a supersaturated, purplish blue color. A few gem dealers prefer stones that are almost pure blue, but tanzanite is not to be equated with sapphire. It is a stone with particular characteristics. Do not turn it into what it is not.

Fortunately, tanzanite crystallizes cleanly, so any stone with obvious inclusions should be priced at a fraction of one that is eye clean. Crystals form nicely so that superior cuts can be extracted. Do not accept stones with obvious shallowness.

Tanzanite that is mounted in jewelry should be treated with respect. The beauty and pleasure that it gives are worth the care. Large stones should be in necklaces, not rings. Rings should be made to provide more than normal protection for the gem.

3 Basics of Diamond Grading

The relative abundance of diamond, the fact that it usually exhibits only yellow, and the standardized way in which it is cut have created a grading methodology that is comfortably precise. The grading of all gemstones is a type of notation that allows people to instantly recognize those stones that are rarer than others. Rarer stones tend to be more beautiful, and beauty is what people desire.

To appreciate the grading of diamonds, it is best to look at them as if they were colored stones. Most diamonds contain some amount of yellow. The main conceptual difference between color grading in other stones and in diamonds is that diamonds are more valuable when they have less color; colored gems are more valuable when the color is more intense. Fancy colored diamonds are an exception to the rule; they are more valuable when the color is intense. All other grading factors have similar importance in both kinds of diamond.

Color, clarity, carat weight, and cut proportions (the four Cs) are stressed when diamond is graded. These four parameters are the main components of grading. It is not enough to simply know what they are. You should also know the method by which they are determined and their importance in ascertaining the price of a diamond. Many retail jewelers and investment companies talk about these parameters as if they can be as accurately measured as time in an atomic clock. Actually, the determination of color is made with a slight amount of tolerance for error. Clarity grading is more a matter of experience than of following fixed and precise parameters. Only cut proportions and carat weight can be measured scientifically; yet, there are those in the trade who legitimately disagree with what is generally accepted as good cut proportions. Finally, other factors, which are not directly addressed in the four Cs, can profoundly affect price including fluorescence, symmetry, and polish.

Color Grading in Diamonds

Other than in the case of the natural fancy colors, color grading is a determination of the lack of yellow in a diamond. On the surface it is a simple concept; in reality, it is not. Many people believe that the color grades they get from jewelry stores are exact, that each color fits within a single point, with no variation, on a line that runs from no yellow (pure white) to much yellow. The reality is that each color grade encompasses a range of yellow. For example, the color G is considered to be in the near colorless range. Yet, a stone can be a high G or close to an F; it can be in the middle of the range; or it can be a low G, close to an H.

The system of using alphabetical letters to indicate the level of yellow in a diamond was invented by the Gemological Institute of America (GIA) and is a highly respected and reproducible grading methodology. For all intents and purposes, it is exact. There are, however, specific situations in which the system cannot meet the grading demands that are put upon it. This does not mean it is a bad system; on the contrary, it would be hard to come up with a better one. The only point to be made here is this: Despite what any company says about diamond color grading, it is not quite as precise as they would have the consumer believe.

The GIA grading system for diamonds is virtually universal; most other reputable grading systems are variations of it. The color-grading system is shown in Figure 20. The GIA chose to

Figure 20
GIA (Gemological Institute of America) Color Grading Scale

	Colorless			Near colorless				Faint yellow			Very light yellow					Light yellow								Yellow		
GIA	D	E	F	G	H	I	J	K	L	M	N	O	P	Q	R	S	T	U	V	W	X	Y	Z	Fancy light	Fancy	Fancy intense

make D color the highest. They felt, with justification, that if the highest color grade for diamond was an A, the system would be abused by unethical jewelers. A D color does not sound impressive unless the system is explained by a knowledgeable diamond salesperson.

The actual operational scale looks like this:

__ d color __ E __ e color __ F __ f color __ G __ g color

When diamonds are color graded, they are compared to pregraded, master stones (the capital letters on the scale). The highest master stone is an E. *Any diamond that falls on or above the E master is a D color.* In other words, there is no D master grading stone. Any stone that falls on or above the F master is an E color. And so on. The difference between each master is slight. Without masters, a loose diamond can only be approximated within two grades. A mounted stone can only be approximated within three grades—with or without masters.

A diamond that falls directly on a master is called a pivotal or transitional stone. When such a stone must be graded, the system has a demand placed upon it that it cannot always handle. The weak link is in the grader, however, and not in the master stones or in the concept of the grading methodology. Technically, if a diamond falls on an E master, it is a D color, although that diamond may be seen as right on or just below the master. Trained, experienced professionals will make few mistakes, but those without intensive training or a natural talent for discerning small variations in color can make an error.

In a one-carat diamond, the difference in price between a K and L color is slight. The difference between a D and E or an E and F, however, can be immense. In finely colored diamonds above one carat, it doesn't hurt to have the stone graded by the GIA. Even if you have to pay the cost of grading, it may be well worth it. For example, in late 1979 the difference in price between a flawless D and an E, one-carat diamond was as much as $30,000!

The important thing in diamond color grading is reproducibility. Reproducibility is the ability of a laboratory to consistently derive the same color grade for a diamond that is resubmitted for grading without the lab knowing it has graded the stone previously. Diamond color grading is much simpler than colored stone grading; therefore, labs such as the GIA have outstandingly high reproducibility.

Even so, they are not perfect. In a highly publicized story in the early 1980s, a well-known department store sold a D color diamond with a GIA diamond-grading report. Upon obtaining a regrading at a later date, the GIA stated it was an E. Ultimately, the department store was forced by the courts to reimburse the buyer for the amount that would have been the price difference between a D and an E at the time of sale. *No laboratory will accept any liability for their grading documents or for what is done with them after they leave the laboratory.* This has been confirmed by the courts and disclaimers appear on every legitimate laboratory document. Whether this should or should not be the case is not open to debate: It is fact.

The choice of color in a diamond purchase depends on (*a*) how much money is to be spent, and (*b*) what purpose the diamond is to serve. Stones used for investment purposes are usually within the top three color grades. The high volatility and cyclical pricing nature of these stones allow for big profits (or losses) over time. Fine jewelry stores normally stock F to J. Mass produced, low-priced jewelry often runs from I on down. The only time colors lower than L are considered of much importance is when stones are three carats and larger. Color grades in the white to yellow varieties can be grouped very generally according to their uses in the gem trade. These listings are not definitive but should be used as guidelines.

1. O to Z Color: Low color and quality. Hard to resell and commonly used in inexpensive jewelry. Moderate to good jewelry demand base. Three-carat plus stones do have a reasonably good market in engagement rings.
2. J to N Color: Middle commercial quality used by many stores, particularly those whose marketing niche focuses on low- to middle-class buyers. Hard to resell unless stone is large. Excellent jewelry demand and strong price support base.
3. G to I Color: Upper commercial grade that is normally stocked by carriage-trade jewelry stores for engagement rings and fine jewelry. Not too difficult to resell in sizes over one carat in a steady to strong market. Good to excellent jewelry demand and relatively strong price support base.

4. D to F Color: Premium colors used in only the most superlative jewelry. Prices can be volatile. Many are used as inflation hedges and long-term stores of value. Easy to resell during inflation; can be virtually impossible to resell in a deflationary market. Very little jewelry demand base.

Fancy colored diamonds are the connoisseur's choice. Most have excellent resale potential except for the more common brownish, grey, black, and dirty or pale green varieties. Pinks, blues, lemon yellows, purples, intense greens, and combinations of pink-orange, orange-purple are premium stones. Prices of these varieties tend to accelerate quickly during an inflationary period and flatten in a deflation. Downward pressure only occurs in a severe recession or depression. The public usually buys one-carat and above stones. Dealers have an active subcarat market among themselves.

The natural, fancy colors are graded according to their intensity and prices will differ tremendously between light, fancy and intense, fancy. Light, fancy yellows are common, while intense lemon yellows (canaries) can carry a high premium. Pinks with the slightest brown tint are far less valuable than pure pastel or hot pink stones.

Clarity Grading

Diamonds form in the earth many miles below the surface. They grow in solid or liquid rock under thousands of tons of pressure and temperatures in the thousands of degrees centigrade. The only reason diamonds do not burn in this environment is because there is no oxygen to create combustion. It is very difficult for nature to provide a diamond crystal with perfectly arranged carbon atoms. A multitude of things are often embedded within the crystal. Many inclusions are created by distortions, reorientations of growth, and imperfections in the diamond's crystal structure. One of the most common misconceptions concerning inclusions involves people calling them flaws. The term *flaw* refers only to inclusions that are so serious they materially endanger the crystal's stability. Most inclusions do not affect the strength of the stone, and those found in better qualities are not visible to the naked eye.

The types of inclusions can range from tiny, pinpoint black spots, to fractures caused by blows to the diamond, to included crystals consisting of diamond and other minerals. Others may be clouds of white pinpoints, feathers, and cleavages. A VS or SI stone is usually more desirable if the inclusions are either (*a*) near the edge (girdle) of the stone as opposed to near the center (table), or (*b*) on the bottom of the stone (pavilion) and not visible through the top (crown). White inclusions are preferred over dark inclusions.

Figures 21 and 22 show the GIA clarity grading system and examples of the types and amounts of inclusions that are accepted for each grade. Every diamond is unique; therefore, these examples are only indicators or guides. Again, each clarity grade is a range of possible combinations and permutations, but no master grading stones are used for reference. Clarity grading must be learned by experience. Strangely, there are fewer debates concerning clarity grading in the trade than there are for color grading although some laboratories have given a few diamonds pivotal or transitional grades. Technically, no inclusions are visible to the naked eye in a diamond until the stone reaches an I_1 clarity grade. Grading is always done with 10-power magnification or greater. Most gemologists use a binocular microscope, magnify the stone 20 or 30 times, locate the inclusions, and then zoom down to 10 power. Inclusions that can still be seen determine the clarity grade. This process makes grading easier and more accurate.

Certain clarity grades are typically found in stones that have specific uses. Again, as with color, the following are only indicators and not ironclad rules.

1. Flawless: Free of inclusions under 10 power. No problems with the surface of the stone including polishing marks, pits, nicks, extra facets, and so on. Almost never used in jewelry. Collector and investor item exclusively.
2. Internally Flawless: Free of inclusions under 10 power but may contain surface blemishes or polishing marks. Seldom used in jewelry although sometimes found in fine pieces.
3. VVS_1 and VVS_2: Very, very slightly imperfect (two levels). Only the smallest inclusions in very small numbers are allowed. A VVS stone is sometimes recut to a flawless or internally flawless stone. To do this the inclusions have to be very near the surface. The recutting will only be done if it will

Figure 21
GIA Clarity Grading Scale

GIA	FL	IF	VVS_1	VVS_2	VS_1	VS_2	SI_1	SI_2	I_1	I_2	I_3

Figure 22
Typical Inclusions in Each Clarity Grade

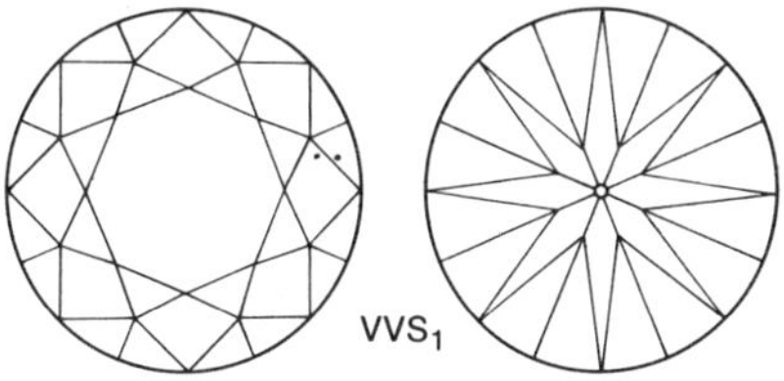

Two small pinpoints near girdle

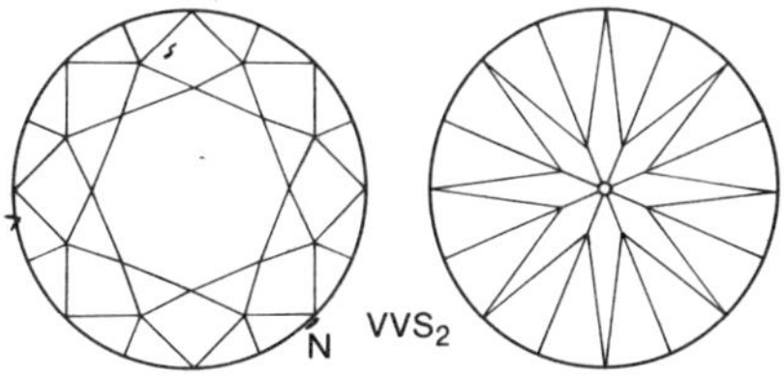

Natural, small nick, and small feather

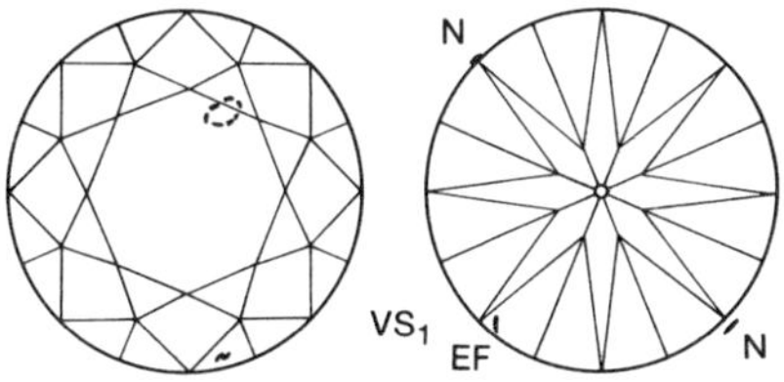

Two naturals, one extra facet, small feather, and faint cloud of pinpoints

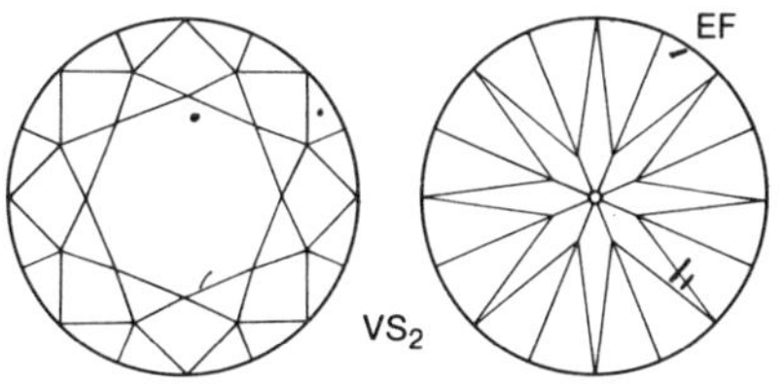

Two opaque inclusions, one feather on table, extra facet, and two small cleavages on pavilion

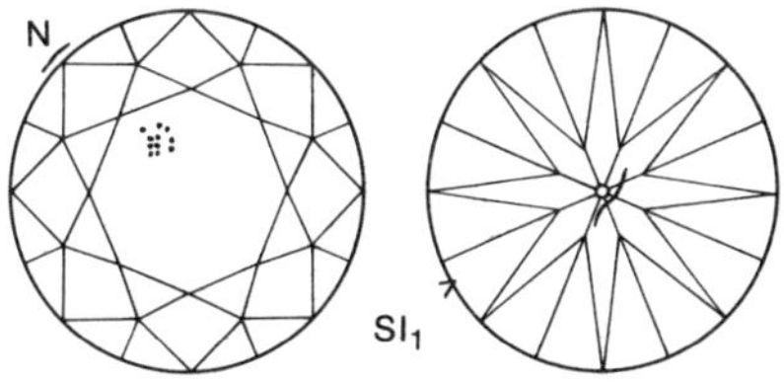

Group of dark pinpoints in table, one natural, nick, and medium feather on pavilion

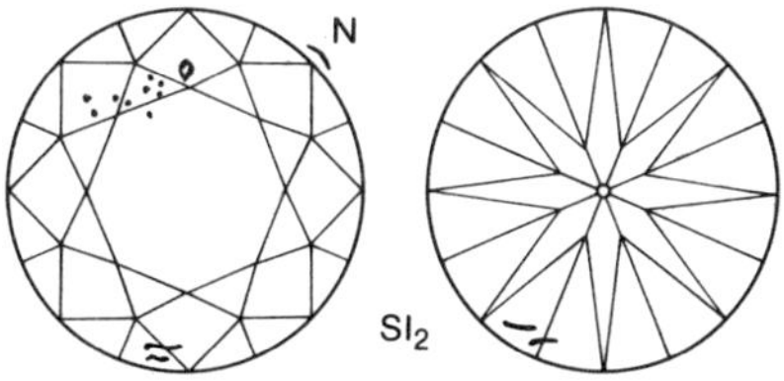

Two cleavages on pavilion, one natural, two feathers, included crystal, and several pinpoints

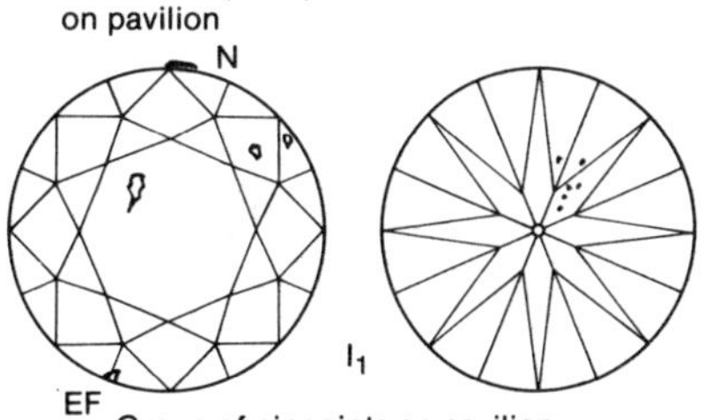

Group of pinpoints on pavilion, natural, extra facet, and three large included crystals

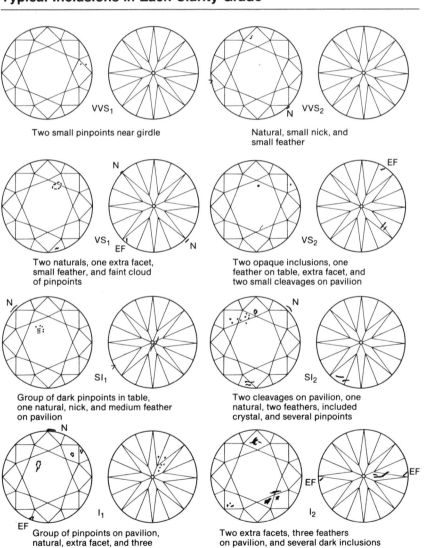

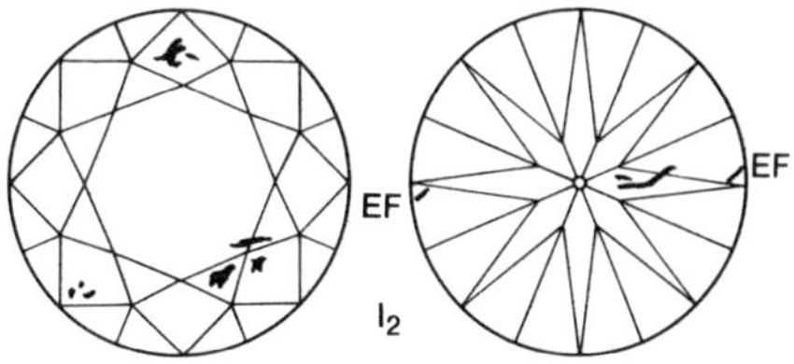

Two extra facets, three feathers on pavilion, and several dark inclusions

increase the value of the stone and not drop the weight below a critical level, for example, each full carat increment. Used in the best jewelry.

4. VS_1 and VS_2: Very slightly imperfect (two levels). Small inclusions only. They still need to be observed with 10-power magnification. VS clarity stones seldom can be cut to IF. VS stones are often used in top-grade engagement rings and high-quality fashion jewelry.
5. SI_1 and SI_2: Slightly imperfect (two levels). More inclusions including small feathers, cleavages, and fractures are allowed in these grades. SI goods will very seldom exhibit inclusions that are visible to the naked eye. Many jewelry quality stones fall into the SI category.
6. I_1, I_2, and I_3: Imperfect (three levels). Used in low-priced commercial jewelry, this imperfect category constitutes the bulk of all cut diamonds. I_1 will have some inclusions that are apparent to the naked eye. I_3 will look very "junky." Imperfect clarity grades are never acceptable to collectors or investors with the possible exception of intense, fancy colored diamonds. Used frequently for earring studs.

Cut Proportions

Cut proportion quality *can* be determined scientifically, yet this aspect of grading is virtually ignored by a good percentage of jewelers and is hardly ever asked about by the public. Perhaps, the combination of the precise nature of determining cut proportion quality and the fact that so many diamonds are poorly cut prompts jewelers to avoid the subject. No one will argue that most diamonds are not well proportioned, and few will counter the argument that well-cut diamonds are more beautiful. In fact, almost any color and quality of diamond can be made to look exciting and brilliant if ideally cut.

At this point many consumers will ask, "If a well-proportioned diamond is so beautiful, why aren't they always cut that way?" There are two honest answers: (*a*) the shape of the rough does not allow for a fine cut, or, more often (*b*) cutters believe the public is more interested in weight than in beautiful proportions. The cutters are right. Given two stones cut from the same rough, a poorly cut stone would weigh more than a well-proportioned stone. While the number of customers who care about proportions has increased, few will say, "That stone is so beautiful, what are its proportions?" compared to the number who will say, "That stone is so beautiful, how big is it?" What most consumers have yet to understand is that two stones with the same weight, color, and clarity can vary up to 30 percent in price depending on cut proportions.

The fact that the public either does not care about cut proportions and/or has been kept in the dark on the subject allows some jewelers to buy very poorly cut stones and sell them at prices that would be reserved for the same quality stone with ideal proportions. Some jewelry chains purposely buy poorly proportioned stones to make bigger profits.

When a diamond is used for investment, its cut proportions become critical and its resale potential may hinge on that factor. Figure 23 shows the structural components of a round diamond. The components of fancy cuts, such as marquise, emerald, oval, and pear, are the same. In these cases, the stone is analyzed from the side by looking down its long axis.

Figure 23

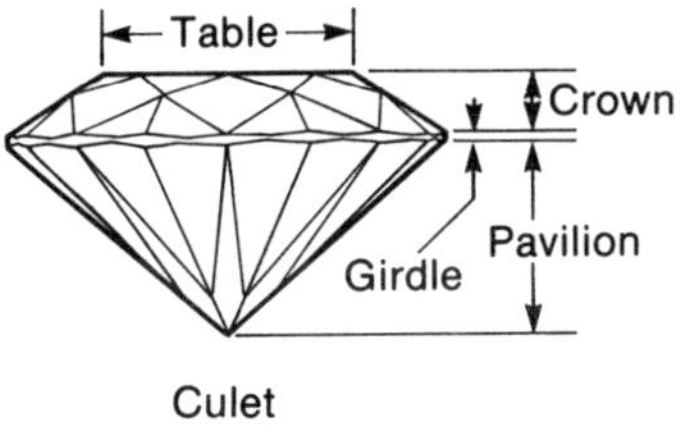

Structural components of a diamond.
These are present in every diamond, no matter what shape.

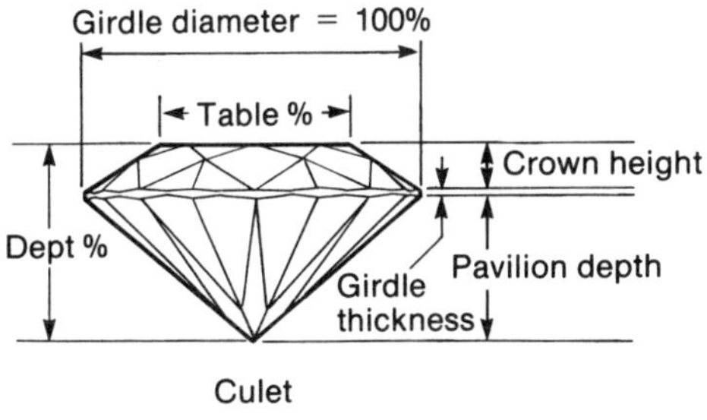

Proportion aspects important to grading analysis.

The Parts of a Diamond

A diamond is divided into three sections: the crown (top part of the stone), the girdle (thin area that separates the top from the bottom) and the pavilion (bottom part of the diamond). In the center of the crown is a large facet called the table. Facets that extend from the table to the girdle are (in order) the star, upper bezel, and upper girdle. The pavilion ends with the culet (facet at the bottom tip of a diamond). The facets that go from the culet toward the girdle are (in order) the lower pavilion facets and the lower girdle facets. The position and relative angle of each of these facets to one another are what gives a diamond a monumental amount of brilliancy and fire or the ugly appearance of a broken piece of glass.

Round diamonds that are considered in the good cut proportion range display the following parameters. Please note, in the trade, fancy cuts are allowed a little leeway from these figures.

Table Percentage This figure is the percentage that the table (flat, top facet) measures compared to the diameter of the stone. The precise, mathematical, ideal table percentage is 53. Trade ideals usually run from 53 percent to 59 percent. Some dealers believe that less than 57 percent is too small and extend the top range to 66 percent. They do this because very few stones fall into the 53 percent to 59 percent range. Thus, by recommending such a narrow range, they are faced with a shortage of diamonds to sell. The 53 percent to 66 percent range is perfectly acceptable for commercial-quality jewelry, but there are objections to expanding the "ideal" figure to 66 percent in the case of superb quality stones. When a person tries to resell a stone with a table percentage above 60 or 62, almost every potential trade buyer will criticize the stone for having a table that is too spread. The hypocrisy regarding cut proportions is often unbelievable.

For stones weighing under one-half carat, it is common trade practice not to provide table percentages. The monetary difference between well- and average-proportioned stones weighing 1/10, 1/5, and 1/4 carats is not huge. For stones over one-half carat, however, there is no reason why the firm cannot give you the correct figure in writing; it is a simple measurement that is no more difficult to give than the square foot storage space in the trunk of a new car.

Depth Percentage This figure measures the depth against the diameter of the stone as a percentage. In ideal stones it is between 59.0 percent and 61.0 percent. Acceptable proportions for jewelry include 58 percent through 62 percent. More than 62 percent or less than 58 percent will be considered outside of preferred trade parameters. Again, this information should be available to the consumer for stones weighing over one-half carat. If a firm does not want to provide this information or the table percentages, or tries to belittle the importance of the figures, they are probably uninformed or trying to push a poorly cut stone on the consumer.

Girdle The girdle is the rim that separates top from bottom. Girdles that are very thick, very thin, or go from very thin to very thick should be avoided. Those that are severely abraded or those with naturals (portions of the outside of the natural rough) that extend into the pavilion or crown facets should also be avoided. Best girdle comments are thin and medium.

Two other factors not directly part of cut proportion analysis but created by the cutting process are polish and symmetry. These factors should not be overlooked, for they, like the rest, influence the price of a stone.

Polish The final action taken in the cutting of diamonds is polishing. Polish on a diamond can be close to perfect, but often it is not. Polish is rated as poor, fair, good, very good, and excellent. On important stones over one carat, a good or better polish rating is important. Poor and fair polish is not acceptable because it represents inexcusable workmanship. These sloppily polished stones will, however, be sold in inexpensive jewelry.

Symmetry Many diamonds do not have good symmetry. Rounds may be lopsided. Emerald cuts may be larger at one end than the other. Marquises can have a crooked axis. As with polish, symmetry ratings include poor, fair, good, very good, and excellent. Parameters for important stones are the same as for polish.

To Review and Create Perspective

Although things like girdle thickness and polish are not terribly important to the overall value of a diamond, each part of the cutting quality and cut proportions is important. All factors reflect upon each other and tell consumers whether the diamond was made for maximum beauty or just so they could have as big a stone as possible. Being cut-proportion conscious enables buyers to get the best-looking stones for their money instead of adding to the profits of firms that sell poorly made stones at prices intended for better made goods.

Carat Weight

The early Mediterranean people believed that carob seeds were of uniform weight. With the invention of accurate weight-measuring devices, we now know that this is not the case. The word *carat*, however, is derived from this early attempt at a standardized weighing system. A metric carat weighs $^1/_{142}$ of an ounce. Therefore, it would take 142 one-carat diamonds to equal an ounce. Each carat is conveniently divided into 100 points. Considering the worth of some diamonds (and colored stones), the carat is a minute weight that can be packed with high value. At early 1985 prices, an ounce of D, internally flawless, one-carat, round diamonds were worth, at wholesale, $2,130,000!

Since the price of diamonds is based on rarity, the greater the weight, the more valuable the stone. One-carat diamonds are between two and four times rarer than half carats, and two-carat diamonds are between two and four times rarer than one carats. Prices based solely on weight also follow this progression. After diamonds reach four or five carats, the price per carat does not increase in the same geometrical pattern despite the increasing rarity. In 20-carat sizes or larger, there may only be a few percent difference in the price per carat from one carat to the next. The price for the stone as a whole is so prohibitive, there are not enough buyers, or stones, to keep the same per carat price differentials as in the smaller stones.

The pricing of diamonds according to size is reasonable with one exception. Those wishing to buy a one-carat stone for jewelry purposes should seriously consider one that is .98 or .99 carats. Although these stones are geologically no less rare than a one carat, they often retail as much as 30 percent lower. There is no reason for this other than psychology. For investment buyers, this psychological factor is important. A .98- or .99-carat diamond will be a disaster; it will rise far less in a bull market and will be very difficult to resell.

Other Factors Influencing the Value and Grading of Diamond

Fluorescence is a type of glow exhibited by some diamonds when struck by ultraviolet light. For many members of the gem trade, blue fluorescence in diamonds is a positive attribute as long as it is not so strong as to make the stone look "oily" or "cloudy." Fluorescent colors other than blue may or may not be considered an asset.

For years there was a premium placed on light to moderately blue fluorescent diamonds. In the last few years, however, the public has shown a marked disinterest in this attribute. This attitude was caused by the surge of "investor information" that came out in the late 1970s. Companies who sold investment diamonds told people that no fluorescence was best. They did this because they didn't have any salespeople who were knowledgeable enough to explain the phenomenon and not because the attribute is bad. In a few short years, the public has absorbed this myth, and beautifully fluorescent stones have been selling at a discount. Because of the intransigent bias of the market, investors should be careful about buying highly fluorescent diamonds. Consumers, however, should again begin to see what extra beauty they can get for their dollars.

A Final Note

When buying an expensive diamond, make sure that all of the above mentioned grading parameters are listed on the sales receipt or appraisal. There are *many* other fine points that can be covered in diamond grading, but understanding these basics will place the layperson miles ahead of the average buyer. (For further details, refer to Appendix C.) Remember, the beauty and value of a diamond is the sum of *all* its parts, not just color and/or clarity. By focusing on one or two grading parameters, diamond buyers are dramatically lowering their chances of receiving a truly wonderful stone.

4 Basics of Colored Stone Grading

White diamonds are valued for their lack of color, all the other gems are valued for their intensity of color. The rapid increase in diamond prices over the last 10 years has prompted consumers to seriously consider colored gems as an alternative to diamonds. One example of this consumer shift is the increased use of ruby, sapphire, and emerald in engagement rings. As the public becomes more familiar with colored stones, the need to understand the basics of grading becomes increasingly important.

World-famous jewelers have offered first-rate, colored stone jewelry for decades. The wealthiest Americans and Europeans have always purchased these items given their awareness that the finest colored stones can be more expensive than the best diamonds. The fact that famous women such as Princess Diana and Jackie Onassis were given sapphire and ruby on their betrothment and wedding days, respectively, is indicative of the upper class' appreciation of these gems. The middle class has only recently been exposed to the beauty and marvelous look of high-quality color. The reasons for this lag in awareness include the facts that (*a*) learning to grade colored stones takes so much time and effort that the average jeweler never bothered, and (*b*) educating the public is difficult, particularly about the finer points; it is easier to sell diamonds than to make the effort in colored stones.

A few years ago, a reputable colored stone wholesaler ran an ad directed at retail jewelers. The caption ran something like this:

Retailer: I don't want to buy any colored stones because I don't sell them.
Wholesaler: You don't sell them because you don't show them.

The ad is true. Jewelers who are now promoting color are doing well, so long as they have a good working knowledge. Moreover, with the incredible rise in the price of some colored stones since the late 1970s, their public appeal has increased. People are now demanding them as never before.

The four Cs are important in colored stone grading. There are, however, more factors to consider. Diamonds have only one color; yellow. Color grading in other stones is more complicated and involves several factors that do not occur in diamond. In colored stones clarity is a more complex issue, and cut proportion assumes a greater percentage of their monetary value.

Color Grading

Every gemologist's job would be much easier if nature made all rubies a pure red, emeralds a pure green, and sapphires a pure blue. Unfortunately, this is not the case. There is no such thing as a pure primary color in naturally occurring gemstones. To verify this fact, pick out a few rubies in a store and look at them carefully. Certainly, the first color to hit your eye will be red, but upon careful examination, you will find that some are redder than others; for example, some are purplish red, pinkish red, or orangish red; some are darker and others are lighter. Every colored gemstone is unique, and its value is determined by the *relationships* between each of its visual components. Many jewelers are not equipped to do both quantitative and qualitative analysis of gems, although a few are venturing into the field and producing extremely fine appraisals and analyses. The best and most accurate work is primarily done by reputable, independent, colored stone laboratories.

The color that a person sees in any gem is comprised of the following three separate elements: (1) primary color, (2) secondary colors, and (3) intensity modifiers.

Primary Color The more primary color in a gemstone, the greater its value. The primary color is the color the eye perceives in greatest quantity, such as the green in emerald. When a stone visually appears to be a perfect balance of two colors (such as the common blue-green of tourmaline), it is not of much value. If the tourmaline is a strong blue or a strong green, it will be more costly. The only important exceptions to this rule are tanzanite, topaz, and padparadscha sapphire. These stones are valued for an intense, virtually equal combination of colors. For tanzanite it is purple and blue; for topaz it is orange and red; and for padparadscha it is orange and pink.

The amount of primary color is often expressed as a percentage of the total color. For example, imagine that all of the above three components comprise 100 percent of the color. The amount of primary will be a specific percentage of those. If the amount of the primary color is exactly 50 percent of the total color, the eye will interpret the stone as being an equal combination of two (or more) colors. If the primary color is below 50 percent, it is no longer the primary color because the others—either singly or in unison—are visually more powerful.

One of the most difficult identification problems for gemologists is in the separation of ruby and pink sapphire. Some rubies are very "pinkish," and the finest pink sapphires are almost "reddish." When does a pink sapphire become a ruby and vice versa? Usually, a consensus can be reached, but a few stones confound the best analysts.

No stone in nature contains 100 percent pure primary color. The majority of stones found in fine jewelry stores have primary color percentages in the 51 percent to 70 percent range. In fact, some stones sold by jewelers contain less than 50 percent "primary" color. An example of this is common, inexpensive "rubies" that are actually very poor-quality purple sapphire; there is not enough red in them to qualify as ruby. Some blue sapphires from Australia often have so much green that they are really dirty green sapphires. To represent these stones as ruby and blue sapphire is fraudulent. The sale of pale, opaque-green beryl as emerald is common but unethical.

Secondary Colors There are three points to remember about secondary colors: (1) they are defined as those with less visual impact than the primary color; (2) they are *always* colors that appear next to the primary color on a color wheel; and (3) the gem trade values some of them over others.

The first point is obvious. If a secondary color were greater in visual impact than the primary color, it would be the primary

Figure 24
Basic Color Wheel
The secondary colors of gemstones will always be on one side of the primary color or the other.

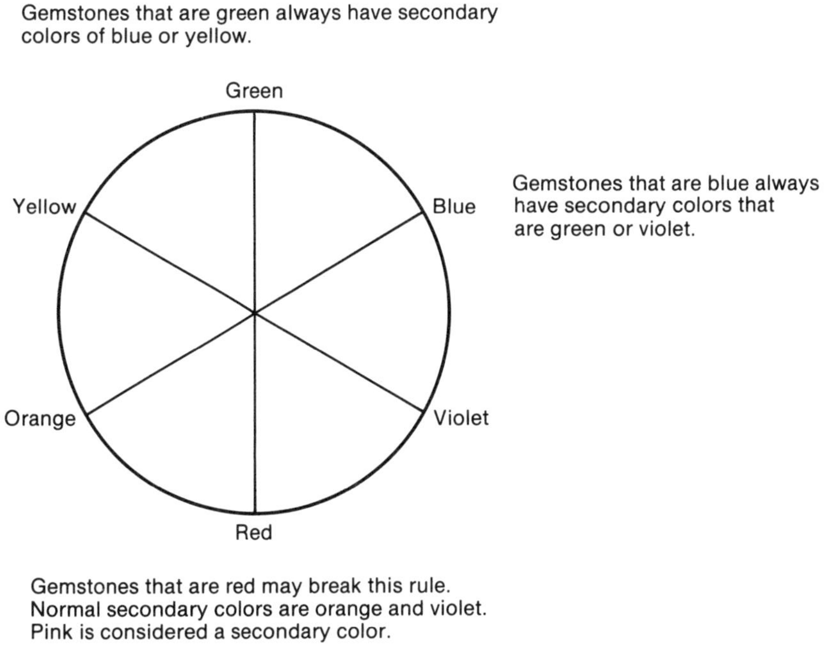
Gemstones that are green always have secondary colors of blue or yellow.
Green
Yellow
Blue
Gemstones that are blue always have secondary colors that are green or violet.
Orange
Violet
Red
Gemstones that are red may break this rule. Normal secondary colors are orange and violet. Pink is considered a secondary color.

color. The second point is interesting. For optical and gemological reasons, the secondary colors will never be far from the primary color on a color wheel. Figure 24 demonstrates this concept. For example, an emerald always has secondary colors of blue and/or yellow. In fact, every green stone will have the same secondary colors! Blue stones will always have violet and/or green, and red stones will always have orange and/or purple. Pink is also considered a secondary color to red. Some gemologists believe pink is diluted red; others consider it a color unto itself. Although there is argument on this technical point, for grading purposes it is easier to assume that pink is a secondary color, along with orange and purple.

The third point is *very* important, particularly for those interested in top quality and for those considering resale at a later date. The trade preference for some secondary colors is not readily discussed with customers for two reasons: (*a*) many jewelers don't know what a secondary color is; and (*b*) most don't particularly care which secondary color is most highly valued. Despite this, two similar stones may have very different prices depending on which secondary color dominates. The most blatant example of this phenomenon is blue sapphire. Experts always value blue sapphire with a violet secondary color more highly than one with a green secondary color. The violet tends to saturate and intensify the blue; the green tends to make the stone look dark and "muddy."

In ruby, purple is considered less valuable than orange or pink. Orangish red sapphires are prized by Europeans while knowledgeable Americans tend equally toward both the orange and the pinkish reds. Green gems are in a class by themselves. There is no particular trade preference. Some like the warmer, yellowish green emeralds while others like the cool, bluish greens. This difference of opinion also exists for other green stones such as tsavorite and tourmaline.

The less the amount of secondary color compared to the primary color, the more valuable the stone. There will always be secondary colors. It is wise to purchase those with the secondaries most prized by the trade since trade preferences are based on a majority bias toward a secondary that increases the beauty of the stone—and beauty is what it is all about.

Intensity Modifiers There are two "colors" present in most gems that do not fall into the primary *or* secondary categories: brown and grey. The presence of either of these "intensity modifiers" will lower the value of the stone. They are called intensity modifiers because of their function. Pure color is the most intense, and any addition of grey or brown will modify its intensity downward. Hence, intensity modifiers! It is very difficult to find any colored stone without some grey or brown, and high concentrations of either will truly deaden the stone's visual color impact. At most, intensity modifiers should constitute only 5 percent of the total color for any top-rated gem.

Tone

Tone is the lightness or darkness of the stone. Most scales of tone are represented numerically from zero (white) to 100 (black), or vice versa. Figure 25 demonstrates a typical tonal scale. Tone is a

Figure 25
Commonly Used Tonal Scale (0 = colorless; 100 = black)

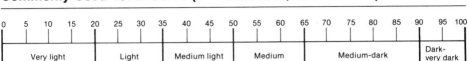

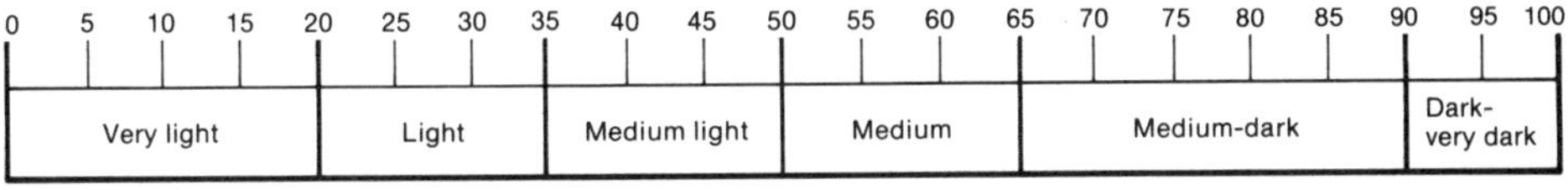

factor independent from color, although it has significant impact on how the color will appear. There is one way to easily visualize how important tone can be to the appearance of a stone. This exercise has to be done mentally because no matter what we actually look at, we not only see color, we also automatically see tone.

As an abstraction, let us assume there is a typical red, as in a fine ruby. It is mostly red, partially pink, and partially grey. This abstraction has no lightness or darkness. If a tonal scale is overlaid on the abstract color, it is found that at zero there is no color showing; it is perfectly white or clear. At a rating of 1, the color is barely visible and extremely washed out. As the color combination is brought up the scale, it becomes more intense. At 75 to 80 tone, the color becomes very intense. At 85 and 90, it becomes more difficult to see because that tonal range is so dark the color does not come through easily. At 95, the color is almost impossible to see. At 100, there is no color; all that is visible is black.

Each specific combination of colors (primary, secondary, and intensity modifiers) has a specific tonal range in which the visual impact of the colors is most intense. The ideal tonal range is different from stone to stone. Indeed, even in the same species of stone, it can vary from one geographical area to the next. For example, in Thailand ruby, the red (plus its other color factors) tends to be most intense at around 75 to 80 tone (medium dark). Burma ruby, however, tends to saturate at around 65 to 70 tone. A fine, gem-quality Burma ruby will sometimes appear less intensely red at 80 than a Thailand ruby even though it has more red primary color!

There are a number of ideal tonal ranges. Fine emerald tends to have intense green color at around 65 to 70 tone. Thailand ruby with a 65 to 70 tone will look washed out. Lemon-yellow sapphire has an ideal range of 55 to 65, while tanzanite becomes more intensely purplish blue at around 80 to 85. Blue sapphire looks intensely blue at 75 to 80 and tsavorite looks greener at 70 to

75. Two things must be remembered concerning tone: (*a*) an ideal tone will increase the price of a stone tremendously no matter what the color combinations, and (*b*) if the tone is too light or dark, the value will fall precipitously. No matter what the color a tone that is too light or dark can reduce the value of a stone as much as 90 percent from what it would cost if the same color combination were at an ideal tone!

Stones of any species with 95 tone are too dark to be pretty, impossible to resell, and need an operating room lamp for the color to be seen. Unfortunately, it is these types of stones that are often sold as superior quality by unscrupulous promoters. If the price of a beautifully colored ruby or sapphire seems too good to be true at a jewelry store, take the stone out of the intense overhead lights. If the stone goes to virtual black in normal light, the tone is far too dark and that is why it is so inexpensive.

One Final Note Many confuse the expressions "the more intense the color" with "the darker the color." Jewelers even misuse and interchange them. Darkness is not a function of color but of tone. Darker is not always more desirable. Intensity is the most important. Most stones seen in lower or medium-priced jewelry are not in ideal tonal ranges.

Clarity Grading

Color and tonal considerations are only the first part of colored stone grading. Clarity is also an important issue, but it generally contributes less to the value of colored stones than to the value of diamonds. Diamonds can occur in a flawless or near flawless state: Most colored stones do not. The amount of inclusions that are tolerated in some species of stones is much greater than in others. In emerald, stones that are considered of high clarity would be considered junk in the same grade in diamond or aquamarine. As a consumer, being sensitive to the inclusion "norms" of various stones is extremely important so that you do not reject a fine specimen, at a bargain price, simply because it is not as clean as a diamond.

Diamond clarity grading is always done with 10-power magnification. Colored stones are graded with the unaided eye. It is true that appraisers will place stones under a gemological microscope, but that is not done for clarity determination. It is done to ascertain whether certain inclusions are dangerous to the stability of the crystal, to determine geographical origin (if possible), to find evidence of the stone being natural or synthetic, or to plot inclusions on a document.

Although there are several accepted clarity grading systems, most follow the format below.

FI __ LI_1 __ LI_2 __ MI_1 __ MI_2 __ HI_1 __ HI_2 __ EI_1 __ EI_2 __ EI_3 __

1. FI: Free of inclusions with the unaided eye.
2. LI_1 and LI_2. Lightly included with the unaided eye (two levels).
3. MI_1 and MI_2. Moderately included with the unaided eye (two levels).
4. HI_1 and HI_2. Heavily included with the unaided eye (two levels).
5. EI_1, EI_2, and EI_3. Excessively included with the unaided eye (three levels).

Although it is not readily apparent, there are the same number of clarity levels for colored stones as there are for diamonds. The LI group roughly approximates the VVS category, while MI is roughly equivalent to VS, and so on. What is extremely important is that the LI group, for example, does not have the same number or size of inclusions as the VVS group. Remember, inclusions in diamond do not become easily apparent until I_1 is reached, but inclusions may be seen with the naked eye in LI. This correlation between the two clarity systems is based on rarity. In other words, LI colored stones are about as rare as VVS diamonds, and so on.

When using this clarity grading system, it is vital to have the inclusion norms of the stone in mind before making a hasty judgment. An MI_1 emerald is probably as geologically rare as a flawless diamond. Eighty percent to 90 percent of all emerald falls into the HI or EI categories. A green tourmaline, by contrast, often occurs in very clean crystals. Anything below an LI_2 is unacceptable in fine jewelry.

The following list indicates what clarity grades are most often accepted as the best.

Beryl, aquamarine: FI to LI_2.
Beryl, emerald: LI_1 (very rare) to HI_2.
Beryl, heliodor (yellow beryl): FI to LI_2.
Beryl, morganite (pink beryl): FI to LI_2.
Chrysoberyl, alexandrite: FI (very rare) to HI_1.
Corundum, ruby: FI (very rare) to MI_2.
Corundum, blue sapphire: FI (rare) to MI_2.
Corundum, golden sapphire: FI (rare) to MI_2.
Corundum, padparadscha sapphire: FI (very rare) to MI_2.
Corundum, pink sapphire: FI (rare) to MI_2.
Corundum, purple sapphire: FI (rare) to MI_2.
Corundum, yellow sapphire: FI to LI_2.
Garnet, demantoid: LI_1 (rare) to HI_1.
Garnet, rhodolite: FI to LI_2.
Garnet, spessartite: FI (rare) to MI_2.
Garnet, tsavorite: FI (rare) to MI_2.
Peridot: LI_1 to MI_2.
Quartz, amethyst: FI to LI_2.
Spinel: FI (rare) to MI_2.
Spodumene, kunzite: FI to LI_2.
Topaz, imperial: FI to LI_2.
Topaz, pink: FI to LI_2.
Tourmaline, regular green: FI to LI_2.
Tourmaline, chrome green: FI (very rare) to MI_2.
Tourmaline, blue (indicolite): FI (very rare) to MI_2.
Tourmaline, red (rubellite): LI_2 to HI_1.
Zoisite, tanzanite: FI (rare) to LI_2.

Like diamond, the relative types and positions of inclusions are important to the overall appeal of the stone. For example, an aquamarine with an LI_2 rating may be priced very close to an FI if the one or two small inclusions are near the edge of the stone or off to the side on the pavilion. Oftentimes, when mounted, a prong may cover the tiny speck of imperfection. An LI_2 aquamarine with a tiny inclusion in the center of the table may be discounted considerably because the inclusion is more obvious.

Inclusions in a colored stone are more often than not an advantage. In this time of troubling synthetics, inclusions are sometimes the only key to determining the natural origin of a stone. Flawless colored stones are always suspect. Emerald, ruby, and sapphire are more highly valued if they come from certain geographical areas. The presence of specific types of inclusions will sometimes positively indicate an origin. For example, Kashmir sapphire is often priced twice as high as its Sri Lankan counterpart. Kashmir stones have a specific type of silking (a needlelike microscopic form of inclusion) that can be observed under the microscope. Color may be indicative of origin, but not a final indication. One mine in Sri Lanka, the Elahara, produces a Kashmir-like color, but its inclusions are different than Kashmir.

Likewise, specific types of inclusions that occur in Burma ruby distinguish it from Thailand ruby. Colombian emerald can sometimes be differentiated from African material through magnification. Value is increased if Colombian origin can be ascertained.

Cut Proportions and Brilliancy

Cut proportions are important in diamonds and subtle dimensional differences will impact on their price. The same is true for colored stones, but the price impact is more marked. Most colored gems do not have as high a refractive index as diamond; therefore, even when perfectly cut they sparkle less. It must be said though that almost any colored stone can have a beautiful sparkle and brilliance when cut well. Unfortunately, most colored gems are cut and polished at or near the mine sites, where weight retention is emphasized rather than beauty. Many superbly cut stones, which will comfortably rest in a collection, investment portfolio, or in a fine piece of jewelry, have been recut to bring out their ultimate beauty.

Because of the standardization of diamond prices and the exacting mathematical nature of their cuts, the increased value that recutting will yield can be calculated. If a colored gem has an exquisite color and a recutting will not drop the stone below a specific, critical carat weight, recutting will invariably increase its price. Of course, a poorly cut Burma ruby that weighs, for example, 1.07 carats cannot be recut. Recutting would drop the weight below a carat. Like diamond, subcarat colored stones cost a fraction of those weighing one carat or a little over. On the other hand, a six-carat, bright golden sapphire that is poorly proportioned can possibly be recut to a four carat and still be worth more money than the original six carat. In some stones, the price can literally double on a per-carat basis because of expert recutting!

How to Determine the Quality of Cut In diamond, all of the critical factors that affect cut are measured in millimeters and transformed into percentages. To do this in colored stones requires that each gem family's ideal cut parameters (based on their individual refractive indexes) be available. Keeping all of these numbers and figures in mind is difficult to say the least. Thus, gemologists have come up with one system for determining the quality of cut proportion for every colored stone.

In diamond, the gemologist takes measurements. If those measurements conform to the parameters of a well-proportioned stone, then, by definition, the stone's cut maximizes the brilliance. The gemologist looks at the cause and assumes the effect. In colored stones, it is the opposite: The effect is measured and the quality of the cut is inferred.

Brilliancy The quality of any gem's cut is evidenced by the amount of brilliancy it possesses. Brilliancy is the ability of the stone to reflect light back to the eye. As with diamond, the only light that comes back to the viewer is that which goes into the stone through the top. If the facets are not arranged correctly, light will leak out of the bottom and sides, leaving gaps in the stone's "sparkle." Stated differently, there will be "dead" areas in the stone. These dead areas are termed *windows* and are very common in many species of gems.

Theoretically, an ideally cut gem will reflect 80 percent to 90 percent of the light that entered the stone back to the viewer's eye. The balance is absorbed. Due to poor cut proportions, this high a figure seldom occurs, but the more light that is reflected back, the more beautiful the gem. Measuring brilliancy is simple. The amount of light that is being reflected back to the eye is measured visually from the culet to the girdle in a 360-degree arc. This measurement is taken while looking straight down at the top of the stone. In many gems, reflections of light from the back facets will only go part way from the culet to the girdle. Sometimes, the reflections will go the complete distance. Also, it is common for a stone to exhibit reflections part of the way in one section and all the way in another. If the reflections go all the way, the stone has a 100 percent brilliancy. If they go part of the way, the distance is measured on a percentage basis.

Actually, two measurements are being taken with this process: the range and the average. The range is expressed from the lowest brilliancy on any area of the stone to the highest. In some cuts, it is possible to have as wide a range as 20 percent to 100 percent. Even without seeing the stone, the figures give vital information. If the stone has a 20 percent to 100 percent range, it could be a long, narrow oval without pleasing proportions. Also, the culet could be off center, creating a less attractive look. If a range is 70 percent to 80 percent, chances are the stone is symmetrical and exhibits a pleasing look.

The average is calculated by looking at the entire stone and determining how much area is reflecting back light; it does not have to be an arithmetic average of the range. If one small section of the stone exhibits a 30 percent brilliancy, the majority of the stone could be reflecting back large quantities of light. Even with a 30 percent to 90 percent range, it is possible to have an average of 70 percent. If the range is narrow, such as 70 percent to 80 percent, the average can be anywhere between the two figures, but not above or below. The closer the range, the better the chances that the average will be exactly halfway between the two.

There are two factors that affect the brilliancy of a stone: how well it was cut, and what the cutter had to work with in the beginning. Many species tend to crystallize in flat or distorted forms. Stones that have been formed by contact metamorphism, such as ruby in Thailand and spinel in Burma, often have a width, length, and depth relationship akin to that of a frisbee. Even with careful cutting, there will be large windows in the stone because the rough was so shallow. Other stones such as aquamarine occur in splendidly formed crystals, and perfect cut proportions can be easily created.

Shallowness is a major cause of windows, the presence of which dramatically reduce the value of a stone. For example, in two, similar, gem rubies, one that has only a 30 percent average brilliancy can cost up to 70 percent less than one with superb proportions that has an 80 percent average brilliancy. Another major cause of windows comes from a cutter trying to deal with a phenomenon termed *color zoning*. Some rough gems, particularly corundum, have areas of varying color intensity or color zoning.

Since color is most important, a cutter will fashion the stone so that the most intense area of color sits in the culet area. This small section of brilliant color is reflected upward and makes the top of the stone look better than it really is. In this case, if the culet is placed in the center of the stone there will be no window—unless the stone is too shallow. More often than not, however, the culet is off center, sometimes dramatically so. Since this lopsided stone cannot evenly reflect light, a window will form.

If you intend to purchase a very high-quality colored stone and are rightfully worried that the stone only has concentrated color in the culet, have the jeweler place the gem in 3.32 heavy liquid. When the stone is viewed from the side, any color zoning will become evident. In the gem trade, stones with evenly distributed color are more valuable than those with small amounts of intense color in particular areas.

Two other factors play a part in the evaluation of cut proportion: proportion and finish. Proportion refers to the overall aesthetic appearance of the stone and takes into account factors such as length to width, symmetry of the girdle, and so on. Finish refers to the quality of the polish.

A Final Note on Colored Stone Grading

The most important thing a layperson can do is to never lose sight of the fact that *all* factors are important in the grading of colored stones. Just because a stone has outstanding color does not mean that it is valuable. Tone, clarity, and cut proportions weigh heavily in establishing the final market price. A ruby that is outstandingly red but has a depth of only 25 percent is going to be inexpensive. Consumers who have been cheated invariably focused on the color grade and essentially ignored all other factors. Do not make this mistake!

5 Gemological Laboratory Certificates

Trying to visualize a gem by just looking at a certificate is like looking at sheet music and expecting to hear the melody.
—Dallas Davenport, The Davenport Organisation

What Is a Laboratory Certificate?

A laboratory certificate is a document that itemizes and analyzes the physical and optical factors that contribute to the visual appearance of a gemstone. The analysis of color, clarity, carat weight, and cut proportions are expressed in verbal and/or numerical form. Most often, each factor is represented on a linear scale to make it easy to see where the stone sits in relation to all possible stones.

Laboratory certificates of both diamond and colored stones are available. Those most accepted in the gem trade are the ones that are produced by independent laboratories. Independent laboratories are not involved in the buying and selling of gems; they make their profit by being as objective as possible about quality analysis and, in some cases, monetary appraisals. Documents created by companies that sell gems, those that are issued with the intent to defraud, or documents that are not highly reproducible, are ignored or discounted by the gem trade. Reproducibility, as you will recall, is the ability of a laboratory to regrade a stone, within a specific tolerance factor, at the same level at which that stone was originally graded. Whenever new grading laboratories enter the market, they are constantly tested by companies. They have a stone graded, wait a few months, and send the stone in again. A market consensus soon develops about the merits or demerits of the laboratory's consistency. Generally, laboratories that have survived for several years show remarkable objectivity, accuracy, and reproducibility.

The system by which each laboratory grades is often of their own invention although the fundamentals, which were discussed previously, are closely followed. Although the length of the ranges for color and clarity may differ slightly from document to document, all diamond-grading reports indicate the amount of yellow color in a diamond and have some specific way of categorizing its degree of clarity. Likewise, colored stone certificates always indicate the level of color, tone, and clarity. All reputable documents indicate, either through simple measurements or by linear scale, the quality of the cut proportion. Because each system is slightly different, it takes quite a bit of practical experience to be able to look at the analysis on one document and project what that analysis would look like on another.

What Is the Proper Use of Laboratory Certificates?

The invention of laboratory grading documents has had a tremendous impact on the gem industry. The Gemological Institute of America developed the first diamond-grading report in the 1950s and these documents were in relatively common use by the 1960s. Most of the colored stone certificates that are currently available were developed in the 1970s. This is reasonable since diamond grading is child's play compared to colored stone grading. Developing a consistent methodology for grading diamonds was easier, and since diamonds are the most popular "precious" stone it was natural that they were first chosen for this kind of endeavor.

Laboratory certificates were created to help in the actual, physical grading of the stone. *They were not created to act as a substitute for the grading of a stone!* The certificates eliminate many of the time-consuming processes that must be used if a gem is to be graded from scratch. Measurements and physical data concerning cut proportions are clear and concise. Perhaps the most important thing they do is identify the stone as natural or synthetic; just finding out if a stone is one or the other can take a considerable amount of time. This information is *objective.* All other information on a laboratory certificate is partially objective, and is only as good or complete as the system used to analyze the stone. A laboratory certificate is like a road map. A map will definitely tell if a car is heading toward Las Vegas instead of Atlanta, but because the car is moving and the map has limitations, the vehicle's *exact* position can only be estimated.

Other than a stone's physically measurable aspects (e.g., diameter and depth percentage), all other analysis of a gemstone, either diamond or colored stone, falls within a tolerance factor. The grades on the document are not specific. Instead, they present a range; the precise grade of the stone being analyzed is somewhere within that range. In the best laboratory certificates, the probability that the exact grade will be somewhere within that range is extremely high. This is confirmed by high reproducibility in grading. The above is an ivory tower approach to examining the nature and purpose of laboratory certificates.

This ivory tower approach is, however, not strictly used by the gem trade. The gem trade uses certificates to help make sales, which is not disreputable in and of itself. The presence of quality laboratory certificates has led to heightened consumer confidence, particularly where high-ticket sales are concerned. The fact that an independent document is being used to support a sales presentation adds the right ingredients, not the wrong ones.

The problem that buyers face concerning laboratory certificates is not with the information itself, but with the way in which the information is used during a sales presentation. Properly used information is always a tremendous advantage to buyers. Improperly used information is one of the most dangerous things a consumer has to face. This danger manifests itself in two ways.

1. The salesperson does not understand the nature and limitations of certificates and either presents the information on them as if it were etched in stone or refuses to use certificates even where appropriate. If salespeople present the information as gospel, they mislead the customer concerning the reality of grading procedures. If they refuse to use certificates where appropriate, they seriously cheat the customer out of usable information. Those who do not use certificates in appropriate circumstances have never taken the time to read the

literature concerning their uses. They invariably have an incorrect preconception that certificates should be perfect. Instead of blaming themselves for their lack of professionalism, they refuse to use certificates on the basis that they are not perfect. Yet, no reputable laboratory has ever claimed to be able to create a perfect grading document!

2. The public tries to short-cut learning about stones by buying the document. In so doing, they reverse the intended process. The document is a vehicle by which to *grade* the stone. Consumers are not buying paper; they are buying a stone.

If both the salesperson and the consumer believe the document is the final word, disaster is the only possible outcome. All reputable laboratories state the limitations of their certificates—either in handbooks or on the certificates themselves. The way in which certificates are represented to the public is a direct reflection on the company's knowledge (or lack of it). A responsible merchant will represent certificates as exactly what they are: documents to assist in the physical grading of the stone.

Since the gem markets are international, one of the primary ways of buying and selling is over the phone. Thus, laboratory certificates are an ideal medium for getting the *general* idea of what a stone looks like to a potential customer. Those who buy on the basis of the certificate alone, without examining the stone, are asking for trouble. For either diamonds or colored stones, the most a *trained* professional can get out of the information on a certificate is about an 85 percent accurate mental image of the gem. The other 15 percent, which is critical, can only be filled in by actual examination. For the public, the accuracy of this mental image will be considerably less than 85 percent.

A secondary but no less important problem, which is caused by the misuse of laboratory certificates, is the focusing on only one aspect of the certificate. Dealers who wish to cheat customers will emphasize only one desirable aspect of the stone and ignore or downplay the poor aspects. Often this is done with stones with high colors but very poor tone, cut proportions, or secondary colors. Dealers do this to obtain a higher price for the stone than the market would normally reflect. In essence, they are defrauding the customer. Uninformed buyers will also look for only one aspect, such as color, and ignore the rest of the information. This problem has been one of the primary reasons people have been cheated when buying gems. *All* the information on a certificate is critical in determining the value of the gem.

There are a few points you should always remember when dealing with stones that have laboratory certificates.

1. Stones worthy of having laboratory certificates are usually quite expensive. Laboratories charge a fee based on the carat weight of the stone. As a rule of thumb, stones under $3,000 do not need a laboratory certificate.
2. Just because a stone has a certificate does not mean it is a good stone. Any stone can have a certificate: One of the most common scams involves the sale of garbage-quality stones that have expensive certificates.
3. All the information is important, not just one or two factors. If all the factors are not taken into consideration, consumers will make serious mistakes.
4. Any gem dealer that sells *exclusively* on the basis of certificate information is to be avoided.
5. If you do not have sufficient training in gems, you should not rely on certificate information. An independent, expert opinion will be needed for your protection.
6. Beware of look-alike certificates. Frequently, a counterfeit will be a perfect copy of a well-known certificate, but a particular initial in the laboratory's name will be different (e.g., BGL instead of AGL, or PGL instead of CGL).
7. Not every laboratory issues reliable grading documents. Therefore, I have included the names and addresses of those that are recognized as honest and accurate.

For complete diamond-grading analysis:

The Gemological Institute of America
1660 Stewart Street
Santa Monica, CA 90406

For complete colored stone-grading analysis:

American Gemological Laboratories
580 Fifth Avenue, Suite 1211
New York, NY 10036

California Gemological Laboratories
3698 A South Bristol
Santa Ana, CA 92704

A Final Note

There are a number of small, independent laboratories in existence. Some do a credible job; others are essentially subsidiaries of unscrupulous dealers. Most of the time consumers will buy a stone with a laboratory certificate for only two reasons: (1) to verify the authenticity and/or grade of a stone because so much money is involved; and (2) because they wish to sell the stone at a later date. In either case the three laboratories recommended above are the best choices. Their record of honesty is excellent, and if resale with a certificate becomes necessary their documents are established and accepted by the gem trade.

6 Understanding the GIA Diamond Grading Report

The basics of diamond grading were explained in Chapter 3. That information was presented as an abstract concept to help you build a foundation of knowledge. In this chapter, the knowledge will come alive as it is applied to a real stone that has an accompanying GIA Diamond Grading Report. The concepts presented will be the normal mental and physical processes that every expert in the diamond trade goes through when determining the quality and value of a stone being offered.

Figure 26 shows a blank GIA Diamond Grading Report on which the word *sample* is written. The GIA has a very strict policy about the reproduction of their grading reports and has graciously consented to supply a blank one for this book. The example that follows Figure 26 is that of a real diamond grading report done by the GIA in 1983. Please mentally transfer the information from the example to the blank sample.

The stone to be analyzed is very large and quite expensive, probably in the neighborhood of $500,000. Regardless of price, however, the same analysis methodology applies to all diamonds.

Figure 26
GIA Diamond Grading Report

GIA GEM TRADE LABORATORY, INC.

A Wholly Owned Subsidiary of Gemological Institute of America, Inc.

1660 Stewart Street
Santa Monica, California 90404
(213) 829-2991

606 South Olive Street
Los Angeles, California 90014
(213) 629-5435

580 Fifth Avenue
New York, New York 10036
(212) 221-5858

DIAMOND GRADING REPORT

SAMPLE

THE FOLLOWING WERE, AT THE TIME OF THE EXAMINATION, THE CHARACTERISTICS OF THE DIAMOND DESCRIBED HEREIN BASED UPON 10X BINOCULAR MAGNIFICATION. DIAMONDLITE AND MASTER COLOR DIAMONDS, ULTRA-VIOLET, MILLIMETER GAUGE, DIAMOND BALANCE, PROPORTIONSCOPE.

SAMPLE

RED SYMBOLS DENOTE INTERNAL CHARACTERISTICS. GREEN SYMBOLS DENOTE EXTERNAL CHARACTERISTICS. SYMBOLS INDICATE NATURE AND POSITION OF CHARACTERISTICS, NOT NECESSARILY THEIR SIZE. MINOR DETAILS OF FINISH NOT SHOWN.

KEY TO SYMBOLS

SHAPE AND CUT . .
Measurements . . . .
Weight . . . .

PROPORTIONS . . .
Depth . . . .
Table . . . .
Girdle . . . .
Culet . . . .
FINISH
Polish . . . .
Symmetry . . . .

CLARITY GRADE . .

COLOR GRADE . . .
Fluorescence . . . . .

COMMENTS:

ORIGINAL

GIA GEM TRADE LABORATORY, INC.

by ______________________

GIA CLARITY GRADING SCALE

Flawless | Internally Flawless | VVS_1 | VVS_2 | VS_1 | VS_2 | SI_1 | SI_2 | I_1 | I_2 | I_3

Imperfect

GIA COLOR GRADING SCALE

D E F G H I J K L M N O P Q R S T U V W X Y Z Fancy Light | Fancy | Fancy Intense

Colorless | Near Colorless | Faint Yellow | Very Light Yellow | Light Yellow | Yellow

NOTICE: IMPORTANT LIMITATIONS ON REVERSE

No Appraisals or Valuations

Source: Courtesy of Gemological Institute of America, Inc.

SHAPE AND CUT: Marquise Shape Brilliant
Measurements: 26.50 × 14.24 × 9.13 mm.
Weight: 20.79 carats

PROPORTIONS
Depth: 64.1%
Table: 63%
Girdle: Medium to very thick; faceted
Culet: Medium

FINISH
Polish: Good
Symmetry: Good

CLARITY GRADE: VS_1

COLOR GRADE: D
Fluorescence: None

There is nothing under the comments section. On the plot of inclusions, which will always appear to the right under "Key to Symbols," the stone has some pinpoint spots, a feather, an extra facet on an upper girdle facet near its tip, and a natural (area of the surface of the rough diamond that is not polished) on the girdle.

Situation

This stone is being offered via the report information only and is being represented as an ideal and superb 20-carat diamond. If the stone is of further interest, arrangements may be made to view it. Pretend to be a gem dealer trying to evaluate the stone for a highly discerning client. If it passes this rigid examination, the stone may be appropriate for your client.

Section One of the Analysis The stone is a marquise shape brilliant weighing 20.79 carats. This size is very rare in any quality. Also, a marquise is a difficult cut to find in this size—an added plus. Its measurements are 26.50 × 14.24 × 9.13 millimeters. The stone is almost twice as long as it is wide, a possible detriment to its physical appearance. Normally, people instinctively appreciate a length to width ratio of 1.66 to 1.00. At this stage of the analysis, however, the length to width problem is not important enough for you to reject the stone, but a mental checkmark must be made. If this stone were available for examination with the report information, it would be proper to measure the stone to see if it matched the millimeter dimensions on the report. This should be done immediately if the marquise is fine enough to warrant a physical examination. (Instead of moving to the proportion section of the report next, many diamond experts would now move their attention from the Shape and Cut section to the Color and Clarity section.)

Section Two of the Analysis The color is D. It can get no better. If a physical examination of the stone were warranted, however, the stone would be graded against an E master. A pivotal grade of D, instead of a "strong" D, may make the purchase doubtful. In this price range, there can be no doubt that the stone will be regraded as a D again.

The clarity grade is VS_1, a very high grade for this size stone. When diamonds are cut, they lose, on average, anywhere from 40 percent to 80 percent of their rough weight. For such a large crystal to be a VS_1 is wonderful.

Closer inspection of the plot or diagram of inclusions (see Figure 27) shows that the one feather (wispy linear inclusion) is on the pavilion of the stone near the girdle. This probably does not show with the stone in a face-up position, which is good. There are some pinpoints in the table and bezel facets, but they are probably not of any consequence. The extra facet is on the crown

Figure 27
Plot of 20.79 Carat D Color, VS_1 Diamond*

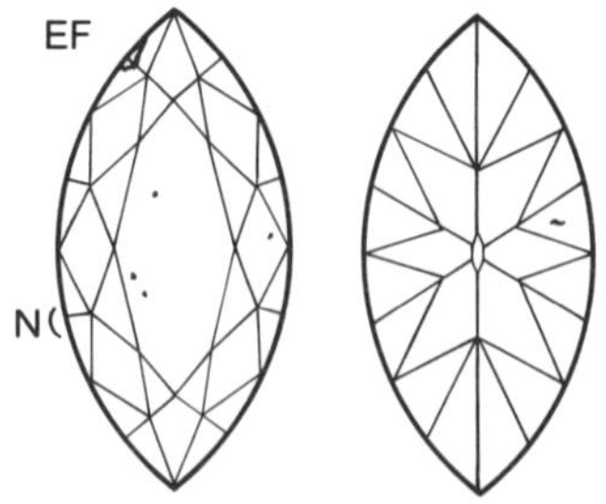

*Please note: Plots on original gemological documents have internal characteristics in red ink. External characteristics are in green ink.

of the stone near the tip, on a girdle facet; this may or may not be unsightly. From the plot, it is hard to know if the cap of a mounting will cover the extra facet. The natural on the girdle doesn't seem to be large. All of these mental assumptions about the clarity and surface features will have to be verified by physical examination. The plot and the information show that they are probably not worrisome.

Under the color grade, the report states that there is no fluorescence. Having no fluorescence is neutral for jewelry and is probably a plus if the stone is going to be used as an inflation hedge or an investment. No worries there.

Section Three of the Analysis So far, the visual appeal of the stone is in question due to the length to width ratio and the extra facet. Other than those factors the stone is very fine. The proportions and finish sections are next. The same parameters for ideal proportions and finish are applicable to every cut of diamond. The fact that this is a 20.79 carat marquise makes no difference in this hard-nosed analysis, although the trade will usually make parameters less severe for pears and marquises than for rounds. For purposes of this example, polish and symmetry will be first. Proportion will be discussed in reverse, from culet to depth percent.

Symmetry in a fancy cut is often not as good as in a round. A marquise is a particular offender in this category. The symmetry here is rated good. The cutter didn't try to squeeze the stone out of awkwardly shaped rough. Polish is also rated good. The stone was finished with care. Very good or excellent would have been better, but on a stone of this size, a good/good is acceptable.

The culet is medium and acceptable. The girdle is medium to very thick, faceted. Medium to thick girdles in a stone this large prevent breakage upon setting. A faceted girdle is common. Examination of the stone will show if the girdle is wavy or has areas that are too thick to allow proper prong placement and eye appeal. Given the good symmetry and polish, this differential in girdle thickness is not substantial.

The table percentage is 63. Given the narrowness of the stone in relation to its length, for the table to be 63 percent, the depth of the crown is probably relatively thin in relationship to the depth of the entire stone. If this were not the case, the crown's angle from the girdle plane to the table would have to be very high. If they were that high, that fact would probably appear in the comment section, but it doesn't. In other words, from a side view the crown will appear thinner compared to the crown of an ideally cut diamond. Technically, the table is not too spread, but the probable thinness of the crown is a worry; much of the stone's weight could be underneath the girdle.

The depth percentage is 64.1—very deep. In fact, it is very deep when compared to many diamonds. Since 59 percent to 61 percent is considered ideal and fine jewelry stones are acceptable at 58 percent to 62 percent, this stone, for all its excellent qualities, has a real problem. In a round stone, a depth percentage of 64.1 will create a large dark spot in the bottom of the stone. The light is leaking out and is not being reflected back to the viewer. In a marquise, the visual problem amplifies itself. The very dark area in this stone is extended into what is called a "bow tie" effect (see Figure 28). Many fancy cuts have this effect to a greater or lesser degree, but it is undoubtedly very noticeable here.

If the stone cannot be recut, either (*a*) the asking price per carat must be *significantly* below that of a better make, or (*b*) the stone is simply unacceptable because of the high standards the client wants to maintain. If the stone is to be used as a piece of jewelry, the bow tie will probably detract materially from its appearance.

Figure 28
Bow Tie Effect Caused by Incorrect Cut Proportions*

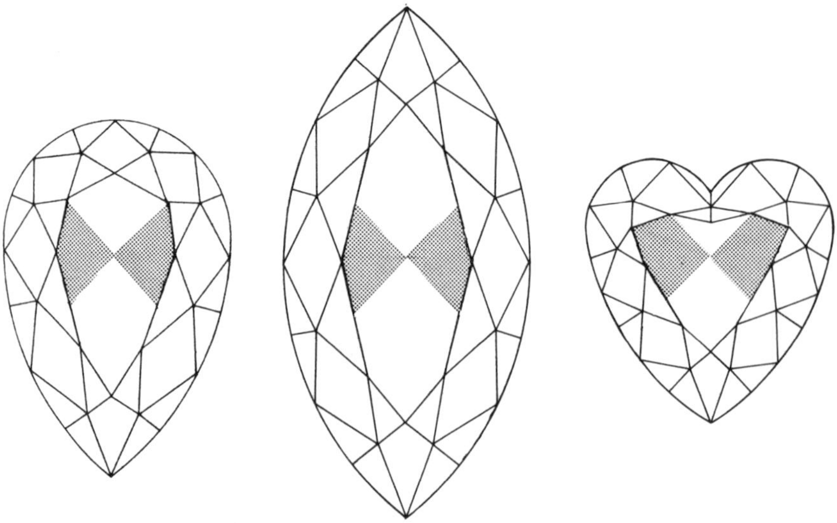

*A prominent bow tie decreases the value of the stone.

If it is to be used as an inflation hedge or an investment, it will be extremely difficult to resell, particularly back to the diamond trade. Because of the depth percentage, the trade will verbally slaughter the stone.

The point here is that *all* the pieces of information on any grading report are of *extreme importance.* There are D colors, but not *all* are well cut. There are high clarities, but not *all* have good colors. And so on. Consumers should not ignore or render unimportant *any* information.

Most people would like to own this stone, depth percentage problem or not. What this example illustrates is how to get the most value and beauty for the money to be spent. Whether spending $1,000 or a half of a million dollars, there are stones in the marketplace that give the best color, clarity, carat weight, and cut proportions for the money being spent. If you were to buy this marquise near the retail list price ($500,000), which assumes good proportions for this size, color, and clarity, you would be making a foolhardy mistake. If you wanted an absolutely superlative stone in this price range, this would not be the one to buy. This stone has to be discounted at least 30 percent under what it would cost if it were well cut!

Finally, this is the kind of consumer oversight that allows jewelers to sell stones they buy at far less than full-list wholesale price for full-list retail price. Therefore, remember that all the grading analysis of any diamond over one-half carat should be available to you. If the jeweler refuses to give it, go to somebody else.

7 Understanding the AGL Laboratory Certificate

There are two excellent colored stone laboratories to choose from: American Gemological Laboratories (AGL) and California Gemological Laboratories (CGL). Both have fine reputations, although their systems for color grading are different. CGL relies heavily on the Munsell color system which is used by industry, paint companies, and the U.S. government. The system is very credible. For most people, however, it takes more study and practice to master the Munsell system than the AGL system. The AGL is a linear, comparative system developed especially for colored gemstones by its president, Caspar "Cap" Beesley. It is also the most accepted by the gem trade. In this section, a vitally important examination and interpretation of three AGL certificates will be discussed. This "walk through" will show consumers, step-by-step, how to read an AGL document. Let it also be known that choosing to use AGL in no way demeans the excellent efforts that have been put forth by CGL; they deserve the attention of consumers as well. (See Figure 29 for CGL certificate.)

CERTIFICATE NUMBER 1
"The 2.22 Carat Investment Disaster"
or
"How to Lose by Not Looking at All the Information"

Figure 30 shows an AGL certificate that describes a 2.22-carat, natural blue sapphire. Before plunging into what quality of sap-

Figure 29
CGL Colored Stone Grading Report

CALIFORNIA GEMOLOGICAL LABORATORIES
3200 Bristol Street, Suite 705, Costa Mesa, CA 92626 • (714) 754-0508

COLORED STONE GRADING REPORT

IDENTIFICATION Natural Tsavorite

WEIGHT 2.49 Carats

SHAPE AND CUT Cushion Mixed

MEASUREMENTS 10.13 x 7.20 x 4.00mm **DATE** 11/12/84

CLARITY MI1 **REPORT NUMBER** SAMPLE

COLOR 5.5 - Good
Color Description Strong Yellowish Green
Munsell Notation 1.25G 5/10
Tone 50
Grayness 25% Gray (4.5)
Light Source Durotest Daylight 65

PROPORTIONS Good
Depth Percentage 55.6%
Brilliance Percentage 40 - 50%
Brilliance Intensity High

FINISH
Polish Good
Symmetry Very Good

FLUORESCENCE
Long Wave None
Short Wave None

COMMENTS:

SAMPLE

Color Grade Scale (CGL)

10	9	8	7	6	5	4	3	2	1
Excellent		Very Good		Good			Fair		Poor

Clarity Scale (CGL)

NI	VLI$_1$ VLI$_2$	LI$_1$ LI$_2$	MI$_1$ MI$_2$	HI$_1$ HI$_2$	HI$_3$ HI$_4$
No Visible Inclusions	Very Lightly Included	Lightly Included	Moderately Included	Heavily Included	Very Heavily Included

Tone/Munsell Value Scale (CGL)

Tone	0	10	20	30	40	50	60	70	80	90	100
	Colorless		Light		Medium			Dark		Black	
Value	10	9	8	7	6	5	4	3	2	1	0

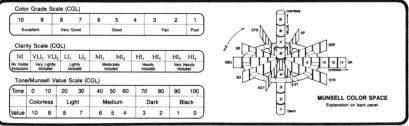

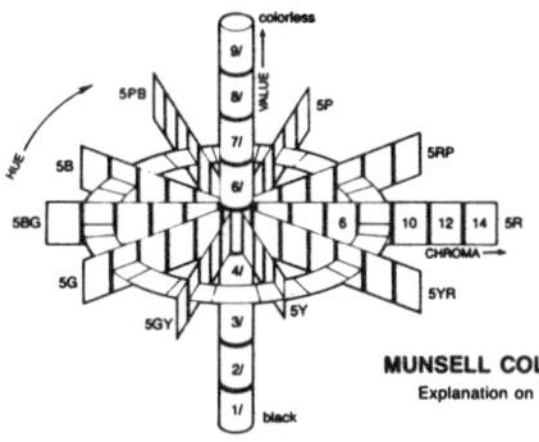

MUNSELL COLOR SPACE
Explanation on back panel.

NOTICE: IMPORTANT LIMITATIONS ON REVERSE

Source: Courtesy of California Gemological Laboratories.

Figure 30
AGL Colored Stone Certificate—Natural Sapphire

American Gemological Laboratories
Olympic Tower
645 Fifth Avenue
New York, N.Y. 10022
(212) 935-0060
(212) 935-0071

Colored Stone Certificate

CERTIFICATE NO: CS 00000

DATE: 28 January 1985

The information contained in this report represents the opinion of American Gemological Laboratories regarding the characteristics of the colored stone(s) submitted for examination.
The conclusions expressed are the American Gemological Laboratories' interpretation of the results obtained from gemological instruments and grading techniques designed for this purpose. Conclusions may vary due to the subjective nature of colored stone analysis. Mounted stones are graded only to the extent that mounting permits examination.

SAMPLE

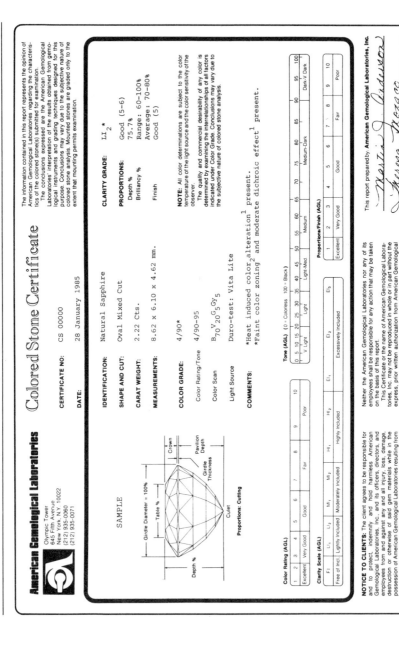

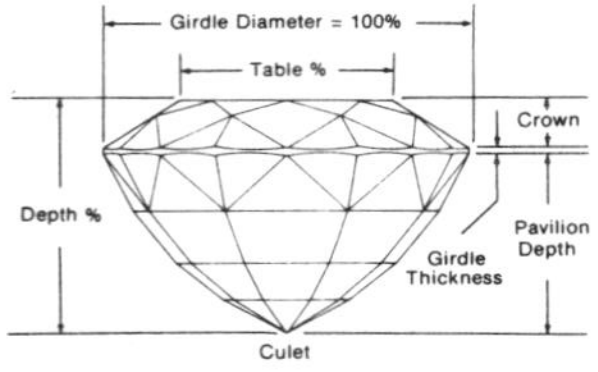

Proportions: Cutting

IDENTIFICATION: Natural Sapphire

SHAPE AND CUT: Oval Mixed Cut

CARAT WEIGHT: 2.22 Cts.

MEASUREMENTS: 8.62 x 6.10 x 4.62 mm.

COLOR GRADE: 4/90*

Color Rating/Tone: 4/90-95

Color Scan: $B_{70}V_{20}G_5Gy_5$

Light Source: Duro-test: Vita Lite

COMMENTS: *Heat induced color alteration[1] present.
*Faint color zoning[2] and moderate dichroic effect[1] present.

CLARITY GRADE: LI_2*

PROPORTIONS: Good (5-6)
Depth %: 75.7%
Brilliancy %: Range: 60-100%, Average: 70-80%
Finish: Good (5)

NOTE: All color determinations are subject to the color temperature of the light source and the color sensitivity of the observer.
The quality and commercial desirability of any color is determined by examining the interrelationships of all factors indicated under Color Grade. Conclusions may vary due to the subjective nature of colored stone analysis.

Color Rating (AGL)

1 2	3 4	5 6	7 8	9 10
Excellent	Very Good	Good	Fair	Poor

Tone (AGL) (0 = Colorless 100 = Black)

0 5 10 15 20	25 30 35	40 45 50	55 60 65	70 75 80 85 90	95 100
V. Light	Light	Light-Med	Medium	Medium-Dark	Dark-V Dark

Clarity Scale (AGL)

FI	LI_1 LI_2	MI_1 MI_2	HI_1 HI_2	EI_1 EI_2 EI_3
Free of Incl.	Lightly Included	Moderately Included	Highly Included	Excessively Included

Proportions/Finish (AGL)

1	2 3	4 5 6	7 8	9 10
Excellent	Very Good	Good	Fair	Poor

NOTICE TO CLIENTS: The client agrees to be responsible for and to protect, indemnify and hold harmless American Gemological Laboratories, Inc., and its officers, directors, and employees from and against any and all injury, loss, damage, destruction or otherwise of said gem materials while in the possession of American Gemological Laboratories resulting from any cause not attributable to the negligence of American Gemological Laboratories or its employees.
The client agrees that this report is for his/her exclusive use.

Neither the American Gemological Laboratories nor any of its employees shall be responsible for any action that may be taken on the basis of this report.
This Certificate or the name of American Gemological Laboratories, Inc. may not be reproduced in whole or in part without the express, prior written authorization from American Gemological Laboratories.
Do not accept copies, alterations or corrections on this document for final transactions.

This report prepared by: **American Gemological Laboratories, Inc.**

Source: Courtesy of American Gemological Laboratories, Inc.

phire is being represented, it is important to understand some of the basics of the document. The following items always appear on an AGL document, and most other laboratory documents.

Certificate Number All laboratories have an individual number for each certificate issued. This number is meant to make research and verification easy. The certificate number can also be used to prove that a counterfeit certificate is being circulated.

Date Designates which day the certificate was issued.

Light Source The AGL uses Duro-test: Vita Lite, a balanced light source. Other laboratories may use different brands, but using a standardized light source is imperative to be able to grade accurately and with high reproducibility.

Signatures Most laboratories have the signatures of one or more qualified graders, usually gemologists. AGL uses two signatures.

The Specifics of the Stone

Identification Natural sapphire. In this sample, AGL has determined the stone to be natural sapphire. If the stone were synthetic, no information other than the weight and dimensions would appear.

Shape and Cut Oval mixed cut. An oval mixed cut is often used in corundum. The stone has an oval shape when viewed from above. The facet structure, however, differs from top to bottom. The crown is cut much like the top of a diamond. The pavilion has a facet structure similar to the picture on the AGL certificate. (See Figure 31.) Whether the cut is mixed or not, the main thing to look for in a stone is the shape. The most common in corundum are cushion and oval. Shapes such as emerald (rectangular), marquise, and pear are discounted against the same quality stone in oval or cushion. The shape that can be more expensive than oval or cushion is round. This shape can command a 10 percent premium over the same quality stone in an oval or cushion. An oval mixed cut, therefore, is perfectly acceptable for jewelry, collections, or investment.

Figure 31
Oval and Cushion Mixed Cuts

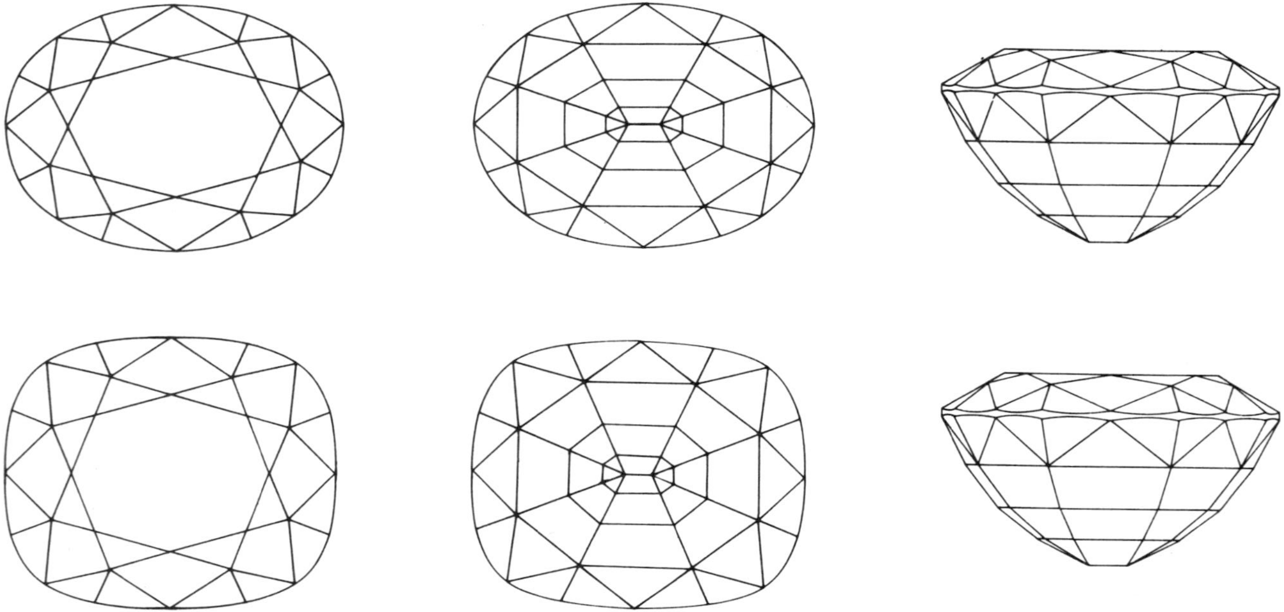

Source: Courtesy of American Gemological Laboratories, Inc. © American Gemological Laboratories, Inc. 1982.

Carat Weight 2.22 cts. Each gemstone has a preferred "international trading size." In diamond or ruby, it is one carat. For sapphire it is two carats. This blue sapphire weighs almost two and a quarter carats. For most purposes, this is a perfect size. It even allows for some slight recutting if it is found to be cut incorrectly. So far, the stone is perfect for any purpose.

Measurements 8.62 × 6.10 × 4.62 mm. All stones are measured in millimeters. This oval stone is 8.62 mm long, 6.10 mm wide, and 4.62 mm deep. These measurements partially tell the observer how well the stone is cut. To interpret the effect of these numbers, it is best to jump over to the proportion section on the right-hand side of the certificate before looking at clarity or color.

Proportions	Good (5–6)
Depth percent	75.7%
Brilliancy percent	Range: 60%–100%; Average: 70%–80%
Finish	Good (5)

The proportion and finish grade are expressed as numbers. On the bottom, right-hand part of the certificate, a linear scale shows where each number stands on a scale from excellent to poor. Proportion is 5 to 6 or at the middle to bottom of the good category. This is an acceptable grade for a fine jewelry stone. It could be a little better for investment purposes, but it must be remembered that corundum is generally cut and polished at the mine site. Proportions are not nearly as exacting as those of diamond. Rarely does one see proportion and finish in corundum better than a 4. To obtain a higher proportion grade, this stone will probably have to be massively recut to below a two-carat weight. Finish is good (5), which is acceptable. Perhaps a little polishing with the loss of a few points of weight could improve the grade.

Depth percentage is 75.7. Corundum has an "ideal" depth percentage in the 70 percent to 80 percent range. The brilliancy range and average are spectacular. The brilliancy ranges from 60 percent as a low to 100 percent as a high. Average brilliancy is 70 percent to 80 percent. Considering that most corundum of decent quality has brilliancy averages in 40 percent to 50 percent range, this stone is exceptional. Its high brilliancy makes this aspect of grading perfectly acceptable for investment, collections, or jewelry.

At this point, a recap is in order. It is a natural sapphire, has an acceptable shape, is in a good trading size, and has good proportions and finish. The brilliancy is excellent. The only demerit the stone has is the 5 to 6 proportion grade, but that is minor considering the high brilliancy.

Clarity Grade LI_2*. Given how high its brilliancy is, it is not possible for the clarity to be too bad. If the stone had large inclusions that blocked the reflection of light, it would be in the HI or EI ranges. It is an LI_2, a superbly clean stone for sapphire. Note that the LI_2 has an asterisk. The comment corresponding to that asterisk is "Faint color zoning and moderate dichroic effect present."

Color zoning is a phenomenon in which there are varying degrees of color intensity within the stone. Sapphire, in particular, can suffer horribly from this effect. Virtually all blue sapphire has some color zoning. In the worst form, prominent areas of blue can be interspersed with colorless zones. A grade of "faint color zoning" is about the best one will encounter in blue sapphire. This comment is a plus; it means the color is evenly distributed.

The stone also has a moderate dichroic effect. The dichroic effect (a form of pleochroism where two optic axes show a different color, e.g. greenish blue and violetish blue) is caused by the double refraction of corundum. Please refer to Chapter 1 for a review of this concept. Faint or moderate dichroic effect is acceptable in fine corundum. There is no real negative to this stone so far. It is very clean, and the color is distributed evenly.

Color Grade	4/90*
Color Rating/Tone	4/90–95
Color Scan	B70 V20 G5 Gy5

The final aspect of this gem to consider is the color. Color is made up of primary color, secondary colors, and intensity modifiers. That total color package is made more or less intense by the tone. Color will be analyzed first.

The color grade is 4. On the color-rating scale, that grade is indicated as very good. Unless a sapphire is exceptional and probably of Burma or Kashmir origin, a 3.5 color is as good as one normally sees. A 4 color, therefore, is an exceptionally high grade. The color scan bears that out. The primary color, blue (B70), is equivalent to 70 percent of all the color in the stone. On top of that, the major secondary color is violet (V20) and takes up another 20 percent of the stone's color. As pointed out before, violet is the preferred secondary color compared to green. The negatives in the color scan are green (G5) at only 5 percent and grey (Gy) at only 5 percent. The scan, then, is very good.

The tone grade is 90, but the actual tone is between 90 and 95. Since tone is expressed in five-point increments, it can be safely assumed that the actual tone is closer to 90 since that is the final grade (as listed in color grade—4/90*). This tone makes the sapphire *very* dark, so dark, in fact, that only a very high-powered light can illuminate the stone intensely enough to show off all its other wonderful characteristics. Blue sapphire, in particular, suffers in this tonal range. In normal light, the stone will appear almost black. In a ring, this stone may be pretty, particularly in sunlight or in a ballroom filled with hundreds of lights. As a collector's stone it is above average, but as an investment stone it is a disaster, despite all its other high-quality components. Trying to resell a stone that is this dark is very difficult. These are the types of stones that jewelers will sell in rings and unscrupulous investment companies will recommend but never want back!

If this stone had a tone of 85, its price would be higher. It would be a beautiful stone if it had a tone of 75 to 80, for the blue would be highly saturated instead of hidden. The difference in price between this stone with 75 to 80 tone and the same stone with 90 to 95 tone is tremendous. The latter would be only one fifth to one fourth the price of the former! The importance of knowing how each separate piece of analysis affects the ultimate price of the stone should hit the reader right between the eyes at this point. Do not ignore *any* information on the certificate or any grading information given by the jeweler!

CERTIFICATE NUMBER 2
"The Very Expensive Frisbee"
or
"How I Fell into the Window of Vulnerability"

The next certificate, shown in Figure 32, is a 1.25-carat ruby. Using the same analytical procedure as was used for the sapphire,

Figure 32
AGL Colored Stone Certificate—Natural Ruby

American Gemological Laboratories
Olympic Tower
645 Fifth Avenue
New York, N.Y. 10022
(212) 935-0060
(212) 935-0071

Colored Stone Certificate

CERTIFICATE NO: CS 00000

DATE: 28 January 1985

The information contained in this report represents the opinion of American Gemological Laboratories regarding the characteristics of the colored stone(s) submitted for examination.

The conclusions expressed are the American Gemological Laboratories' interpretation of the results obtained from gemological instruments and grading techniques designed for this purpose. Conclusions may vary due to the subjective nature of colored stone analysis. Mounted stones are graded only to the extent that mounting permits examination.

SAMPLE

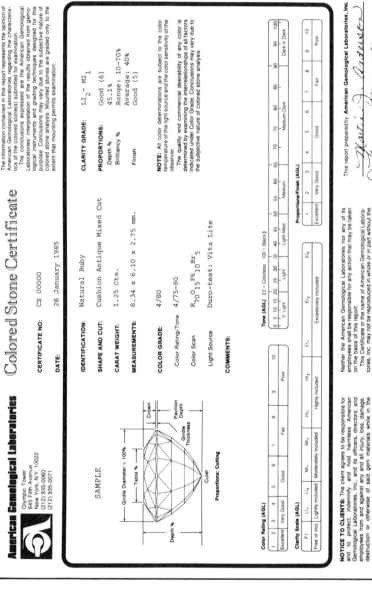

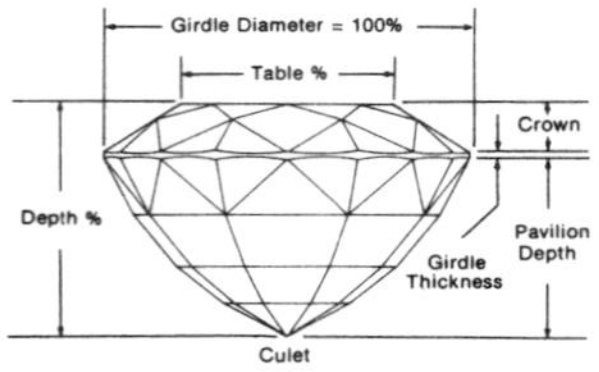

Proportions: Cutting

IDENTIFICATION: Natural Ruby

SHAPE AND CUT: Cushion Antique Mixed Cut

CARAT WEIGHT: 1.25 Cts.

MEASUREMENTS: 8.34 x 6.10 x 2.75 mm.

COLOR GRADE: 4/80

Color Rating/Tone 4/75-80

Color Scan $R_{70}O_{15}Pk_{10}Br_{5}$

Light Source Duro-test: Vita Lite

COMMENTS:

CLARITY GRADE: LI_2 - MI_1

PROPORTIONS: Good (6)

Depth % 45.1%

Brilliancy % Range: 10-70%
Average: 40%

Finish Good (5)

NOTE: All color determinations are subject to the color temperature of the light source and the color sensitivity of the observer.

The quality and commercial desirability of any color is determined by examining the interrelationships of all factors indicated under Color Grade. Conclusions may vary due to the subjective nature of colored stone analysis.

Color Rating (AGL)

1	2	3	4	5	6	7	8	9	10
Excellent		Very Good		Good		Fair		Poor	

Tone (AGL) (0 = Colorless 100 = Black)

0	5	10	15	20	25	30	35	40	45	50	55	60	65	70	75	80	85	90	95	100
V. Light				Light			Light-Med.				Medium			Medium-Dark					Dark-V. Dark	

Clarity Scale (AGL)

FI	LI_1	LI_2	MI_1	MI_2	HI_1	HI_2	EI_1	EI_2	EI_3
Free of Incl.	Lightly Included		Moderately Included		Highly Included		Excessively Included		

Proportions/Finish (AGL)

1	2	3	4	5	6	7	8	9	10
Excellent	Very Good		Good			Fair		Poor	

NOTICE TO CLIENTS: The client agrees to be responsible for and to protect, indemnify and hold harmless American Gemological Laboratories, Inc., and its officers, directors, and employees from and against any and all injury, loss, damage, destruction or otherwise of said gem materials while in the possession of American Gemological Laboratories resulting from any cause not attributable to the negligence of American Gemological Laboratories or its employees.

The client agrees that this report is for his/her exclusive use.

Neither the American Gemological Laboratories nor any of its employees shall be responsible for any action that may be taken on the basis of this report.

This Certificate or the name of American Gemological Laboratories, Inc. may not be reproduced in whole or in part without the express, prior written authorization from American Gemological Laboratories.

Do not accept copies, alterations or corrections on this document for final transactions.

This report prepared by **American Gemological Laboratories, Inc.**

Martin J. Anderson

Theresa Morace

Source: Courtesy American Gemological Laboratories, Inc.

the problem with this stone is easily found in the cut proportions and not in the tone. The color and tone of this gem are very nice. The color is 4, highly saturated in the 75 to 80 range (ideal for Thailand stones), and the scan reflects a strong red (70 percent) and secondary colors of orange (15 percent) and pink (10 percent). There is only a tiny amount of intensity modifier—brown (5 percent). Clarity is good at LI_2 to MI_1.

Corundum, unfortunately, frequently forms in flat, tabular crystals; they are very shallow when cut. This stone is a perfect example. The depth percentage is only 45.1 percent, far removed from the ideal 70 percent to 80 percent. The brilliancy range is 10 percent to 70 percent; the average is only 40 percent because the shallowness allows light to leak out of the bottom of the stone in huge quantities. This gem has an enormous window, and from the side it looks like a very expensive, red frisbee.

This type of gem is sold as fine quality (often at excessive prices) by unethical investment companies and jewelers who do not know any better. Its certificate is used to point out to the buyer: "Just look at this color and tone!" But ignore the fact that the stone can skip across the water with no problem!

The only way this ruby can be made to look good is to mount it in jewelry. Even then, it will not sparkle much and will look like a red blob. Although these high-color, shallow rubies are sold frequently in jewelry stores, the price should be low because they are priced as such in the wholesale market. Just as in the previous example, the price of this ruby is about one fifth to one fourth the price it could be if it had the cut proportions of the 2.22 carat sapphire above! Shallow stones simply will not make the grade—in either the collector or investment market. When purchasing any stone that is being represented as fine, look to see what kind of window is present. Most stones will have a small window, but large windows are unacceptable in fine gems.

CERTIFICATE NUMBER 3
"The Burma Boomer"
or
"Send All Unwanted Ones to This Author"

This stone, shown in Figure 33, is superb. Its Burma origin will possibly price the stone as much as 100 percent higher than a Sri

Figure 33
AGL Colored Stone Certificate—Natural Sapphire (Burma)

American Gemological Laboratories

Olympic Tower
645 Fifth Avenue
New York, N.Y. 10022
(212) 935-0060
(212) 935-0071

Colored Stone Certificate

CERTIFICATE NO: CS 00000

DATE: 28 January 1985

The information contained in this report represents the opinion of American Gemological Laboratories regarding the characteristics of the colored stone(s) submitted for examination.

The conclusions expressed are the American Gemological Laboratories' interpretation of the results obtained from gemological instruments and grading techniques designed for this purpose. Conclusions may vary due to the subjective nature of colored stone analysis. Mounted stones are graded only to the extent that mounting permits examination.

SAMPLE

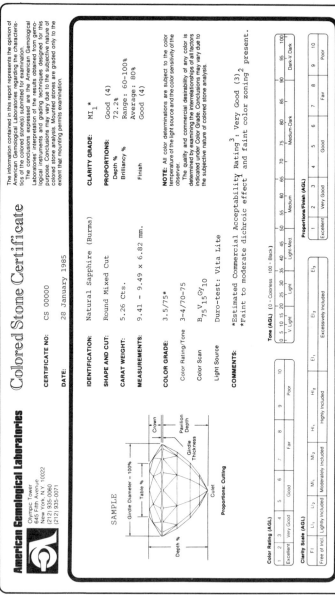

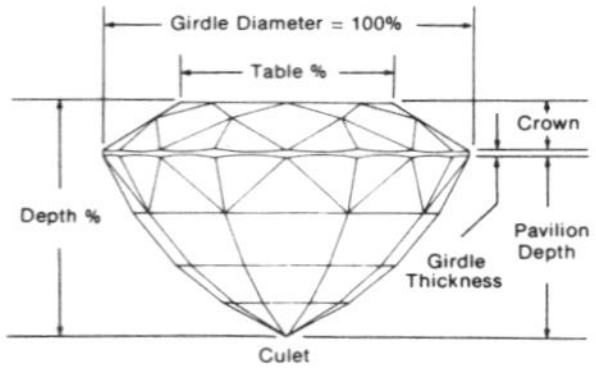

Proportions: Cutting

IDENTIFICATION: Natural Sapphire (Burma)

SHAPE AND CUT: Round Mixed Cut

CARAT WEIGHT: 5.26 Cts.

MEASUREMENTS: 9.41 - 9.49 x 6.82 mm.

COLOR GRADE: 3.5/75*

Color Rating/Tone 3-4/70-75

Color Scan $B_{75}V_{15}Gy_{10}$

Light Source Duro-test: Vita Lite

COMMENTS: *Estimated Commercial Acceptability Rating[3]: Very Good (3)[2]
*Faint to moderate dichroic effect[1] and faint color zoning[2] present.

CLARITY GRADE: MI_1*

PROPORTIONS: Good (4)

Depth % 72.2%

Brilliancy % Range: 60-100%
Average: 80%

Finish Good (4)

NOTE: All color determinations are subject to the color temperature of the light source and the color sensitivity of the observer.

The quality and commercial desirability of any color is determined by examining the interrelationships of all factors indicated under Color Grade. Conclusions may vary due to the subjective nature of colored stone analysis.

Color Rating (AGL)

1	2	3	4	5	6	7	8	9	10
Excellent		Very Good		Good		Fair		Poor	

Tone (AGL) (0 = Colorless 100 = Black)

0	5	10	15	20	25	30	35	40	45	50	55	60	65	70	75	80	85	90	95	100
V. Light				Light			Light-Med.			Medium				Medium-Dark				Dark-V. Dark		

Clarity Scale (AGL)

FI	LI_1	LI_2	MI_1	MI_2	HI_1	HI_2	EI_1	EI_2	EI_3
Free of Incl.	Lightly Included		Moderately Included		Highly Included		Excessively Included		

Proportions/Finish (AGL)

1	2	3	4	5	6	7	8	9	10
Excellent	Very Good		Good			Fair		Poor	

NOTICE TO CLIENTS: The client agrees to be responsible for and to protect, indemnify and hold harmless American Gemological Laboratories, Inc., and its officers, directors, and employees from and against any and all injury, loss, damage, destruction or otherwise of said gem materials while in the possession of American Gemological Laboratories resulting from any cause not attributable to the negligence of American Gemological Laboratories or its employees.

The client agrees that this report is for his/her exclusive use.

Neither the American Gemological Laboratories nor any of its employees shall be responsible for any action that may be taken on the basis of this report.

This Certificate or the name of American Gemological Laboratories, Inc. may not be reproduced in whole or in part without the express, prior written authorization from American Gemological Laboratories.

Do not accept copies, alterations or corrections on this document for final transactions.

This report prepared by: **American Gemological Laboratories, Inc.**

Source: Courtesy American Gemological Laboratories, Inc.

Lankan sapphire of the same quality and size. It is large, over five carats, and is a round mixed cut—a premium shape. The stone has everything going for it; not one thing is wrong. Brilliancy is outstanding. The proportions and finish are a 4. The Estimated Commercial Acceptability (ECA) rating is a special comment that AGL gives when a stone's appearance warrants more than just a straight color grade. The color grade is a fantastic 3.5, the ECA is a 3. The high-cap 3 over the ECA designates that the stone has better areas of color than 3.5. Having better areas of color, however, will not necessarily increase the grade. Other excellent factors must be there for the stone to get that boost. The stone will be priced between a 3.0 and a 3.5 color. Finding a buyer for this stone in a moderate to strong market will be a piece of cake. Everyone who buys and sells fine gems would love to own it.

A Final Tip Every commercial-grade colored stone will have some quality aspect(s) that depart from the "ideal." There is no way a consumer can walk into a jewelry store, buy a $1,500 ruby ring, and expect to receive a superlative stone. The concepts that were presented in this section should do two things for you:

1. When buying commercial-quality jewelry, keep all these factors in mind. It will make shopping easier so that you can buy the most beautiful stone for your money.
2. When buying a superb colored stone, keeping these factors in mind will prevent your being "taken" by an unscrupulous company that tries to have you focus on just one fine aspect of the stone and ignore other vital data. Any colored stone with a price of $10,000 or more should have an accompanying independent laboratory certificate. The information provided will tell you much of what you need to know to analyze the components of the stone via the document, despite what any dealer or jeweler claims. Always remember, it is the *stone* that is being purchased, *not* the piece of paper.

8 Improving the Rainbow

On the counter sat an incredible 10-carat, pear-shaped, pink-red precious topaz. The color was so intense, it practically glowed. It was marvelous to look at, the kind of stone you see at the Tucson Gem & Mineral Show, the largest trade show of its kind in the world. The wonders of nature displayed there reach out to tickle the desire for ownership. The year was 1980, the price was $1,500 per carat (dealer price), and the stone certainly seemed worth the money. The inexperienced salesman was so anxious to make the sale, he said, "If you think that is something, I have a lot of the same quality stones." He pulled out a large parcel, with stones ranging in size from 3 to 20 carats—all *exactly* the same color. The chances of nature producing that many stones of that particular rare color were billions to one. The stones had been irradiated and heat treated, hot off the X-ray machine and out of the oven. My admiration of the single stone turned into the nervous question, "Is the induced color stable, or will it fade?"

It is estimated that up to 80 percent of all colored stones found in jewelry stores are treated in some way to either improve the color and/or lessen the visual impact of inclusions. Treating gemstones is an art and has been going on for decades. Everyone who has studied gemology within the last 20 years is aware of the fact that stones may be cooked in ovens (heat treated), oiled, dyed, irradiated, lasered, bleached, impregnated with plastic, or surface coated. Although some of the processes are as old as the jewelry business itself, virtually none of this information has been disseminated to the public. Why? The industry has been scared to death to present this information, for it cannot always know if a stone has been treated.

There are certain questions to be answered: (1) Are some of the processes of the "laboratory" the same processes that nature accomplishes over millions of years? (2) If they are, does that make them acceptable? (3) Are there ways of improving color and clarity that do not occur in nature? (4) Is the process permanent or is it unstable?

Actually, it is not the can of worms it seems, but the gem industry has stuck its head in the sand for decades concerning this issue. The subject of treatment can be presented intelligently and cogently. The real problem faced by jewelers today is not whether they are able to present the information to the public. It is the fear of what the public will do when they realize they have been misled all these years. The view has been, "If we don't bring it up, we won't have to deal with it." It is only within the last few years that the industry has begun to internally deal with the problem and there has been considerable infighting over what should or should not be publicly disclosed.

Presently, Federal Trade Commission rules *require* disclosure of gem treatment to the public. Yet, the jewelers who actually abide by this requirement are so few, they are almost nonexistent. It has only been the development of the investment oriented gem companies and the rapid development of accurate colored stone certificates that have brought these facts to public scrutiny. When truthful dealers started telling the public that virtually all aquamarine is heat treated, and laboratory certificates began proclaiming that blue sapphire had undergone the same treatment, traditional jewelers were caught with their pants down. The bull market in stone prices from 1977 to 1981 was the major catalyst in getting this type of information to the public. If this quality conscious buying frenzy had not occurred, the whole issue would likely be being whispered about in the back rooms of jewelry stores to this day.

The trauma the jewelry industry is going through about disclosure of stone treatments is tantamount to the trauma of being involved in a nasty divorce. Some trade associations that are involved in the debate are similarly torn. Lacking consensus, different groups are power struggling to try to get their ideas into the industry. Traditional retail jewelers are generally bewildered.

Most want to be honest, but apart from their fear of suddenly revealing that most of the stones they sold were treated, many do not have the experience, knowledge, equipment, or initiative to find out which were and which were not.

Of all the criticisms that can be leveled against the gem industry, its failure to disclose stone treatments to the public is the most valid. For example, in late 1984, a major trade magazine conducted a poll to find out how many jewelers always disclosed treatments to the public. Of the 204 respondents, 38.2 percent said they always do so; 37.3 percent said it depended on the treatment; 18.6 percent said they gave the information only if asked; and 5.9 percent said they never disclose treatment. These are not bad percentages in light of what was mentioned earlier. In the same article, however, retailers gave the following information: Of those that sold black onyx, only 28.4 percent sold dyed black onyx. Of those that sold tanzanite, only 13.4 percent sold heat-treated material. Of those that sold emeralds, only 21.7 percent sold oiled gems. The truth is that almost 100 percent of all black onyx is dyed; 100 percent of all tanzanite is heat treated; and it is believed that almost 100 percent of all emeralds are oiled!

The same trade magazine sent a "mystery shopper" to 12 stores in the northeast United States a few months after this initial article. Their findings? Not one store voluntarily told the shopper about treatments. In fact, several of the salespeople said that treatment shouldn't concern the shopper, or that there was no such thing, or that there were treated stones but *they* did not carry them. The jewelry industry may well continue to hide from the issue, but consumers, collectors, and investors have the *right* to know. Once explained, the caveats become much clearer and more manageable.

Below are some of the types of treatments used on gemstones. More exotic ones exist, but these are the ones commonly encountered.

1. Bleaching.
2. Surface diffusion.
3. Dyeing.
4. Heat treatment.
5. Impregnation.
6. Irradiation.
7. Lasering.

8. Oiling.
9. Sugar treatment of opal.
10. Surface coating.

Bleaching

Some gem material can be made lighter through the use of chemicals. This process, bleaching, is used primarily on pearls. The use of bleaching in pearls is probably extensive for those that can use a slight improvement; bleaching can improve the evenness of color. The finest pearls are natural in color or very lightly bleached; their prices correspond accordingly. Bleaching pearls is acceptable for the consumer because no amount of the process can improve pearls to the point that their prices will jump dramatically. The most favored pearls in the United States are those with an intense pinkish cast and high luster. In South America, yellow and golden pearls are the most highly prized. Natural black pearls are universally expensive and appreciated. Bleaching would only tend to lower their value. Elephant ivory is often bleached to remove grey and brown.

Surface Diffusion

Through the use of heat, a chemical is forced into the surface of a stone. Blue sapphire has appeared on the market that has an intense blue caused by a diffusion process. *Surface diffusion is unacceptable.* It can be seen with the use of a gemological microscope. The intense color only appears on the surface of the stone; it does not penetrate deeply. Other stones whose color will improve through surface diffusion include all other corundum, ruby, and fancy-colored sapphires. The danger of buying a diffusion-colored sapphire occurs when jewelers do not carefully check the stones that they buy for inventory. Going to a jeweler who is a gemologist or has one on the premises will help alleviate this danger. Remember, all color diffusion processes are an attempt to defraud the consumer, whether the jeweler knows about it or not!

Dyeing

Many stones are known to be dyed. Dyeing involves the soaking of a porous stone in a colored solution, with or without heat, for varying periods of time. Stones that are commonly dyed include calcite, lapis lazuli, chalcedony, ivory, quartz, serpentine, shell, pearl, and jadeite. Dyeing is acceptable in a few of these and is absolutely *not* acceptable in others.

Calcite is hardly ever used for jewelry. Lapis lazuli is so commonly dyed that its price reflects the assumption that it has undergone this treatment. Lapis that has not been dyed and possesses an intense blue color is more expensive than the dyed variety. Ivory is often dyed, frequently to bring out details in carvings. Shell is dyed, but since it is often an inexpensive material, this is not a critical issue. Dyed pearls are usually sold as such to the retail jeweler, but jewelers often don't tell customers that this is the case. Commonly dyed pearls include the fashionable freshwater type; bluish, golden, and pinkish casts are often put into these. Most black pearls in jewelry stores are dyed. Dyeing is not acceptable in jadeite. Fine emerald green or lavender jadeite is very rare and costly. Dyed jadeite, which mimics these very expensive stones, is actually pale jadeite (just a few dollars per stone). Selling dyed material as if it were natural is an attempt to defraud the public. The threads of the coloring agent, however, can be identified through the use of a microscope.

Heat Treatment

Of the major treatments, heat is the most common. It is a dangerous form of treatment in which destruction of stones is commonplace in the ovens. As they move toward their melting point, many stones explode and shatter. A number of stones are often treated in this way. They include: blue sapphire, yellow sapphire, golden sapphire, ruby, aquamarine, topaz, some varieties of quartz, zircon, and tanzanite. In all probability, every type of crystalline stone has been at least experimentally heat treated. The effects and consequences of heat treatment on each of these stones are listed below.

Blue Sapphire Heat treatment produces a permanent color improvement, improves clarity, and is acceptable. Heat tends to remove silking and has been commonly used for many years. Price matrix charts for blue sapphire always reflect the assumption that they have been heat treated. Very fine gems that can be shown not to have been heat treated cost 10 percent to 30 percent more than the heat-treated variety.

Yellow and Golden Sapphire Heat improves color, although there is some debate about color permanence in the super heat-treated yellows. These stones are so intense, they often exhibit flashes of orange. Nonheat-treated yellows and goldens are usually more pastel and soft looking in color; goldens often have areas that exhibit a light greenish tint. Heat also improves clarity. While the process is acceptable, collectors and investors will pay a premium for natural stones, particularly fine goldens.

Ruby Heat treatment in ruby is not as common as in sapphire, although it is apparent on careful examination that some Thai rubies have been "fried" to the melting point. This may improve color but it melts obvious inclusions into less visible ones. Since the process is becoming more common, there will come a point when natural gems will be valued higher than cooked ones. At this time, the difference in price between heat-treated and natural ruby is not as critical as in sapphire.

Aquamarine Virtually every aquamarine has been heat treated. In its natural state, most aqua has a moderate to strong green secondary color. The cooking process drives out most of the green and enhances the blue. Since all aqua has been treated, the process is acceptable as well as permanent. Actually, it has been done for so long, natural colors would probably be ignored by the buying public.

Topaz Virtually all varieties of topaz have been heat treated; many, however, have also been irradiated. The cooking process in topaz is not as well understood as it is in corundum, although the stability of the ensuing color is believed to be good. Heat improves color randomly. Severe color instability has also been demonstrated when topaz is irradiated. Blue topaz, a very popular stone, is 100 percent heat treated and is sometimes irradiated. This combination process appears to be stable for this color. Natural, rough material is very pale to almost colorless before the process. Heat treating of topaz is acceptable unless the color fades. When purchasing very fine and expensive topaz, a consumer is wise to obtain a two-week refund guarantee while the stone sits in daylight—unless the jeweler has already run the same test.

Quartz Of the most expensive varieties of quartz, amethyst is often heat treated, and citrine is always heat treated. Actually, citrine is very pale amethyst that has been cooked, which produces its popular, golden-whiskey color. Better colored natural amethyst, when cooked, will sometimes become more intense in color. Citrine wouldn't exist unless poor quality amethyst was heated, so the process is acceptable as well as permanent. Heat-treated amethyst is difficult to identify as fine, grape popsicle-colored natural stones do occur. There is no clear way, unfortunately, to distinguish the cooked from the natural. For those who want the best natural amethyst, estate pieces, which contain fine Russian material, will ensure a good stone.

Zircon Zircon is not used extensively today, although it had considerable popularity 40 to 50 years ago. The stones show wear and become unsightly over time. The most popular zircon is bright blue. These stones do not usually occur in nature. Rather, they are created by heat treating. Heat treating is acceptable.

Tanzanite Natural tanzanite tends to be a brownish color or brown with some bluish overtones. The exquisite color of tanzanite would not exist without heat treating. The process is permanent and perfectly acceptable.

Impregnation

Highly porous stones, such as turquoise, are sometimes impregnated with clear or colored plastic, wax, or similar material to make the stones stronger and enhance the color. This is a common process for inexpensive jewelry stones. Other stones subject to this process are jade and lapis lazuli. The process is not acceptable for those who want a fine, natural stone.

Irradiation

This is one of the most controversial of all treatments, primarily because gemologists do not always know what its effects will be. Irradiation is often done in conjunction with heat treatment. Other than in blue topaz, irradiation is often considered unacceptable, particularly if the color is unstable. Some stones, such as lavender jade, may be irradiated to permanently improve their color. While dyeing can be identified in jade, no test exists to differentiate irradiated lavender from natural lavender. It has been suggested that intense, natural colored, lavender jade has its color because of its proximity to radioactive elements (uranium) in the earth. This color forming process normally takes a few million years due to the low level of radiation, but the atomic reactor or X-ray machine can reduce eons of time into minutes or hours.

Detection of irradiation treatments is in its infancy, but progress has been made. Most suspect are stones of Brazilian origin such as topaz and tourmalines. If the color is stable after a stone has been in the sunlight for a while, the stone is probably natural; or, whatever process was used is permanent and stable. In this case, the stone is acceptable.

Diamonds have been irradiated for many years to create fancy colors such as golden, green, brown, and yellow. The process is permanent. The stones used for this process are a very low color grade in their natural state. The irradiated stones mimic the astronomically expensive natural, fancy colors, but tend to be metallic looking. Pastels typify natural colored diamonds. Separation of cyclotron irradiated diamonds from natural colors can be done by using a spectroscope.

Lasering

One of the newest types of treatments, lasering, is used to remove unsightly black inclusions from diamonds. The laser cuts a hole to the inclusions. The diamond is then soaked in acid to remove the black area. Under microscopic examination, the hole the laser makes and the cavity where the inclusion existed are easily visible. Lasering helps the appearance of the diamond, but after this treatment the stone must be graded on the same clarity level it was originally. Lasering *must* be disclosed. It is an acceptable treatment and any independent laboratory or appraisal analysis will disclose its presence. Jewelers who do not disclose lasering are committing fraud by representing the stone as natural and possibly at a higher clarity grade than it really is.

Oiling

This process is most commonly associated with emerald. It is estimated that 90 to 100 percent of all emeralds have been treated in this way. Clear oil is used frequently and is acceptable. The oil fills in surface indentations and cavities, making the stone look more desirable. It may also improve the color. Over the years, the oil will disintegrate and the emerald may become pale. Reoiling will bring the stone back to its original state. Green oil, however, is not acceptable, particularly in very fine stones. Rubies are sometimes treated with red oil; this is not acceptable.

Sugar Treatment of Opal

Given the same quality of color play, naturally occurring opal with a dark body color is more expensive than opal with a white body color. The terms *semiblack* and *black* are generally used to represent these more valuable and rare stones. The body color of an opal may be made darker by soaking the stone in a sugar solution. Treatment with sulfuric acid after drying turns the sugar dark, producing a more desirable-looking stone. Sugar treatment is unacceptable and can be identified. It is an attempt to defraud the consumer. When buying expensive black opals, always obtain a written guarantee from the jeweler that the stone has not been treated in this way, or have the stone verified as natural from a laboratory before purchasing it. Black opals are also created in other ways, including burial in manure while being cooked over charcoal!

Surface Coating

Surface coating is a fancy term for painting the surface of a stone with a chemical that enhances its color. Coating has been used on diamonds to turn them into "fancy colors," and many colored stones have been coated. Coating can often be taken off with solvents and can be identified in the same way as surface diffusion. Again, the danger is that jewelers may not carefully check incoming stock in which case they may offer this type of treated stone unknowingly.

Although at first these treatments may seem hard to understand, the bottom line is that many are quite common and are acceptable to both the gem trade and the public. The real problem is not that treatment occurs, but that few in the trade wish to discuss it. Acceptable treatments are not cause for issues of confidence in a jeweler if the consumer understands what they are and how they are used. A question concerning nonacceptable treatments directed to a competent jeweler will evoke an honest answer and/or a guarantee of nontreatment based on specific, reliable tests. Customers should avoid *any* company that claims its stones are never treated or that treatment does not exist. Such companies are either ignorant or they are being purposefully deceitful. In neither case is the customer well served.

9 The Pricing Cycles of Gemstones

Introduction

Understanding the information in this chapter is *vital* to those who buy important jewelry, fine collector stones, or investment-quality gem material. Without a grasp of the following concepts, the chances of paying too much, buying at the wrong time, or trying to resell into an illiquid market are very high. The impact of the information presented does not materially affect those buyers of fashion jewelry that costs a few hundred dollars, but understanding the economics of the gem market will be very interesting to them and will allow them to take advantage of the situations that create downward pressure on pricing. Excellent bargains may be found—even in the lower price ranges.

The prices of all gemstones began to move in cycles in the mid-1970s. The effects of these cycles on commercial-grade jewelry prices are incremental. At the retail level, they have a very gradual impact. Once an item is put in inventory, it keeps the same tag price until prices shift with such magnitude that the jeweler is forced to change them. A jeweler will change them in only two circumstances: (1) when prices for gems and/or precious metals have moved up so much on a percentage basis that the current tag price is at or below replacement cost; or (2) when prices have moved down so much that the jeweler has to compete with new inventory in other jewelers' showcases.

In the fine jewelry, collector, and investment markets, price changes are absorbed and passed on much more quickly. A 10 percent increase in the wholesale price of a $100 ruby can be absorbed, but a 10 percent increase on a $10,000 ruby is significant. The finer the quality and the higher the trading velocity for each species of stone, the more exaggerated the price change to the public.

The mid-1970s marked the end of a 30-year, stable era in gem and precious metal prices. The world's currencies began to float against one another, inflation became the primary way for politicians to buy votes, and massive, Third World debt became a dangerous problem to the international banking community. These situations caused the gem world to go slightly crazy, and the popular media treated the resulting increases in prices for diamonds and colored gems as if they were a previously unheard of phenomenon. They were incorrect.

The single most important factor that differentiated the gemstone bull market of 1976 to 1981 from previous bull markets was the presence of global communication capabilities. Given the standardization of grading and ease of identification that had been developed for gemstones, the proliferation of accurate price lists, and the global increase in investment capital, this market seemed totally unique. For these reasons, it *was* a different market—but only in its efficiency. Many societies have placed high values on gemstones, thereby driving prices to stellar heights only to have those prices tumble when the crisis passes.

From the earliest civilizations, gems have been a medium by which large quantities of wealth could be stored or moved. Gemstones have historically been used by the wealthy as a hedge against disintegrating currencies. The rarer and finer the stone, the more quickly it rose in terms of paper money. The only reason gemstones have not been recognized as playing a more important role in the economics of past and present troubled societies is that they are private, confidential, and anonymous. While governments copiously record their own follies in economic and social mismanagement, individual actions remain largely private and unknown.

The world's gemstone source markets quote prices per carat in U.S. dollars. This is not new. For years, virtually every major gem has had its price fluctuations pegged to American currency. From just after World War II through the early 1970s, this made sense. Low price volatility was a way in which gems could be positively marketed to the public; a strong underlying foundation and an image of stability were good selling points. "Diamonds Are Forever" was the symbol of this concept. It was believed that diamonds *are* forever, not only because of their durability and beauty but also because they reflected the stability of the U.S. dollar. DeBeers initially pegged the price of diamond rough to the U.S. dollar shortly after World War II at which time U.S. currency was the strongest in the world. The cartel continues to use the dollar as the basis for any price changes in rough diamond. On balance, DeBeers' methods have worked. Only in the last 10 years has the U.S. dollar fluctuated greatly.

What Causes the Prices of Gemstones to Increase?

There were two important factors that created stability in the prices of gemstones before the mid-1970s. First, as discussed above, prices for gems were quoted in U.S. dollars. In countries with weak currencies, the price of gemstones would go up in relationship to the local currency, but there was an automatic gain against the depreciation of that currency: payment in U.S. dollars. The number of units of the local currency that were equivalent to the dollar would adjust daily through the exchange rate. As long as the dollar was stronger than any other currency, the price for gems in the major consuming countries, particularly the United States, remained stable. This situation promoted consumer confidence and formed the foundation upon which DeBeers built its empire.

The second stability factor was that the industrial countries had not inflated their currencies enough to vitally damage the value of their money in relation to the dollar.

Inflation is a monetary, not a price phenomenon. When the money supply increases at a faster rate than the amount of goods and services produced, each unit of currency buys less. Global inflation was growing during the 1950s and 1960s, but not nearly to the extent of the 1970s and 1980s. Some countries had serious inflation problems in the 1960s, but the major industrial countries had inflation relatively under control. Even if the dollar fell in buying power by 4 percent or 5 percent, the effect of that fall on the pricing of the bulk of commercial jewelry and gemstones was minimal. Over a period of several years, there was a significant difference in price, but it was felt gradually by consumers.

Diamonds and colored stones needn't *ever* increase in price more than the inflation rate of the U.S. dollar. What causes gemstones to rise at faster rate than inflation is the relative level of interest rates. If the inflation rate is less than the interest paid on loaned money, gems are of little interest except as items to be used for adornment. If the inflation rate moves ahead of interest paid on loaned money, traditional and so-called safe investments such as bonds, T-bills, and CDs become surefire losers. The traditional capital markets offer nothing to the investor who is in this situation. Figure 34 shows when U.S. T-Bill rates yielded a negative return against inflation. During those negative return periods, many gemstones increased in value and did so in relative proportion to the amount of the negative return.

If there were enough high-quality gemstones to meet demand in these situations, the prices of stones would not increase rapidly. But the fact is, there are not *nearly* enough high-quality stones to meet the demand during a wholesale slaughter of the traditional capital markets. At such times there are more buyers and money than available stones. Therefore, the price increases give positive returns against the inflation rate and overwhelmingly beat the "traditional" investments.

Figure 34
Real Interest Rates (T-bill rates minus inflation)

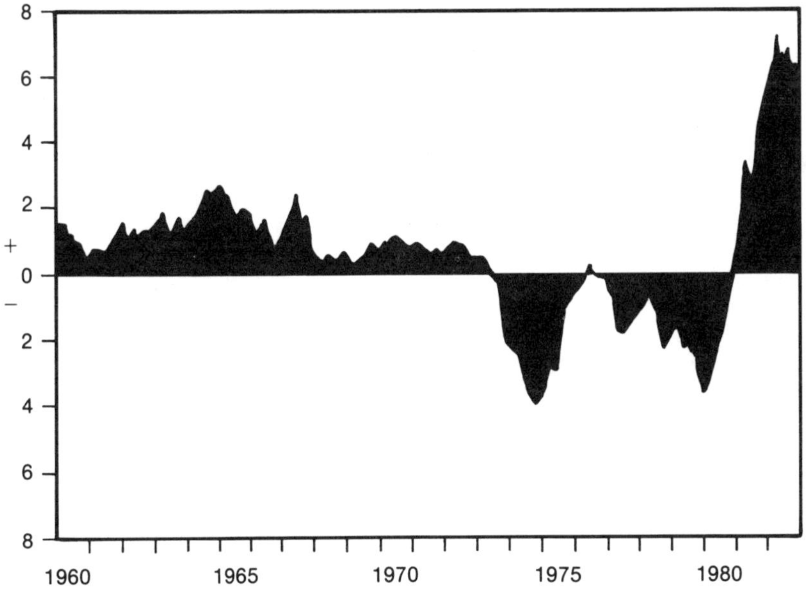

Source: John A. Pugsley, *Interest Rate Futures: The Ultimate Inflation Hedge.*

The situation can reverse itself, as it did in 1980 for diamonds and in 1981 for colored stones. As the inflation rate drops, traditional investments begin to yield positive returns, people do not invest in the finest stones, and demand collapses except at the jewelry level. Prices follow accordingly. *As long as the major currencies of the world, particularly the U.S. dollar, remain inflationary and unstable, the prices of fine gemstones will move in cycles.*

The Pricing Cycles of Gemstones Are Not All the Same

This overview is only a fundamental outline of why diamond and colored stone prices move in cycles. The gem markets of the world are not economically homogeneous. Since this is the case, stones will exhibit different price behavior given the same economic stimuli.

Diamonds are only one of 20 commonly traded gemstones, but they are generally thought of as comprising a market unto themselves. All others are lumped into one general category: colored stones. This is a valid way of thinking about gemstones and there are many reasons why people mentally organize the gem world in this fashion. Not the least important is in the comparative economic structures of the two markets: They are quite different. Although there are some exceptions to the rule, broadly speaking, the diamond market is a credit market and the colored stone market is a cash market. Because of this, the way in which prices in these two markets react to various economic conditions differs.

The diamond market is comprised of two submarkets: the market for rough (uncut) stones, and the market for polished stones. The rough market is essentially a cash market while the polished market is essentially a credit market. The one that directly affects individual buyers and sellers is the credit market. The dividing line rests between the giant DeBeers cartel and the rest of the diamond industry.

By contrast, the bulk of the international colored stone market is of a cash nature. The only area of the market *dominated* by credit is that of sales to retailers by local wholesalers. All else is pretty much cash and carry. Mining, cutting, and exporting are often carried out at or near the mine sites instead of being funneled through a long, snakelike distribution channel as with diamonds.

The Diamond Market

The mining and rough marketing sector of the diamond distribution chain is a cash market that is controlled by the DeBeers cartel. Over the last 40 years, the cartel has effectively controlled the price and distribution of 60 percent to 85 percent of all the world's uncut diamonds. What they don't mine themselves or in cooperation with governments, they buy from independent miners. DeBeers sets prices for rough. Independent miners of diamond rough usually price their material in the open market at or near the price that DeBeers demands from its customers.

DeBeers is often described as a "benevolent monopoly" that ensures the stability of prices for the world's consumers. In fact, they are aggressive in their quest for domination of the market and have crushed many who have tried to compete with them. Their diversification into other areas over the last three decades has provided them with the cash and power to effectively force the Soviet Union and certain African governments to see things their way. The only reason they have not replaced the cutters, wholesalers, and retailers who work for other companies with their own people is because those businesses do not have a large enough return on the capital invested to suit them.

The marketing arm of the DeBeers mining conglomerate is the Central Selling Organization (CSO). It sells diamond parcels called *sights* in London 10 times a year. The approximately 300 buyers are called *sight buyers*. These buyers may either accept or reject the parcels that are offered to them; they generally accept lest they be excluded from future sales.

DeBeers does make a considerable effort to give each sight buyer what is needed. Large stones go to New York, middle sizes go to Tel Aviv, and tiny stones go to India. DeBeers's attempt to make labor costs uniform on a per carat basis is also accompanied by a no haggle price policy. The price of the sight is the price: There are no exceptions.

The first part of a diamond's journey from the earth to the jewelry store occurs within a cash market. Sight buyers pay for the parcels of rough in full. When sight buyers sell to the world's cutters, the economic structure of the market changes dramatically; it becomes a credit market. Cutters often borrow money from banks or demand payment terms; for example, payment in full in 30, 60, or 90 days. In turn, wholesalers often borrow money to buy from cutters or take payment terms and retail jewelers do the same. Ninety- to 120-day payment terms are not unusual. In 1984, a diamond wholesale company was offering 18-*month* credit terms! Occasionally, members of the distribution pipeline will pay cash, but delaying payment is usual. DeBeers is smart: They will not accept credit terms. If they did, they would be connected to a system that is as unstable as a house of cards.

DeBeers Does Not Control Pricing in the Polished Market

Before January of 1980, one of the most common slogans heard from flippant diamond salespeople was, "DeBeers controls the diamond market. They have never lowered the price of rough; therefore, diamonds cannot go down in price." When the collapse came, people were shocked. Many publicity-seeking investment dealers were saying, "I think this is only temporary, the worst is over." They kept on saying it until the entire polished diamond market hit bottom in June and July of 1982. During that period, the price of a one-carat, D, flawless diamond fell from $60,000 plus per carat to around $12,500 per carat—a 79 percent slide in value. Since the $12,500-per-carat price had been reached in late 1977 and early 1978, the market had gone full circle in approximately five and one-half years. Some people had warned against the myth that DeBeers controlled the polished market, but few listened. The only individuals who made money bought before 1979 and sold back to the market at the end of 1979 or in early 1980. The earlier they bought, the more money they made. The longer they held on after early 1980, the more money they lost. Figure 35 shows a price history of D, IF, one-carat, round diamonds.

It is true that DeBeers, which controls the rough but not the polished market, has never lowered the price of rough. If consumers can understand what happened to the price of polished diamonds from 1977 through 1982, that understanding will do two things: (1) revolutionize their image of the diamond market, and (2) create an understanding of how the pricing cycles of diamonds work. This will make it clear when to buy, when to sell, and when to wait.

Many laypeople believe that polished diamond prices are directly sensitive to inflation and/or interest rates, but the situation is slightly more complicated.

Figure 35
Price History Curve of 1-Carat, Round Cut Diamond (D color, IF)*

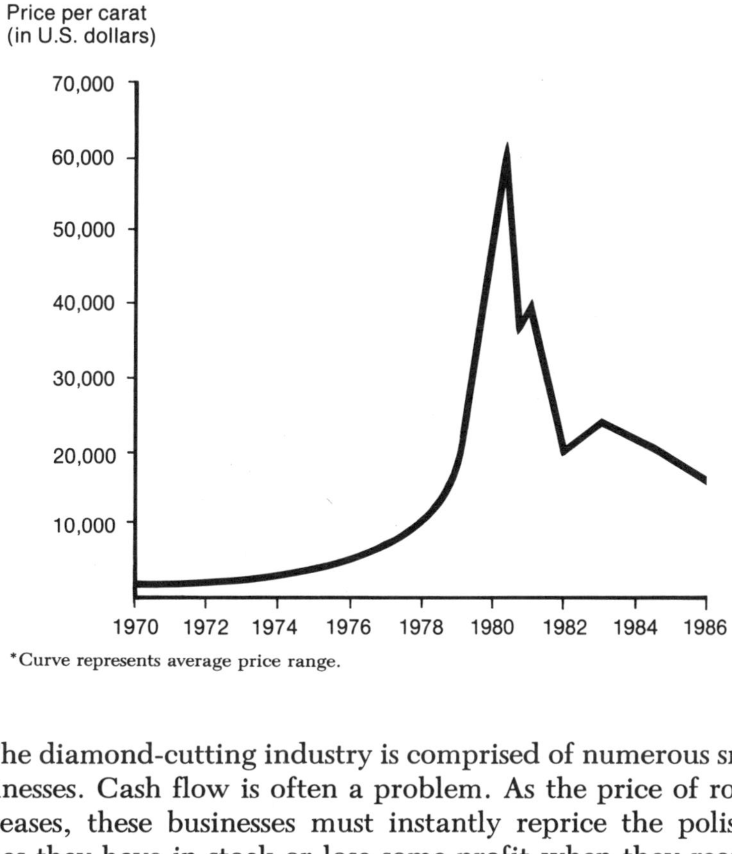

*Curve represents average price range.

The diamond-cutting industry is comprised of numerous small businesses. Cash flow is often a problem. As the price of rough increases, these businesses must instantly reprice the polished stones they have in stock or lose some profit when they reorder rough at a higher price. When the U.S. dollar is stable, business is good and diamond sales at the jewelry level continue at a regular pace. Since DeBeers adjusts the price of rough according to inflation fluctuations in the U.S. dollar (real inflation, not the politically manipulated consumer price index), a minimal upswing can be passed on through the distribution pipeline. Although cutters are continually borrowing money to buy new rough, they are paying off old loans with steady sales. Thus, even after their interest and overhead expenses, they are making a profit. What happens, however, in a full-scale bull market caused by high, double-digit inflation in the U.S. dollar?

The Investor and the Cutter: A Fairy Tale

This is the story of an investor who knows nothing about diamonds. It is also the tale of a typical cutter who is trying to make money in his business. Any similarity between this story and real people is completely intentional.

The year is 1977. The investor is beginning to get worried about inflation. His traditional, safe investments are not yielding what they used to. Literature has been sent to him proclaiming that the price of the finest one-carat diamond, which was $1,000 in 1970, is now $7,000. It will continue upward because inflation is going to get worse. The investor is cautious. Never jumping the gun, he needs to see more price increases to believe that the trend is real.

In the same year a cutter is enjoying good business. Back in 1970, he carried very few fine stones in his inventory; commercial grade was all that he sold on a regular basis. But the demand for fine stones is up and he is buying more expensive rough. He feels some vague apprehension because fine rough is moving up at a faster rate than commercial material and he is borrowing more money but owns fewer stones. If fine stones keep selling, however, he will make money.

By 1978, the price of a D, IF, one-carat, round diamond jumps to $10,000. The investor starts getting interested, but thinks there is no sense buying in a panic. He decides to talk to some of his friends: They know as much about the diamond market as he does. He continues to wait.

Meanwhile, the cutter is racking up orders for one-carat, high-quality diamonds. Inflation is up and he has to borrow considerably more to buy the rough. Despite the profit he made in 1977, it is not enough to compensate for the demand and increased price of rough. Business is good, but profits are on paper. The only thing to do is buy more.

In early 1979, the investor decides that his returns in traditional, safe investments are negative. He has to get into something that keeps ahead of inflation. The voluminous sales literature and hype brochures he has received on diamond investing finally convince him that diamond prices cannot go down. The best one-carat diamonds are selling for $28,000 each. "Perhaps," he thinks carefully, "an increase of $1,000 to $28,000 in eight years is a trend. I'll buy."

By this time, the cutter has found he can make more profit by selling his goods directly to the public. The investor comes to the cutter and purchases a one-carat, D, IF diamond. The cutter is also convinced that the dollar will never get out of its tailspin and that prices will go up forever.

By mid-1979, the cutter is buying more expensive rough on credit than he is selling. He feels he can stock up and beat the inevitable price increases. He has some apprehension because interest rates have moved into the double-digit area. They are twice what they were back in 1977. But despite the recent surge in interest rates, diamonds continue to climb and all caution is thrown out of the window.

By the end of 1979, the investor's diamond has skyrocketed in value to over $50,000 and liquidity is good. It seems everybody wants his stone. Feeling the giddiness, he slyly decides not to sell. If diamonds never come down, the worst he can do is almost double his money in one year.

During this time, the cutter is working 14 hours a day. He stretches his credit to the breaking point. Rough is getting hard to find, particularly in the top qualities. Commercial-quality stones, with which he built his business, are a pain in the neck. They make low profits and he has very few in inventory. Interest rates are around 20 percent, but the public is still buying diamonds at breakneck speed.

In January of 1980, the price for the best quality D, IF, one-carat diamond tops at $63,000. Suddenly, the buyers start drying up and the cutter has already bought a considerable quantity of rough. Feeling that the situation is temporary, he refuses to lower the asking price.

Meanwhile, the investor is unaware of the sales slowdown because the hype mongers keep on talking. Money markets are beginning to balloon as they grab the high interest rates and inflation is slowing and starting to reverse: The public will not borrow at these astronomical rates.

The market continues to fall through 1980. As each date approaches for repayment of past loans, the cutter begins to worry. His business in commercial goods had been steady, but he now has no inventory. The only way to convert the inventory emphasis is to unload his finest stones. He begins to cut prices a little, then a little more, and finally he is taking offers. He needs cash and fast!

The slide continues; interest rates remain high. By 1981, the price of the investor's diamond has dropped to $38,000 and the bid–ask spread is widening. He waits, hoping that his copious research, which consisted of memorizing the sentence, "Diamonds don't go down in price," will be right.

By late 1981, the cutter is in a major panic. He is selling his one-carat, D, IFs for as little as $20,000—well below his cost—just to stave off bankruptcy. The investor, if he can find a buyer, can get $15,000 for his stone, which means he has already lost $11,000. By mid-1982, the cutter has lost a fortune and is back to selling commercial-quality quarter carats. The investor cannot find a buyer. In his desperation, he finds a firm that will buy any diamond for cash; they buy the stone for $7,000.

The investor files a complaint with the FTC against the cutter for fraud. He writes letters to popular financial newspapers and magazines complaining about how he was cheated, while the cutter is barely scraping by during the slowest period in diamond sales within the last 30 years.

For those who lived this story—and there were many—it was not a fairy tale, but a nightmare. If both the cutter and the investor had been able to figure out how an alternative money form such as diamond would act given the economic scenario that was unfolding around them, neither would have lost. However, one did not do his homework and the other had no understanding of how his industry worked. The pertinent facts that can be gleaned from this story are as follows:

1. During times of currency crises, diamonds are an alternative form of money. Their prices will rise faster than the inflation rate because a considerable quantity of money that is ignoring the capital markets will chase a few high-quality stones.
2. Prices will continue to rise as inflation increases—despite increasing interest rates. This will continue as long as the public's belief in higher *future* inflation is greater than their perception of the quality of current returns on interest-bearing vehicles. Theoretically, if interest rates are 30 percent and people believe that inflation will go even higher, they will continue to buy diamonds. A cutter can continue to borrow at ever-increasing rates because the public is absorbing the cost. The critical juncture for diamond prices occurs when the public moves to a positive perception of traditional investment vehicles. Just before this point, diamonds should be sold, not purchased or held.

3. As soon as the public believes that (*a*) inflation will slow down because high interest rates have been able to strengthen the currency's value, and (*b*) they can once again earn interest through traditional investments, they will stop buying. The volatility in the price of fine diamonds, then, is directly proportional to the strength of perceived negative or positive returns on traditional investments.

Even if a consumer is interested in purchasing a commercial two- or three-carat diamond for adornment only, it is obviously better to purchase in a pricing trough than during the peak of a bull market. When the prices of gem-quality stones skyrocket, the commercial market rises as well. The price of large, commercial-quality stones also fell a significant percentage between 1980 and 1982.

The Colored Stone Market

Part of the reason that the distribution pipeline for diamonds can be solidly entrenched on a credit basis is because the market is huge. Diamonds are the most plentiful of rare gems. The finest quality colored stones, by contrast, are extremely rare and their source supplies are small. These two factors create an entirely different economic structure than that of the diamond market.

For example, when a diamond-bearing pipe (the remainder of a volcanic core) is located, geologists can predict within an acceptable range how many carats and of what quality can be obtained within a given time period. Taking samplings and making extrapolations may take several months, but the result is a mine that can actually have a "production schedule" within realistic expectations. Colored stone sources are often very small, sometimes taking up just a few square feet; others may extend for many acres. A few are known to cover several miles, but there is no uniformity to the amount and quality of the stones within the formations. There are several consequences of this geological condition.

1. Most colored stone mining companies are small and independent.
2. Venture capital for the mining operation is often supplied by one or just a few people.
3. Initial capital investment is severely restricted pending the outcome of the overall run-of-the-mine quality.

4. Inexpensive hand labor is preferred over machinery. In the event that the deposit gives out quickly, the quality of the stones changes negatively, or world demand drops, major overhead can be reduced by simply laying off workers.
5. Transactions are primarily cash in nature; very little credit is extended. And if credit is offered, it is often of short duration. Credit will only be allowed if proof of available funds exists.
6. Much of the world's finest and most popular colored stones comes from countries with unstable or oppressive governments where the rarest gems are considered an alternative passport out of the country. Prices, therefore, are usually inflexible for better goods unless the world's economy is so bad that discounts are necessary for people to stay in business.
7. The "cartels" that can be formed in any major, colored gem-producing area are informal. The closest thing to DeBeers in the colored stone market is a small hierarchy of Bangkok ruby dealers, several Colombo gem dealers, and a loose clique of Colombian emerald dealers. These small "associations" will generally give pricing indications to the rest of the market and establish price-base resistance levels, but they cannot control the price of rough the way DeBeers does.
8. Virtually all of the rough material is cut and polished at or near the mining area. In diamond, it is much easier to discern what the quality of a finished stone will be by studying the rough. Colored stone rough is often coated with a "rind" and it is difficult to know what the quality of the cut gem will be. To prevent a fine gem from sneaking out of the owner's hand in the guise of a visually poor piece of rough, the stone is cut before it is sold.

In the previous section, the difficulties that the diamond cutter had in managing his capital outlay in a credit-entrenched market was described. During the same period—1977 to 1982—what happened to the colored stone dealer was very different. His ability to cope with an accelerating, long-term, high interest rate situation was better.

Like the diamond cutter, the colored stone miner/cutter was in a good position from 1977 through 1979. Prices for the best goods were increasing at a faster rate than the commercial variety. His main problem was in obtaining superb stones. The typical Thai ruby miner simply had to step up his production. He might hit a pocket of gem material and be able to meet the increasing demand, or he could mine for days and only come up with the lowest commercial quality. As a result, prices for upper level stones became inflexible. By 1979, the anticipation of more inflation caused prices at the source to increase at a faster rate than prices to the U.S. public. It was common for a U.S. dealer to go to Bangkok, buy ruby and sapphire, sell it in the United States, and go back in three months only to find wholesale prices higher there than current U.S. prices.

Again, there were too many dollars chasing too few goods. The situation was even more pronounced in colored gems than in diamond. The overall quality of the colored stones sold to the American investing public was much lower than that of diamond. Only a handful of top-grade stones was available at any one time. Thus, investors consistently settled for high commercial or lower quality stones.

Perhaps the most interesting aspect of this comparison between the two markets is that the diamond cutter was in a position to selectively purchase finer diamond rough and ignore commercial material. The colored stone dealer, because he was mining his own, had to wade through tremendous quantities of commercial material in his quest for better quality. The diamond cutter imbalanced his inventory while the colored stone dealer filled his inventory with an abundance of every quality.

When increased interest rates put the skids on diamond purchases in early 1980, prices for the best colored stones continued to rise. The colored stone dealers would not discount fine goods. Those investors who had missed the bull market in diamonds (or had been burned by buying in December of 1979) saw the most amazing thing in all of investment history: a tangible price rise during deflation and record-breaking high interest rates!

Many investors and gem dealers believed that colored stone prices were totally immune to the effects of high interest rates. Most saw the reason for this phenomenon being the incredible rarity of fine gems. In a way they were right, but they only had part of the story. The key to the difference in the price reaction phenomenon rests in two areas.

1. Because source dealers primarily sell for cash and not on credit, they can weather the monetary drain even during slow periods. It is only after prolonged periods that they must start cutting prices.

2. Since the source dealer has a full and well-balanced inventory toward the end of a bull market, he will start cutting the lower priced merchandise first. The lower qualities are more readily available and there is always a chance that the slowdown may cease. The diamond cutter will slash prices on the best stones so that he can move back into the commercial market, while the colored stone dealer will only discount the best stones when business absolutely demands it.

Figure 36 shows the rate of change against a 1978 base price for gem ruby and sapphire from 1978 to 1985 against the rate of change for the 12-month moving average of U.S. T-bills CPI. Compare this to Figure 37. While diamonds collapsed immediately, fine ruby and sapphire drifted down in price. Lower quality ruby and sapphire, shown in Figure 38, fell faster in price than the premium material.

Figure 36
Price Change History of 1-Carat Thailand Ruby, Top Gem Quality, and 1-Carat Sri Lankan Sapphire, Top Gem Quality (percentage of 1978 base)
Notice how long top gem ruby and sapphire maintained their value despite accelerating interest rates. It took four to five years of high interest rates before prices started down. Compare to Figures 37 and 38.

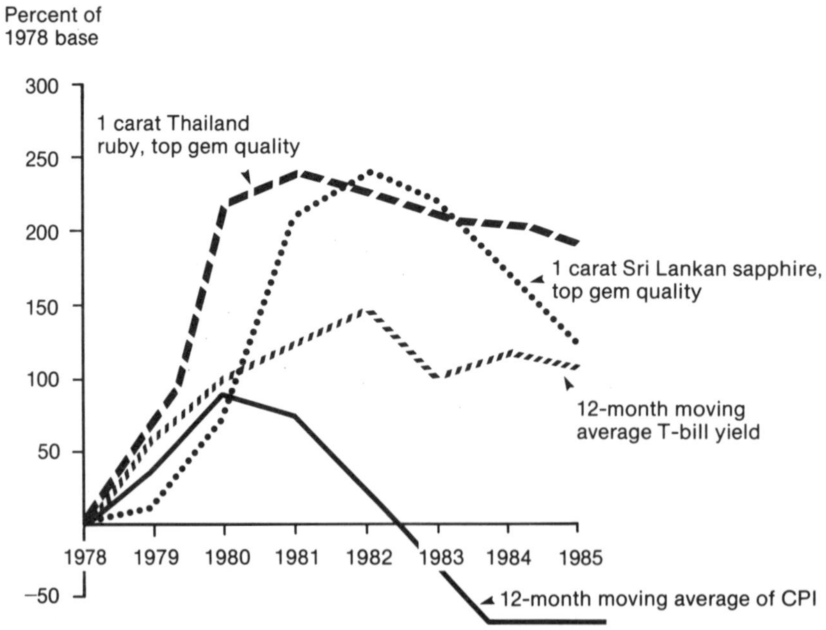

Figure 37
Price Change History of 1-Carat Round Diamond—D, IF (percentage of 1978 base)
Notice how diamond collapsed as interest rates rose and sustained high levels. The CPI fell against the ever-strengthening dollar. Lower quality, one carat diamonds are less volatile than this rate of change curve.

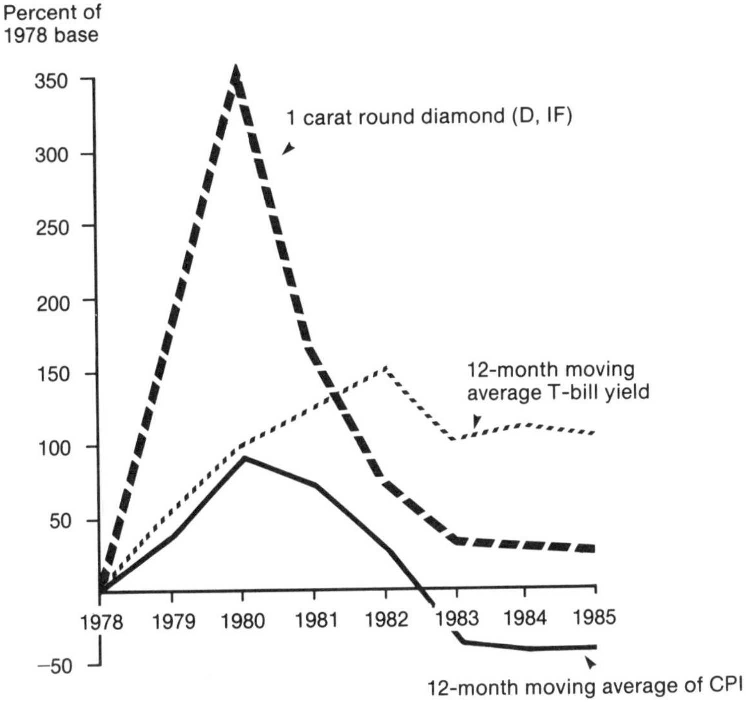

Certain colored stones, particularly those in the capital gains category, have been relatively unaffected by interest rates. In Figures 39, 40, and 41, the rate of price change compared to a 1978 base through 1985 for pink sapphire, tsavorite, and red spinel is compared to the same interest rate situation. The augmenting factors for these stones is increasing popularity, a price per carat that is affordable by many, and incredibly short source supply. Whether this trend will continue is unknown. Historically, markets always reverse at some point, but since these stones weathered the 1980 to 1983 high interest rate period, it may be that they will continue to rise through another four- to six-year cycle before a correction occurs. Tanzanite, which has been compared eco-

Figure 38
Price Change History of 1-Carat Thailand Ruby, Upper Commerical Quality, and 1-Carat Sri Lankan Sapphire, Upper Commercial Quality (percentage of 1978 base)
Notice how fast upper commercial quality prices fell compared to top gem (Figure 36).

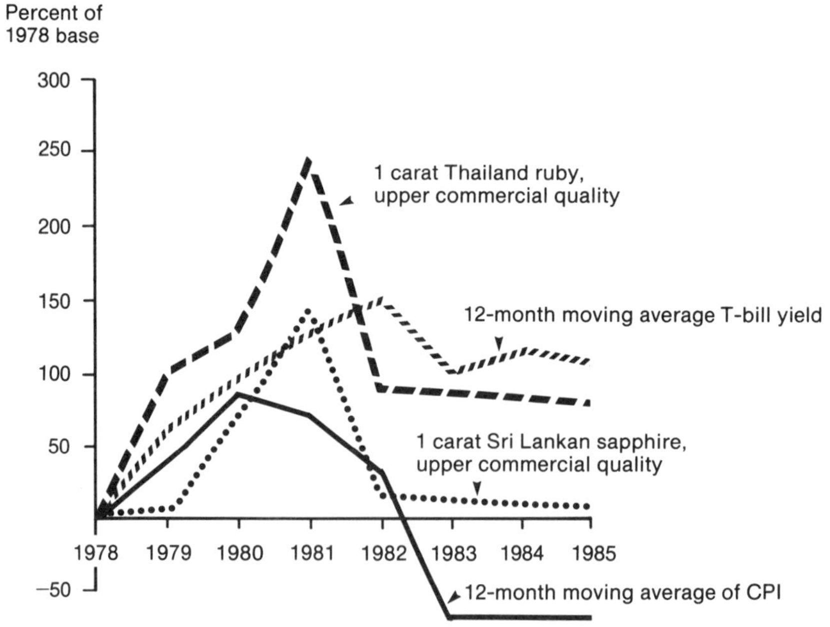

nomically to these three stones, showed some weakness in 1983 and 1984.

Figure 42 shows the same parameters for gem-quality Colombian emerald. Its rate of change has been minimal throughout the entire high interest rate period, the almost perfect stone for storing value.

A Final Note

The conclusions about the analysis of gem-quality diamond and colored stone price histories and their reactions to changing economic situations are based on past trends and cycles. There is a high probability that these general observations will hold true in the future, but it is only a probability. There is a chance that

Figure 39
Price Change History of 2-Carat Pink Sapphire (Burma), Gem Quality (percentage of 1978 base)
Notice how gem, pink sapphire continued to climb against sustained high interest rates.

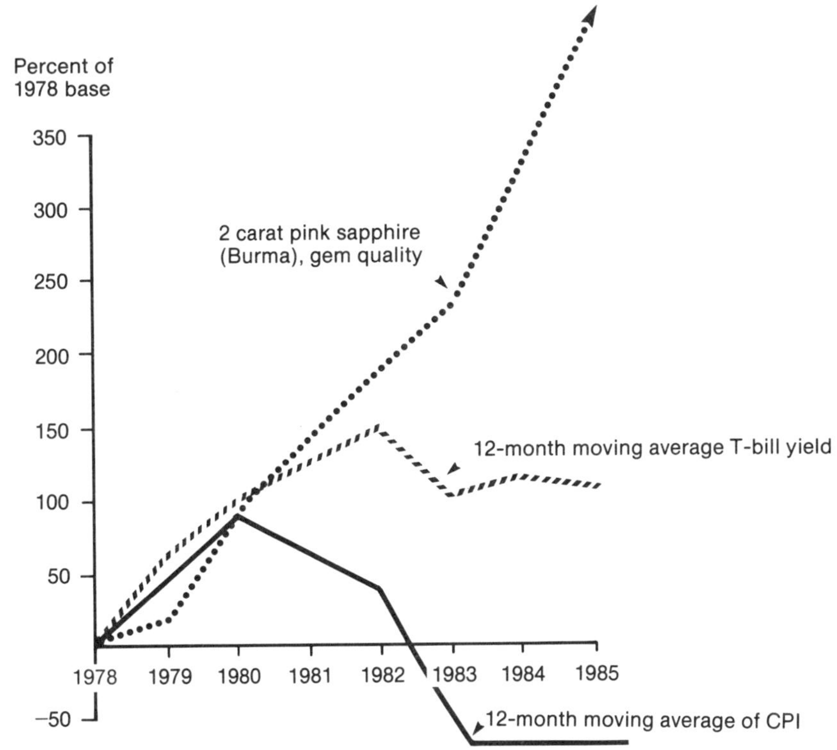

stones may not react in the same way given similar conditions. In 1984 there was a group of bankruptcies in Bangkok that was caused by customers not paying their bills. Obviously, the tradition of not extending credit had been broken by at least a few dealers. Many diamond cutters are aware of the mistakes that were made during the last bull market, and will try hard not to repeat them. Finally, the big ticket consumer, investor, and inflation hedger of the future will be considerably more informed than in the past. The market, therefore, will be more selective and smaller. This alone could make stone prices react quite differently than they have in the past.

Figure 40
Price Change History of 1-Carat Tsavorite, Top Gem Quality (percentage of 1978 base)
Tsavorite ignored high interest rates as it soared upward.

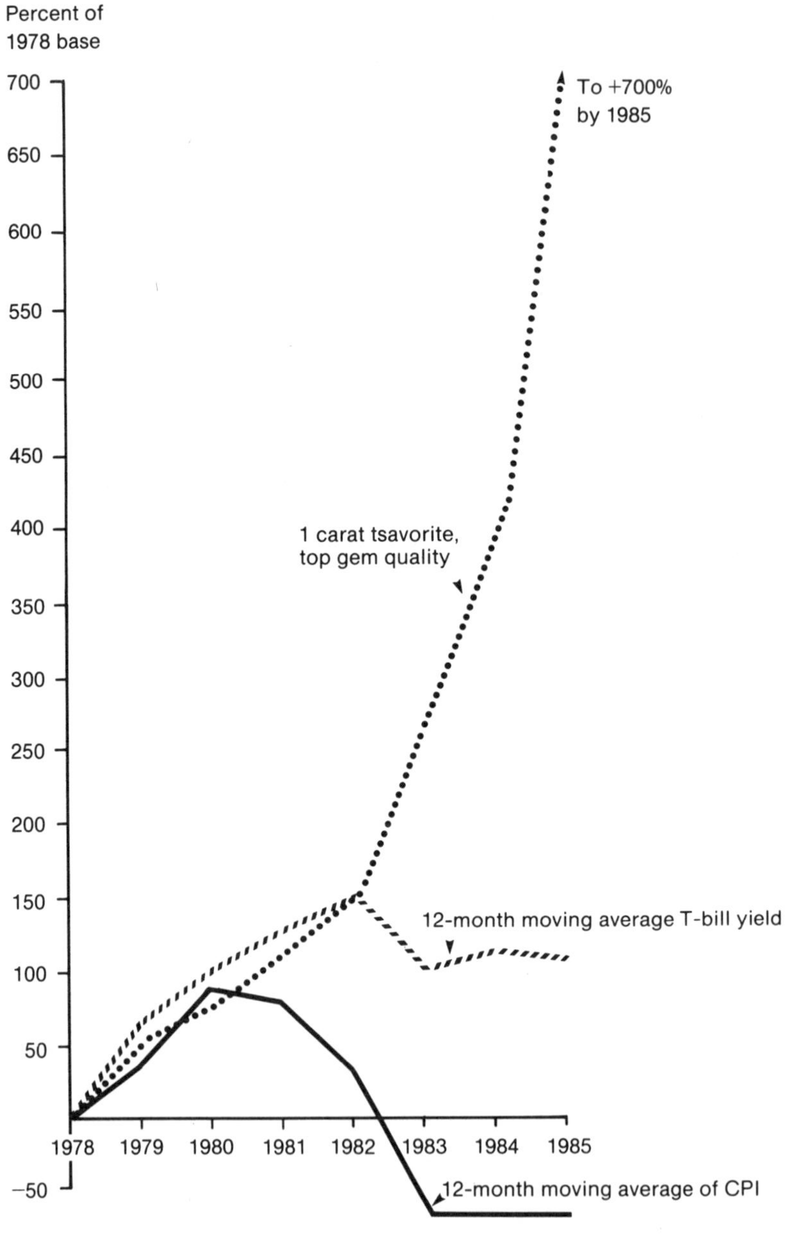

Figure 41
Price Change History of 2-Carat Red Spinel, Gem Quality (percentage of 1978 base)
Notice how gem red spinel soared against sustained high interest rates.

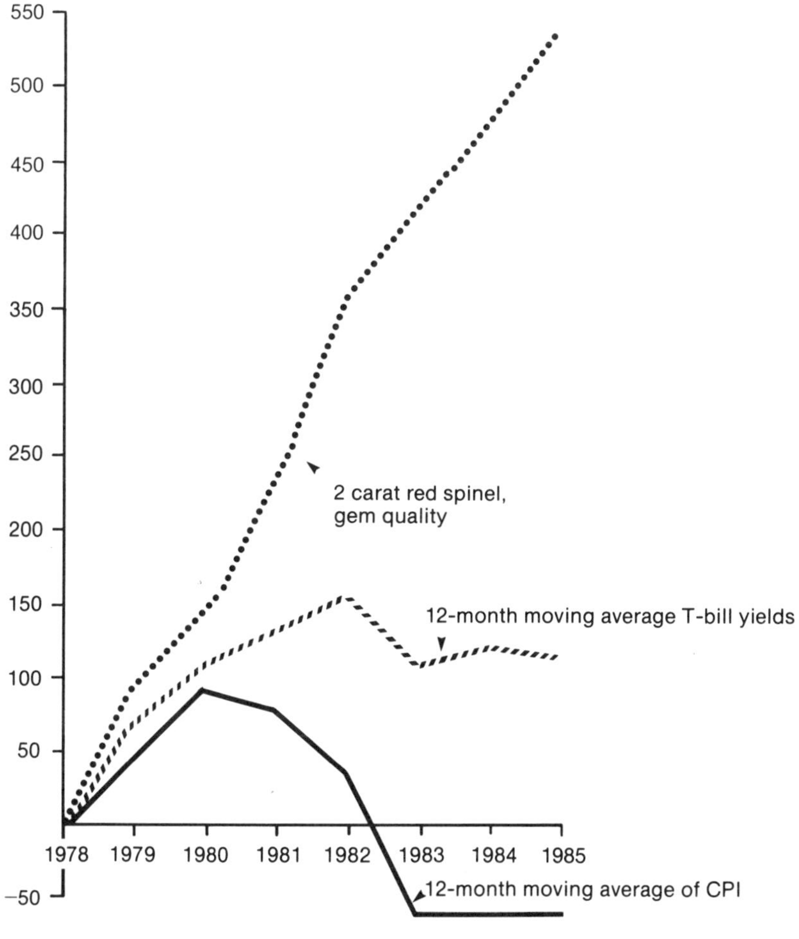

Figure 42
Price Change History of 1-Carat Colombian Emerald, Gem Quality (percentage of 1978 base)
Notice how top-quality Colombian emerald has stayed relatively stable in price.

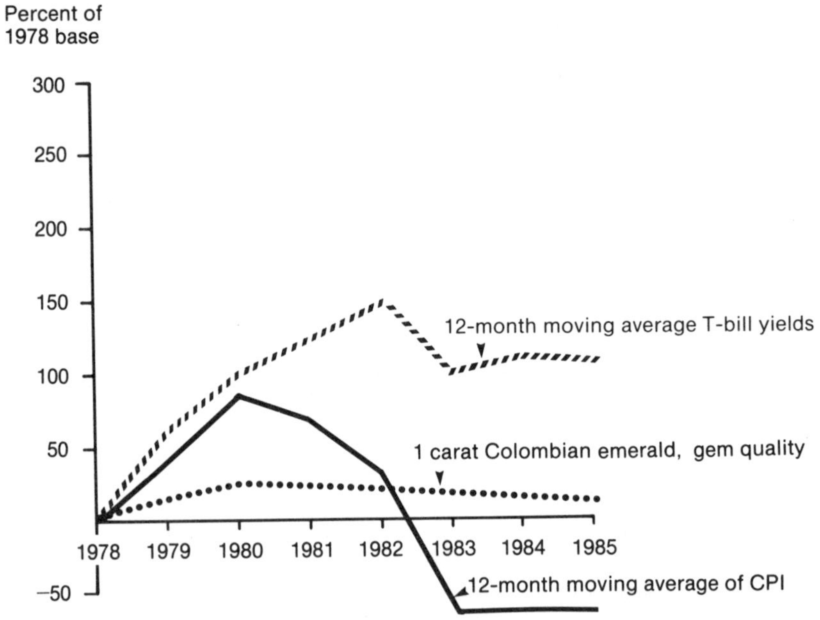

10 Is Gem Investing for You?

In the beginning of the book, it was advised that establishing a dual purpose for gem and jewelry purchases is a prerequisite for those who wish to obtain the most value and beauty for the money that is spent. Creating a dual purpose helps a consumer to learn about concepts such as quality analysis, market cycles, and prices, all of which are important to a prospective purchase. Establishing that dual purpose, however, is not tantamount to buying gemstones strictly for investment. Admittedly, the dividing line between buying for both adornment and a secondary financial goal, and straight investing is thin. Both goals need the same information. The concepts that make consumers shrewd buyers are the same as those that make gem investors successful.

Buying gemstones with the specific intention of making a profit at a later date is not easy. Like every other investment medium, the gemstone market has its intricacies and pitfalls. Gem investing is neither panacean nor utopean. It takes the same effort, accumulation of knowledge, and market savvy that make people winners in commodity, stock, and bond trading. Any claims to the contrary are so much hot air.

During the last 10 years, thousands have entered the gem investment arena. Many lost money in the years after they purchased, or were defrauded at the outset. For these reasons, it has been claimed that gemstones are not a good investment. Yet, historically, few investment mediums have created the type of profit potential and as strong an inflation hedge as have fine diamonds and colored stones. Any investment that can move from $1,000 to $63,000 in only 10 years must be considered magnificent. And any investment that can turn $900 into $9,500 in nine years has to be ranked highly. Since these examples are true for diamond and tsavorite, respectively, what then is the problem?

Quite frankly, the problem is ignorance and greed. Approximately 85 percent of all the investors who bought gems thought they could do so without having any knowledge of the medium, paying attention to market cycles, or creating a liquidation plan. About 15 percent made profits because they did their homework before buying. It makes no difference what hype mongers say. The ultimate responsibility for money invested rests with the investor. People should not cry if they miscalculated about the direction that commodities, stocks, or interest rates would take. Any risk has its consequences. The same is true for gem investing. Very simply, those who knew what they were doing made money and those who didn't lost their shirts.

At an international investment conference, I conducted an informal poll of people who had invested in gems. Those who had lost money, who were stuck with stones in a down market, or who simply couldn't find a buyer had, *without exception,* done one or more of the following:

1. Bought the wrong quality of stone.
2. Bought the wrong type of stone.
3. Paid too much.
4. Bought at the wrong time.
5. Failed to set up a liquidation plan in advance.
6. Refused to watch the market carefully.

Successful investors had done none of the above. If there had been no source of accurate information concerning these markets, then sincere sympathy would be in order. But there were numerous sources, some of them available to the public as early as 1978! The late 1970s and early 1980s produced a large amount of accurate information. Numerous, straightforward, honest publications were (and are) available at a nominal cost. For many years it has been common practice for stock and commodity investors to spend several hundred dollars per year for market information. Yet thousands of people put money—sometimes small fortunes—into gem investments (and fine jewelry) without seeking even *one* source of independent, quality information concerning those markets. Moreover, each of the six reasons why gem investors have lost money can be expanded upon.

Bought the Wrong Quality of Stone For some inexplicable reason, when honest gem dealers tell people that a certain type and quality of stone is very rare and hard to obtain, they don't believe them. Because of their disbelief, people end up settling for less than the highest quality stones. It is estimated that approximately 50,000 people in the United States invested in colored stones between 1978 and 1982. In the entire world market, there are possibly not more than 50,000 stones encompassing the whole spectrum of species that can adequately qualify as "investment" or "superb" gem quality. A good proportion of the stones that do qualify are not for sale; they are in collections or in premium jewelry. The true winners either did not buy at all because nothing of superior quality was being offered, or they bought the best. All others bought less than universally desired stones and suffered accordingly.

Bought the Wrong Type of Stone The lack of knowledge among gem investors is staggering. People have purchased or traded valuable property for stones that haven't a chance of keeping up with the inflation rate. Even in the best qualities, some stones cannot make money for the investor because they are (*a*) too common, or (*b*) too rare to have a trading market.

You have to wonder why a woman in Ohio sent a check for $25,000 to a company she did not know to buy approximately 60 carats of Malayan garnet that were worth about $20 per carat. Not only did she drastically overpay, but no reputable consultant or gem dealer had ever recommended this stone as an investment. No reputable dealer had ever given a speech proclaiming the investment virtues of commercial-quality amethyst, yet a man in Wisconsin traded valuable real estate for thousands of carats of this kind of material. These are not isolated incidents, as you would discover if you made a casual perusal of the popular press of the last five years. In-depth, economic studies of diamonds and colored stones have been done for at least eight years and have shown conclusively which gems have the best potential for overall price appreciation. Analysts in the gem industry are beginning to wonder if some people know how to read.

Paid Too Much The majority of stones that are traded in the international investment markets can be graded on some type of consistent, standardized scale. These standardized grades, within a certain tolerance, have a legitimate price attached to them and this price information has been available to the public since the mid- to late 1970s. With this proliferation of information, how can anybody dramatically overpay for gemstones? There is only one reason: Investors are penny-wise and pound-foolish. They will not pay between $50 and $100 dollars per year for regular price information (which is a tax deductible expense in the United States), but they will readily give $10,000 to the first person who puts on a good dog and pony show. If a stock on the NYSE is priced at $50 per share, would average stock buyers pay $800 per share? Of course not. They would check the price in *The Wall Street Journal*. Potential buyers can do the same by using the best gem newsletters.

Bought at the Wrong Time A seasoned investor knows that when a price climbs from a historical low to an unbelievable high in a very short time, a price correction will be made sometime in the near future. This line of reasoning is the basis of almost every fundamental and technical pricing study of commodities and stocks. Yet, some of the same people who accumulate thousands of dollars every week in the grain pits or the stock markets totally disregarded this basic fact in gems. Instead of buying diamond in 1977 or 1978, they jumped into the market in late 1979 and early 1980. Instead of buying ruby in 1978 or 1979, they waited until the prices peaked in late 1980 and early 1981. Serious analysts in the trade wonder if these people have some kind of death wish.

Failed to Set Up a Liquidation Plan in Advance Those who did buy the right stone, at a fair price, at the right time, often did not set up a liquidation plan. Therefore, when the market became hot and they had made profits, they didn't know where to sell. Although the gem markets have no organized exchanges like commodities, there are a number of ways to resell stones. These outlets are listed later in the chapter. Analysts are not sure if investors believed that an angel of mercy would develop an exchange for private buyers and sellers or if they just never thought about the practical nature of reselling a tangible investment. To exclusively depend on the dealer who sold the stone originally for resale is foolish. Superb gems are salable most everywhere. Even if the original company is still around, what is the guarantee that it will be able to find a buyer? Rare and fine gems are internationally traded commodities and their sale has to be approached on that level. The time to sell is when everybody is buying. Did anybody seriously believe that hype ridden investment companies would be around to resell *after* the peak of a bull market? The answer, of course, is no. They are enjoying their villas in San Moritz.

Refused to Watch the Market Carefully During the height of the gem bull market, one of the best catch phrases for identifying a gem investment firm with incredibly little expertise was, "You'll have to hold your investment for at least three to five years." The credible companies said, "Gemstones have to be viewed as a long-term investment. Emergency liquidation of the position should not be necessary to your financial security. Due to the volatility of the economy, receiving continuous market information is vital to your financial well-being. Price swings may become so great that resale may become prudent sooner than expected."

The difference in the approaches is dramatic. Why three to five years? Did some publicity-seeking investment company pull those numbers out of a hat? Three to five years was claimed to be the holding time only because the companies didn't understand the market or the nature of the investment, and they hadn't done one lick of research. The other approach is as reasonable as is possible. Those investors who live on catch phrases and old wives tales loved the three to five year time frame. It gave them a rationalization for becoming lazy about monitoring their investment. Of course, if they were smart enough to buy diamonds in 1978, by the time three to five years had rolled by, they had lost whatever real profits had been possible.

It is true that the world's monetary systems are geared to cyclical inflation; therefore another bull market in gems will come. It may be next year, or in 5 or 10 years. Nobody can predict the future, but if the investing public doesn't learn to pay attention to the harsh lessons discussed above, the unscrupulous investment companies will not only retire to the French Riviera after the peak of the next cycle, they may be able to buy it!

How To Sell

One of the common questions people ask is "How do I sell my investment stones or unwanted jewelry?" While reselling diamonds and colored stones is not as easy as selling a silver futures contract, it is not as difficult as you might think. Keep the following points in mind:

1. There is no public trading market for gemstones; therefore, it will probably take time to find a buyer. Auctions are about the closest thing to a public trading market. The time involved to sell can run from just a few hours to several months, depending on what is being sold, if there is an immediate customer, the price being asked, and the number of contacts the selling agent has on file.
2. A fee will be involved. Nobody will sell a stone for free. Sometimes an up-front fee will be charged that may be applied to the final bill. Some firms will charge a percentage of the realized amount. Others will charge a flat fee in advance or upon completion of the sale. Since all other investments have liquidation fees (e.g. brokerage charges), this should not come as a surprise. Often brokerage or consulting fees will run from 5 percent to 20 percent of the realized amount, depending on the piece. Generally, the finer and more expensive the item, the less will be the percentage.
3. Although it is possible to sell a stone to another individual, there are very few opportunities to do this. A company that has access to a large number of private and trade buyers is best. Companies in this category include:
   - **A.** Alternative gem companies that specialize in buying and selling fine goods for clients on a regular basis.
   - **B.** Retail jewelers or wholesalers who have a rebrokering service and are active and well known in the gem trade.
   - **C.** Auction houses that have specialized departments for gems and jewelry and are known for their premium offerings.
   - **D.** Independent consultants who are not gem dealers but actively trade superior material for their clients.

The following companies offer resale programs for individuals wishing to sell stones and jewelry. They have proven track records, are respected in the gem trade, and usually are most effective in finer quality goods.

Category A: Alternative Gem Companies

Dallas Davenport
The Davenport Organisation
822 Lafayette Road
P.O. Box 164
No. Hampton, HN 03862
800-258-0853

Richard Harig
Harig Financial Services
The Harig Companies
29 E. Madison, Suite 200B
Chicago, IL 60602
312-641-0641

Robert Genis
National Gemstone Corporation
P.O. Box 42468
Tucson, AZ
800-824-6876

Steven Lindsay, Mayor Gross
Lindsay + Wasser, Inc.
20 W. 47th St., Room 904
New York, NY 10036
212-719-1733

Category B: Retail Jewelers and Wholesalers

Will Hurwitz
Colonial Diamond Brokers
9 W. Patrick St.
P.O. Box 674
Frederick, MD 21701
301-663-9252

A. J. Puckett
Precision Gems
955 Lomas Santa Fe
P.O. Box 1047
Solana Beach, CA 92075
212-719-5727

Category C: Auction Houses

Sotheby's
1334 York Avenue
New York, NY 10021
212-606-7000

Christie's
Park Avenue and 59th Street
New York, NY 10021
212-546-1000

Category D: Independent Consultants

David Marcum
The Marcum Exchange
P.O. Box 606
Geneva, IL 60134
312-232-1583

A Final Note on the Psychology of Investment

To decide whether you should invest in gems, you *must* be able to answer all of the following positively. If you cannot answer positively, there is a high probability that you will lose capital invested in this area.

1. I need an investment that is private, portable, and does not necessarily leave a monetary or documented trail.
2. I enjoy the beauty of gems more than I want to make money on them. It is a proven fact that those who invest in gems for the sole purpose of making money often lose.
3. I am willing to take time and make a serious effort to learn about gems, to actively get to know trade people, and to moni-

tor the market on a regular basis. I am willing to spend as much time as I would put into another investment of the same monetary importance.

4. My investment portfolio is large enough to enable me to invest without needing the funds in an emergency. I am not investing in gems to be able to send my children to college or to lay the groundwork for a comfortable old age.
5. A good gem portfolio will cost at least $10,000 (one or two stones). For a diversified portfolio, the cost will be between $25,000 and $100,000, maybe more. I can, at least, properly afford the bottom figure. Ideally, only between 5 percent and 10 percent of *net, investable, liquid funds* should be considered in this case, not the combined value of liquid funds, house, car, art, income property, and other illiquid assets.
6. I am willing to be patient. I am willing to pay for a consultant if I am not sure. I have the strength to withstand sales pressure and to stand aside if the price is too high. I am psychologically and monetarily capable of sustaining a total loss just in case I really blow it.

Although these points may sound demanding, they are vital and basic to *any* high risk or tangible investment. If they sound intimidating or frightening, put your money into something else.

11 Markups in the Gem and Jewelry Business

The greatest misconception the public has concerning jewelers is that they make unconscionable profits. In reality, nothing is further from the truth. The U.S. auto industry makes more net profit in a good year than the entire U.S. diamond market makes in gross sales over the same time period! Although many people think jewelers have no competition, most do not realize that each jeweler is competing with other jewelers, furriers, art galleries, luxury car dealers, antique dealers, and a host of others. It is common for a three-carat diamond sale to be lost because a husband opts for a mink coat or a cruise.

The markups used by the traditional retail jeweler are similar to those used by any other retailer, including those who sell furniture, clothing, and chocolate chip cookies. Actually, designer clothing and chocolate chip cookies have a higher average percentage markup than most jewelry. Reputable gem investment firms sometimes have a lower percentage markup schedule than the average jeweler because they specialize only in the finest and most expensive stones. Department store markups are similar to those of retail jewelry firms. The largest percentage markups in jewelry come from catalog houses that have to cover the cost of printing and postage as well as the cost of merchandise, and from jewelry store chains that cater to lower- and middle-income customers.

A person who is trying to decide where to buy jewelry is in a Catch 22. The finest jewelry companies invariably offer high-quality merchandise at a reasonable price. Unfortunately, these firms intimidate the public with their "posh" image and are therefore frequented by the wealthy, those who think they are wealthy, and a few smart shoppers no matter what their income level. The chains that cater to the less princely endowed are the ones with the greatest volume of business. The reason they do so well is because they advertise an allegedly lower price and the reason they advertise so frequently is because they make a much higher percentage markup and subsequent profit on merchandise than fine jewelers! The question that consumers have to ask is: "Do I want mediocrity and to pay the firm a higher profit, or do I want high quality and to pay essentially the same price or a little more and give the firm a smaller profit?" Most consumers, unfortunately, opt for the first because they have not learned to be quality conscious.

The following is a case in point. Several years ago, I was working as a salesman at a very fine jewelry store. A customer came in and wanted to look at 14 karat (K) gold neckchains. He had already bought one, but he had the option of returning it if he changed his mind. Actually, what the customer wanted was to gloat over his "good buy." The jeweler from whom he had purchased the chain had had chains on sale at 52 percent off. Without commenting, I took an identical chain from the showcase. Then I took the customer to a digital gold scale. First I put the customer's chain on the scale; next he put my store's chain on the scale. The weight of each was so close to the other, that hardly a quarter of a pennyweight (1/80 of an ounce) separated the two. I asked, "What did you pay for the chain?" "Two hundred-fifty dollars. How much is yours?" "Two hundred-ten dollars." Of course, the customer's jaw dropped. I said, "Did you ask, '52 percent of what?' It is obvious that your chain was at least double the regular price before it was marked down. Please notice that the polish on ours is higher, a sign of better workmanship and manufacturing care." Needless to say, the customer returned the sale chain and bought the "full price" item. What he thought was a steal turned out to be a bum deal.

This example is *not* an isolated incident. Phony sales and advertising that only emphasizes price are a plague upon the industry. The situation will only change when consumers become knowledgeable and realize they are being defrauded.

Who Makes What?

If people in the gem business cannot make a profit on what they sell, they might as well sit in a chair and watch TV during the day. They cannot, however, charge too much or they will be driven out of business by competition. Likewise, if they charge too little, they will not be able to pay their bills. In either case, the result is the same.

According to recent statistics, the average jeweler, during a successful year, will net between 8 percent and 11 percent of gross income after taxes. The jewelry business is not quite as lucrative as the public believes. There are approximately 32,000 jewelry stores in the United States, and the median, gross, yearly sales total for each is somewhere around $400,000. At a 9 percent net profit, that amounts to only $38,000. The average firm is not exactly climbing up the Fortune 500 list!

Let us assume that a jeweler has done a good job and has turned dollar inventory over once during a particular year. Of $400,000 in gross sales the jeweler has netted $38,000. Let us also assume that to replace inventory, it will cost $200,000 or half the total gross receipts. The other $162,000 in income was paid out for insurance, salaries, security devices, and other overhead. If prices are stable for precious metals, diamonds, colored stones, and watches, the jeweler can either pocket the profit or reinvest the $38,000 and build inventory by 19 percent when he or she buys again.

Now let us assume a different scenario. Inflation is moving up rapidly, as it did in the late 1970s. Gold has doubled, diamonds are up 30 percent, and colored stones have risen 20 percent, with gem-quality stones up 35 percent on average. What happens? The jeweler loses money when restocking with the same quality merchandise. Strangely, if metals and stones go down in price, the same thing happens. For this jeweler to compete with the jeweler down the block who has just purchased new merchandise, he or she has to discount pieces already in stock. The result? Another money loss. This example is not presented to convince consumers to weep for the jewelry industry. It is, however, a good indication to the consumer of what jewelers are up against in a volatile economy—the kind we have been in for several years. Jewelers don't make unconscionable profits, and it takes a knowledgeable person to make a good living at selling gems, unless, of course, that person is successfully defrauding the public via phony sales and overpriced merchandise!

Virtually all retail jewelers have a standard cost-overhead package that includes salaries and commission (if applicable), rent, the cost of replacing merchandise, advertising, insurance, security equipment, repair shop costs, and postage. There are many other minor expenses such as display props, outside appraisal services (if applicable), and buying trips. One of the reasons jewelry is expensive is because of loss due to theft and burglary. As gems have become more expensive through inflation, crime against jewelers has risen tremendously. Thus, insurance costs have risen manyfold in the last few years. Unfortunately, this cost must be passed on to the consumer.

For jewelers to stay in business, they must mark up their jewelry an unvarying, specific amount over cost. The author, after spending many years in the retail business and three years as a research consultant and publisher in the gem business, went undercover as a salesman in 1983 in a carriage trade store. The primary goal was to analyze jewelry markups. The store chosen is one of the most successful guild (upper quality merchandise) firms, and is part of the world's largest retail jewelry company. It was believed that its markups would be representative of the industry as a whole. The company's incredible historical success was due to its being competitive in order to be profitable. The outcome of the undercover work supported the author's previous experience and understanding of markups, a result of his having worked behind the counter for eight years.

The following markup schedule is an average. Some jewelers will charge a little less or a little more. The term to be understood is *keystone.* A keystone markup is 100 percent over the cost of the merchandise. For example, if a ring costs a jeweler $500, a keystone markup puts the price to the public at $1,000. If the $500 ring were keystone plus 20 percent, it would be sold at $1,200. Triple keystone is three times the cost. This markup occurs in very low-priced jewelry, for example, thin, 14K, chain bracelets.

Two things must be emphasized about these markups: (1) this markup schedule is fair and absolutely necessary for a jeweler to stay in business. The markups are applicable only to jewelry used as adornment; first-class stones often have different markups. Unlike a grocery store, which has a lower markup but considerably higher volume, all luxury items are priced to the public at approximately the same markup or higher; and (2) at these markups, a jeweler will make 8 percent to 11 percent net profit in a good year. If a jeweler offers 20 percent off, he or she will break even after all costs of doing business. Because of this, any sale that features more than 20 percent or 25 percent off is likely to be phony. Unless the jeweler is going out of business, he or she will lose money at any legitimate discount higher than 20 percent.

Solitaire Diamond Engagement Rings

1. One-carat plus diamonds, any shape or quality: Keystone.
2. Subcarat diamonds, any shape or quality: Keystone plus 20 percent.
3. Plain wedding sets or sets with accent melee (tiny diamonds) with one-carat plus center diamond, any shape or quality: Keystone on diamond. Keystone plus 50 percent on mounting.
4. Plain wedding sets or sets with accent melee. Subcarat center diamond, any shape or quality: Keystone plus 20 percent on diamond. Keystone plus 50 percent on mounting.

Loose Diamonds

1. One-carat plus diamonds, any shape, any quality: Keystone.
2. Subcarat diamonds, any shape, any quality: Keystone plus 20 percent.
3. Melee (.01 to .10 carats): Triple keystone.

Diamond Solitaire Pendants and Stud Style Earrings

1. One-carat plus diamond pendant: Keystone.
2. Subcarat diamond pendant: Keystone plus 20 percent.
3. Two-carat plus total weight earrings: Keystone.
4. Sub-two-carat total weight earrings: Keystone plus 20 percent.

Wedding Bands

1. Plain 14K or 18K white or yellow gold: Keystone plus 20 percent to 60 percent.

Gold Fashion Jewelry (No Stones)

1. 14K or 18K white or yellow gold: Keystone plus 20 percent to 60 percent.

Colored Stones

1. Loose or mounted ruby, emerald, and sapphire under $1,000 cost to the public: Keystone plus 20 percent.
2. Loose or mounted colored stones other than those listed above under $1,000 cost to the public: Keystone plus 40 percent.
3. Loose or mounted ruby, emerald, and sapphire over $1,000 cost to the public: Keystone.
4. Loose or mounted colored stones other than those listed above over $1,000 cost to the public: Keystone plus 20 percent.

Memorandum Goods (Those That Are on Temporary Loan to the Jeweler)

1. One-carat plus diamonds, any shape or quality: Keystone.
2. Subcarat diamonds, any shape or quality: Keystone plus 20 percent.
3. Any colored stone, loose or mounted: Keystone plus 20 percent to 60 percent.

Miscellaneous (Giftware, Watches, Porcelains, Crystal, China, Silver)

1. All: Keystone; the exception is Rolex watches where the cost is 55 percent of retail.

There are exceptions to these averages. Some jewelers use a sliding markup scale. The more expensive the piece, the less percentage gross profit. This policy is easier to implement for free-standing stores or for jewelers in nonshopping mall locations. In malls, stores often have a base rate of rent. Once gross sales move over a specified amount, however, rent becomes a percentage of gross sales. That amount can be as high as 8 percent to 10 percent. In this situation, it is difficult to use a sliding markup scale.

Other jewelers wear two hats. They have an average markup structure for jewelry as indicated above, but for investment buyers and serious collectors, they have a different markup schedule. Shopping mall jewelers have to set up another company which is based outside of the mall to avoid the percentage of sale clause in their rent contracts. A 20 or 30 percent markup will not make a profit if they have to pay the mall a percentage. Actually, there are numerous retailers who successfully compete in the lower markup area of top-quality stones.

Other Markup Schedules

Before the mid-1970s, the only place the majority of people could purchase any gem or jewelry was from the retail jeweler. The higher inflationary cycles that have occurred over the last 10 years have spawned a new breed of "jeweler." These are the so-called investment or alternative gem firms.

These companies originally sold only loose diamonds and colored stones, usually with laboratory certificates, to investors. Since the 1980 collapse in diamond prices, the reputable, surviving companies have shifted their emphasis. They not only offer the finest diamonds and colored stones, but also superbly crafted jewelry, rare collector stones, objects de virtue, mineral specimens, and high commercial-quality jewelry.

A caveat is in order here. Just because a company is an investment company or an alternative gem firm does *not* mean it has met the kind of standards mentioned above. The downward spiral of the investment gem business has weeded out many who were in it for a quick killing. They have since gone on to real estate, insurance, and commodity scams. There are, however, companies still bilking the public. Some do their marketing through phone solicitations, others through the mail. Be very careful! Shopping is vital and much of the material in this book can be used to test the quality of these companies. Currently, the only reasonably comprehensive list of these companies available to the public is the annual Gem Investment Company Survey. It can be purchased from *Gem Market Reporter* for $5 at P.O. Box 39890, Phoenix, AZ 85069.

A few individuals have set up practice as professional consultants and do not carry any inventory. They are hired by the public and paid for their services on a hourly or mutually agreed upon fee. This type of service is new to the public. It is one of the best, particularly if the client wishes to purchase a major stone or piece of jewelry. For example, if a person is looking for a $20,000 emerald ring, the consultant can find the stone, often directly from the source, and locate an appropriate mounting. The consumer pays the wholesale cost *only*, plus the consultant's fee. An emerald ring that would have a standard retail cost of $20,000 could be had for 40 percent to 45 percent less using this system!

When the gem investment market first began, markups for fine and rare stones were all over the board. Some of the highest profile diamond investment companies were selling stones at a higher price than most reputable retail jewelers. Others had markups of 25 percent, 30 percent, and 40 percent over cost. The same chaos reigned in the colored stone investment market. Certainly, those who used phone solicitations had to pay salespeople at least a 10 percent to 20 percent commission for everything they sold. Coupled with overhead, insurance, and so on, markups could be very high.

The surviving, reputable companies in this area are extremely competitive. With retailers setting up special divisions for investors and collectors, investment companies now have to buy correctly and sell at the right price. These firms are typified by the following: (*a*) relatively inexpensive office space, high security, and little or no walk-in traffic, (*b*) few employees; most are one- to three-person operations, (*c*) little advertising; rely on referral business, (*d*) an expert gemologist, often part of the company, (*e*) often do not accept credit cards or have credit accounts; consumers pay by fully cleared funds only, and (*f*) only cater to discerning clientele and members of the gem trade.

A recent study of these companies indicates that their average prices to the public are as follows:

Diamonds

1. Premium quality diamonds over one carat, any shape: 10 percent to 25 percent over dealer list price (the price that retailer jewelers pay).
2. Commercial quality diamonds over one carat, any shape: 20 percent to 50 percent over dealer list price.
3. Premium quality diamonds under one carat, any shape: 20 percent to 50 percent over dealer list price.

4. Commercial quality diamonds under one carat, any shape: 30 percent to 60 percent over dealer list price.

Colored Stones

1. Premium quality ruby, emerald, and sapphire. Varies from 10 percent for very expensive, fine and world-class goods to as high as 50 percent for smaller, easily replaceable stones.
2. Premium quality colored stones other than those mentioned above: 10 percent for very expensive, fine and world-class goods to as high as 50 percent to 60 percent for smaller, easily replaceable stones.

How Does the Consumer Obtain the Best Price?

It should be obvious at this point that there are many companies, both within and outside the traditional gem trade, that can give excellent prices on stones and jewelry. The ability to compete effectively sits in both "markets." There are three things that consumers must do to ensure that they get the best price. The more expensive the item, the more important are these steps.

1. **Knowledge.** Before buying, it is important to get a grasp of what a fine stone looks like in your area of interest. Without this, the first "pretty" looking stone will seem the best. Companies do not often stock fine diamonds and colored stones. Although the best one in inventory may look superior to others, it may only be an average or slightly above average stone. Major museums sometimes have superior stones on display. Familiarity with stones breeds confidence. If you live in an area that does not have fine jewelry stores or access to a better investment company, plan to travel to one that has the kind of stone desired. The best companies will often allow prepayment for the merchandise and send the item on approval, with a refund option. At this point, if you are unsure of your buy, you can take it to an independent appraiser or consultant who is knowledgeable about the type of stone being purchased. Before buying, read, look and ask questions. A customer who is interested in a $10,000 plus item should talk to an independent consultant first.

2. **Shop and Compare.** Any company that is worth its salt is going to know that an expensive purchase is not an "impulse" buy. They will expect people to comparative shop. This can be accomplished in a professional manner by following the guidelines in the last chapter on how to be a good customer.
3. **Know Prices.** One of the weakest areas of knowledge for laypeople is in prices. If a person usually patronizes a local, corner jewelry store, the prices asked for very fine or world-class diamonds and colored stones will probably put him or her into a catatonic trance. Ten or 20 years ago, the consumer had an impossible time trying to find out if the quoted prices were fair. The unscrupulous jeweler loved it. Today, there is *no* excuse for customers not knowing in advance what stones will cost. There are a multitude of informational newsletters that regularly report the price of gemstones, and they are available for a nominal cost. Whether putting together a top-flight portfolio costing hundreds of thousands of dollars, getting that long-saved-for $15,000 sapphire ring, or buying that moderately priced and very important engagement ring, not having this information at your fingertips is being penny-wise and dollar-foolish.

Buyers have a plethora of reliable publications to choose from, not only for pricing but for consumer tips, economic analysis, and world news concerning liquidity and supply and demand trends. The most important of these include:

Gem Market Reporter
Kurt Arens, Editor
P.O. Box 39890
Phoenix, AZ 85069
602-252-4477
1 year, 12 issues, $98; six months, $55

Gemstone Price Report/PreciouStones Newsletter
Jean Francois Moyersoen, Editor
Ubige s.p.v.d.
Avenue Louise, 221
Brussels 1050, Belgium
(02)-648-07-11
1 year, 12 issues, $270

The Marcum Report
David Marcum, Editor
P.O. Box 606
Geneva, IL 60134
312-232-1583

1 year, 12 issues, $89; three-month trial, $25

Always remember, finding a bargain is wonderful and lucky. The most important thing any layperson should work for—and expect to get—is excellent value for the money spent.

12 Appraisals

What Is an Appraisal?

An appraisal is a document that analyzes and describes a piece of jewelry or a loose gem and puts a monetary value on the described item. Appraisals are most frequently issued by jewelry stores, independent appraisers, and in some cases, independent gemological laboratories.

Appraisal documents are often used as proof of the description, quality, and value of an item in the event of loss. Other legitimate uses include: proof to tax authorities of the value of an item in estate evaluations or museum donations; proof of the value for barter purposes; and proof of the value when selling to other individuals or to gem dealers.

The important concept to remember is that the gem appraisal business is not directly regulated by government. This is as it should be: Governmental interference in anything usually results in chaos. The IRS has tried to crack down on disreputable appraisers, but their inexperience in the field has resulted in the indiscriminate harassment of the industry, particularly in the area of museum and nonprofit organization donations. There are appraisal associations, but the level of expertise required to join varies considerably. Although the majority of appraisers are honest, know their business, and have high credibility, there are some who use their appraisal documents to commit fraud. It is this minority that seriously endangers the public. It is for this reason also that the consumer must know what constitutes proper and improper appraisals.

The majority of appraisals are submitted to insurance companies to either describe the item so that the company can replace it in the event of loss, or to allow the company to compensate the owner with money in the event of loss. The escalation in the price of diamonds and colored stones over the last 10 to 15 years has made it imperative for insurance companies to replace, which they can often do well below the normal price to the public, rather than compensate.

What Constitutes an Improper Appraisal?

Since an appraisal is most commonly used as proof of ownership and value, complete and accurate work are needed. If this is not done, the owner may be seriously shortchanged if the gems and/or jewelry are lost. Insurance companies have no interest in the quality of an appraisal. They are interested in obtaining premium payments.

Too many times, appraisals show up that look like this: "One engagement ring in 14K yellow gold containing a round diamond weighing 1.00 carats. The stone is fine white and clean. Value = $5,500."

To the layperson, this may appear to be a good description of the ring. After all, it was sold to him or her as a fine white and clean stone. It does weigh one carat. The ring is 14K yellow gold. What then is wrong with the appraisal?

If the ring is lost, the owner will find out that plenty is wrong. A typical insurance company would rather replace the ring than give up $5,500, and they can purchase a replacement from whomever they wish. Since the insurance agent's main job is to save the company money, that agent will find the least expensive ring that fits the description. Chances are, the replacement ring will never compare to the original.

The following faults in the appraisal will be used against the customer by the insurance company:

1. The ring is 14K gold, but how is it made? Is it cheaply made or is it a hand-crafted wire mount? The wire is far more expensive, and is made solidly. The cheaply made piece could be full of air (porosity) and have less gold than the original. What was the price of gold when the ring was purchased? How much gold was in the ring? Without the proper description, the insurance company will go with the less expensive mounting.

2. The diamond is round, presumably a brilliant cut. What are the proportions? Is the stone beautifully cut with fine symmetry and finish? The insurance company does not know or care. It is a round stone and that is all that matters. The least expensive round in any quality is cut poorly. That is what the customer will receive if the diameter and depth, depth percentage, and table percentage are not described. If they are described, and the stone is finely made, the insurance company is obligated to replace it with a similar quality stone. The one-carat weight is definite, so that will be maintained.
3. The diamond is fine white. What does that mean? To some carriage trade jewelers, a fine white is between an F and an H color (GIA scale). To others, a fine white could be an H, or I, or J! Chances are, the insurance company will buy a stone that faces up white in a mounting—an I or J. But what if the customer paid for a G color originally?
4. The diamond is clean. The same problem arises. One jeweler may think that VVS is clean; others may think that VS_2 or SI_1 are clean. Since SI_1 is clean to the unaided eye, the insurance company will probably opt for that.

The worst case scenario is that the owner had a handmade, wire mount ring with a finely made, round, brilliant diamond of G or H color and VS_1 clarity. He or she receives a cheaply cast ring with a poorly proportioned stone in a J color and SI_1 clarity. The insurance company replaces the ring for $2,300 and the owner has paid premiums on a $5,500 ring!

What Should Be on a Proper Appraisal?

The following are on every proper appraisal. To totally protect yourself, *demand* them!

1. The buyer's or owner's name and address.
2. The date the appraisal was issued and the signature(s) of the appraiser(s).
3. A brief verbal description of each stone or piece of jewelry. If the item is over $2,000, a picture is to be attached. Some jewelers do this as a matter of course; others will issue an appraisal on an item worth $20,000 and never photograph the piece. Customers should demand photos: They help in accurate replacement—if the time comes.

4. The mounting and the metals comprising the piece are fully described. Is the mounting die struck, cast, or handmade? The karat content and weight of the mounting (in pennyweights or grams) is listed. If it is platinum, this will be stated. For a piece that is a combination of white and yellow gold, or platinum and gold, the document will adequately describe which parts are made of which metal. The per-ounce price at which the metal was sold will be listed. The types of settings represented will be described. Possibilities include: four and six prong, bead set, hammer set, pavé, channel set, bezel, and fishtail. The type of clasp is stated: spring ring, French box lock, sister hook.
5. The weight for major diamonds is listed to the hundredth of a carat; for example, 1.53 carats. The cut type of each stone is stated. Is it round (single or full cut), emerald cut, pear shape, marquise, oval, or some other? Measurements in millimeters of each major diamond appear, including length, breadth, and depth. The cut proportion for each *major* stone is itemized including depth percentage and table percentage (mountings sometimes makes this impossible to do accurately). Finish quality is mentioned, particularly on very fine stones. The degree and type of fluorescence will be indicated, if present. For small side stones or pavé, it is customary to list the number of diamonds and total weight; for example, nine round full cuts weighing a total of .63 carats. The aggregate, average color and clarity will be itemized; for example, the nine round full cuts range from G to H color and VS_2 to SI_1 clarity.
6. For major, colored stone jewelry, the parameters will be the same for mountings, cut styles, measurements, photos, and weight. Identification of the stone is important; for example, natural or synthetic. Also included on *major* colored stones over $2,000 are primary color, secondary colors, intensity modifiers, and tone. The average brilliancy is listed to indicate the quality of cut proportion. The depth percentage is sometimes listed. With the wide range of qualities in most colored stones, these latter factors are important for proper replacement if that should become necessary.
7. Finally, the type of instruments used in determining the identification and quality of the stone(s) are itemized; for example, polariscope, refractometer, leverage gauge, loupe, and so on.

What Does the Monetary Value Mean?

Many appraisals describe gems and jewelry in a sloppy way, but the monetary value ascribed to the piece is often the most-abused aspect of the document.

Placing an accurate value on gems or jewelry is more art than science. Identification and quality analysis are primarily objective. Monetary values are an estimate or educated judgment. Stores that issue appraisals on items they sell have no difficulty in arriving at a price. They use the price at which the customer purchases the item. Notice how few jewelers perform appraisals on items they do not sell. That in itself shows it is no easy task.

What is it worth? Although this may sound flippant, any gem or piece of jewelry is worth exactly what somebody is willing to pay for it. To a starving peasant, a superb, 10-carat, Kashmir sapphire is worth diddly-squat; he can't eat it. To the C.E.O. of a major company, it may mean much in terms of the compliments his wife receives from fellow executives. For a wealthy individual in a country torn by warfare, it may be worth as much as his or her life.

Fortunately for appraisers, the bulk of jewelry sold worldwide is not as rare as a 10-carat Kashmir sapphire. Most jewelry can be duplicated with stones that look very much like the original. Commercial to fine stones have an international trading market and as long as some kind of cogent grading system is employed in evaluating them, appraisers can determine a stone's value within a specific tolerance.

Those who produce complete, accurate, informational appraisals will be more accurate in their monetary valuations. The discipline needed to definitively categorize a stone's quality creates a monetary fence around that stone. If a stone is XYZ quality, its monetary value will be within a specific range that is limited by that XYZ quality. Careless descriptions often lead to inaccurate monetary valuations.

The values most commonly placed on appraisals fall into two categories. One is the price the customer paid. Whether that price is low, average, or high can only be determined by comparing that item to the same or similar items offered by other firms. The second type of value is that which an independent appraiser gives on an item never before seen. That value, if accurate, is indicative of the average retail replacement price that the customer would have to pay to obtain another piece. There is a high probability that 10 qualified appraisers will place slightly different values on the same piece. If they know market pricing and jewelry store markup schedules, however, the prices will differ, at most, 10 percent to 15 percent either way. To be able to be this consistent, they must see a constant stream of merchandise and obtain the latest price-listing publications on a regular basis. They, like the consumer, must keep abreast of price trends.

Appraisal Abuses and Fraud

Jewelers who issue appraisals on the merchandise they sell provide a valuable service to the client—if the document does what it is supposed to do. Some jewelers, however, use the in-house appraisal as a phony selling tool. Salespeople will sometimes say, "This item is worth a lot more than what I am selling it for. To prove it, I'll write an appraisal for 50 percent more than your price. I just can't replace it for the price I am quoting!" In black and white, this quote appears as phony as a three dollar bill. Yet, day after day some variation of this theme comes across the counter to customers. It is an attempt to make clients feel they are getting a better "deal" than they really are.

Nobody is likely to sell something on which they don't make a profit. If a stone is more valuable than what they sell it at, why are they selling it for less? This is one of the oldest psychological tricks in the book. If a jeweler uses this line or writes an appraisal for considerably more than what was paid, terminate the sale and walk out. There is no need to pay extravagant insurance premiums because you were conned.

The kind of appraisal abuse described above is minuscule compared to some of the scams that are used in the gem business. One of the shames of the industry is the appraiser who uses what are known as "multiples." Instead of making a legitimate valuation based on normal industry markups, the appraiser multiplies the wholesale value by five, ten, a hundred, or more times! In 1983, there was a group trying to trade 10,000 carats of corundum for real estate. The corundum, which can be purchased for $1 to $20 per carat as an aggregate, was valued at $32 *million!* This was the most outrageous case of multiples ever witnessed by the author. Multiples, unfortunately, are frequently encountered.

What Makes a Good Appraiser?

A good appraiser has four positive attributes: gemological knowledge acquired academically and through working in the field; a good color sense; current pricing information; and the proper gemological instruments. All four of these attributes work for the good of the consumer if experience and integrity characterize the appraiser. A gemologist degree does not necessarily ensure good appraising since some appraisers may lack color sense, experience, or integrity. Groups such as the American Society of Appraisers, the American Gem Society, the United States Appraisers Association, the International Society of Appraisers and the National Association of Jewelry Appraisers try to maintain quality standards.

Finally, the consumer should know that appraisers are generally split into two camps when it comes to fee structures. Some charge a percentage of the value (usually 1 percent) of the piece being appraised; others charge by the hour or agree upon a specific flat fee in advance. Those who charge by the hour or use the flat fee are considered the fairest. Charging a percentage of the value penalizes those who have fine jewelry and encourages overevaluations. Ultimately, if an appraiser ascribes a value to merchandise, it is *his or her* responsibility to be able to prove that the monetary values reflect the current market average.

13 Potpourri: A Compendium of Analytical and Observational Notes

Polygon

Polygon is a communication network that links jewelry retailers, wholesalers, manufacturers, and others through the use of a keyboard, a video screen, and a printer. Messages are sent using a telecommunications satellite. The system was in development for four years. In 1984, it went on-line as the most advanced system of its type in the gem industry.

The purpose of Polygon is to allow subscribers to buy and sell gemstones in a flexible manner via their terminals. The system is a great advance for the industry because before its installation, the phone was the primary method of locating a stone. Polygon subscribers may broadcast a universal message to all other subscribers itemizing what they need or what they wish to sell. Others may buy, make offers, or ask for the merchandise to be sent on loan for their consideration.

Polygon is cost effective for those who own high-volume jewelry stores, for wholesale gem dealers, and for those who specialize in very fine goods. As the system expands, the benefit to the consumer, collector, and investor will be great. Although consumers may not be able or want to pay the regular $475-per-month rental fee (as of early 1985), those who have resale programs for the public can effectively advertise to a select buying audience. Once the system opens to foreign dealers direct supplies to jewelry stores, collectors, and investors may be possible.

Already, the system's "open outcry" style of offering merchandise has lowered bid-ask spreads and has helped prevent the unscrupulous from selling overpriced merchandise. The ultimate benefit to the public of this system will be indirect but substantial.

Synthetics

Consumers sometimes worry about receiving synthetic gemstones in place of naturals. They are overreacting. Many synthetics can be detected by a few, simple, gemological tests, although some take more equipment and expertise. Only in a couple of instances, such as separating Japanese synthetic amethyst from natural material, do detecting synthetics present a real problem in the laboratory. Many jewelers and gem dealers, however, have difficulty identifying hydrothermally grown corundum, ruby in particular. Although gemological laboratories can differentiate Kashan and Ramaura brand synthetic ruby from its natural counterpart, jewelers are at serious risk when trying to identify this material. Obtaining a laboratory analysis is vital when purchasing very expensive ruby and sapphire. With other stones, the public needs to be aware that they exist, but not frightened. Reputable companies make sure the stones they represent are natural.

Barter

In this day of heavy taxation, the urge to return to barter is strong. For items such as video recording equipment, cars, furniture, artwork and real estate, gemstones offer an almost ideal form of barter. Unfortunately, this ideal is hardly ever realized and people constantly get stuck with stones that are worth less than what they were told and/or are such poor quality that they can't be resold.

One of the worst abuses in this area has been with gems used for real estate swaps. These exchanges began between 1981 and 1983 as high interest rates destroyed the real estate market. Some desperate sellers took gems in trade for their property. There were two major mistakes made by those who were burned.

1. They did not establish a common level of liquid value. If the real estate was worth (on a bona fide appraisal) $100,000,

they simply accepted this as the "retail" figure. This retail figure was matched to the retail figure on the gem appraisal. Ultimately, the "retail" figure is unimportant.

The important question is: What is the most, yet reasonable amount of cash that can be obtained from both? If a building has a retail cost of $100,000, but has a realistic "fire sale" cost of $60,000, the gemstones received have to be able to be sold at a "fire sale" price of $60,000. *The retail price on the gem appraisal does not matter.* It could say $60,000 or $20 million. Traders can protect themselves by forcing the person offering the gems to demonstrate that they will bring $60,000. An independent consultant will be able to discern if the stones can be easily sold for that amount, if the offering party cannot provide the proof. If the people offering the gemstones do not want a third party opinion, or will only approve one that they believe in, stay away from the trade. Common sense should prevail here.

2. In some cases, the stones received were worth far less than the level at which the trade took place. Some were totally unsalable. In a few cases, the value *was* in the stones, but they were of commercial quality and only a gem dealer could dispose of them over time. The person who traded the real estate should have gone after a limited number of stones of superlative value and desirability to make ease of resale possible. If offering agents want to trade amethyst, blue topaz, poor- or average-quality ruby, sapphire, peridot, or similar stones, this is an attempt to unload unwanted and unsalable merchandise for the real estate. Barters that have worked in high-ticket trades always involved stones such as gem padparadscha, Burma ruby, Kashmir sapphire, and high-quality diamonds. If the person is convinced that his bag of amethyst is so valuable, tell him to sell them, turn them into premium tsavorite, gem red spinel, and D, internally flawless diamonds, and offer those instead. *If he cannot liquidate the stones and convert them, neither can the person who owns the real estate.*

Some U.S appraisers have become infamous for creating appraisals in which the wholesale price of gemstones is marked up many times. All of the honest appraisers know the identities of these con-artists. They are paid a high fee for this kind of fraud.

Always remember, *just because appraisers are gemologists and have credentials covering their walls does not mean they are reputable or honest.* There is no governmental body that regulates them. The best protection in a barter situation is to have an independent consultant adjudicate the trade, someone who is not connected with either party and does not sell gemstones.

Syndications

For those wishing to buy and sell gemstones as an extra form of income, but lacking the time or expertise to do so, syndications are a possible solution. Syndications are groups that pool their money for the specific purpose of financing gemstones so that a gem dealer can buy underpriced items and resell them on behalf of the group. Syndications are common within the gem industry; very expensive stones are often owned by more than one dealer. The dealer receives a brokerage fee for the reselling service, and the syndicate splits the profits based on each individual's investment. In the best situations, this form of "investment" can reap excellent capital gains for the group and substantial brokerage fees for the dealer. In the worst situations, it can be a nightmare. To create a successful syndication group, adhering to the following guidelines is imperative:

1. The money raised by the group must be totally committed; nobody should need that money for any daily or emergency purposes. This investment is risk capital *only!*
2. A written agreement must exist between members of the syndicate and the dealer. These documents are to be totally legal and binding.
3. The initial monies are to be held in a liquid, interest-bearing vehicle prior to making a commitment to purchase gems. The dealer should not have access to the funds. He or she is to inform the group when a bargain comes along, after which the group makes the decision to release the money to the dealer.
4. The group is not to expect immediate returns on the inventory purchased, although there is the possibility that it could be resold quickly. The dealer is to report on a regular basis regarding the status of the merchandise. Monthly reports to the group should suffice.

5. The dealer's percentage of the sale and the range of possible profit that the dealer may work within is to be stated in writing during the initial purchase. The dealer is to provide accurate records of sales, profits, and costs of doing business with each sold item.

Limited Partnerships

The last bull market in gems proved that many people have no ability to buy and sell stones on their own. They lack knowledge, time, contacts, and an ongoing commitment to the investment. Limited partnerships are a possible answer for those who wish to take advantage of an upcoming bull market without having the responsibility of direct ownership.

Limited partnership shares are usually offered by financial planners. The concept is simple. The general partners (those who have formed the partnership) buy the stones and/or other assets, and manage the daily activities of the partnership. Assets are acquired for the limited partnership after purchases of shares by the limited partners (the public) exceed a predetermined minimum amount. The public buys shares based on a prospectus, a document that tells potential limited partners what is going to be purchased, how large the partnership will be, when liquidation of the assets will happen, and includes a host of other rules and regulations. The general partners are responsible for the eventual resale of the partnership's assets. In theory, the original investment plus a profit for each share owned is returned to the original buyers upon liquidation of the partnership. The whole concept is very similar to buying a share of stock in a company except, instead of profit coming from doing daily business, the public is simply betting that the value of the gems and/or other assets will increase enough to make a profit upon a one-time resale.

The concept is excellent. The limited partnership is like a large syndication, except that the gems are not bought and sold during the life of the partnership. Rather, they are liquidated at some predetermined date or dates.

There are many caveats for the public here and they cannot all be listed. A prospectus is a legal necessity for the offering of limited partnerships. It is mandated by the government to force general partners to fully disclose their current and future actions, as well as to protect the public from the unscrupulous. Instead of just doing these simple things, however, any prospectus easily competes in size with the Tolkien trilogy, has the excitement of a turtle race, and is rarely read by the public because of its legal jargon. What is said in these documents, however, is vitally important and can make the difference between failure and success. There are two very important questions that the public has to ask concerning each gemstone limited partnership prospectus.

1. How much does the market have to go up before the limited partnership breaks even? The question people should ask *before* they buy shares is: How much of the capital will go into gemstones and/or other assets? That information is given in the prospectus. Not all of the capital will go into assets. The financial planner gets a sales commission as does his broker-dealer. Sometimes, the general partners get a sales commission as well. The cost of printing and advertising, and start-up costs are reimbursed to the general partners out of this money. There are also legal fees. In some cases, the value of the assets has to escalate considerably for the partnership to break even.

   In 1983 and 1984, there was a gemstone and hard-asset limited partnership offered in the United States. It was comprised of a combination of colored stones, bullion, and numismatic coins. Upon careful reading of the prospectus, the author found that of the $1 million minimum funding, over 40 percent of the equity was going into nonassets! That meant the gemstones and other assets had to appreciate 66.6 percent just for investors to break even (and that does not include the 15 percent performance fee the general partners were to take upon dissolution of the partnership!).

2. How is the buying accomplished and what parameters dictate the type, quality, and cost of assets within the partnership? In the same partnership discussed above, the general partners were charging the limited partners 3 percent for buying a little over $300,000 worth of precious metals. That can be done with one or two phone calls—an outrageous overcharge! Moreover, they planned to physically take delivery of the bullion and pay storage charges instead of holding commodity warehouse receipts. And this is not the worst.

   The gemstones to be purchased were not clearly defined as to range of quality, size, type, or level of liquidity. One of the general partners was a gem dealer. An independent expert was not hired to choose from the multitude of bargains in the international marketplace. Under the provisions of the prospectus, the stones could all come from the general partner's inventory; the prospectus allowed him to sell to the partnership at a 20 percent markup from cost. The cost figure was derived, through some unexplained formula, from retail values that appeared on an independent gemological laboratory's grading and evaluation reports. What markup schedules did this laboratory use? When were these reports made? Changes in the prices of stones make it imperative for buyers to know when the stones were purchased. The prospectus didn't answer these questions. Certainly, the offering was legal, but the fine print showed that it could be difficult for a limited partner to make a profit. The general partners were getting a lot of money up front.

If approached with this type of offering, do not reject it out of hand, but have someone read the prospectus who can clarify the situation. Ideally, a gemstone limited partnership should have most of its payments and fees to the general partners on the back end. If the general partners were right about the market, they would win along with the limited partners. A heavy up-front load drastically lowers the chances for limited partners to make a profit, even in a reasonably good market. Gems should be purchased for the partnership by an independent expert who has no inventory to sell for a *flat, one-time fee.* The gems should be placed directly into the partnership at the true cost.

Protection from Scams

Along with the heady increases in gem prices within the last 10 years have come the inevitable scams. Gem scams always have two components:

1. **Intentional giving of false information.** Firms involved in scams mislead the public with either false claims concerning past price appreciation or current prices, and/or unfounded predictions of future price appreciation. They also give false geological, gemological, or economic information.
2. **Lull the public into a trusting and interesting mood.** In so doing, the firm can take money without giving much or any-

thing in return. This part of the scam manifests itself by the firm either: (*a*) selling unconscionably overpriced stones to people who have been duped by false information; (*b*) taking valuable gems from people ostensibly to sell at higher than real market prices and then disappearing with the goods; (*c*) switching low-quality stones for high-quality stones that people already possess; or (*d*) taking people's money and never delivering the stones.

The diversity and number of scams are incredible. Thus, people must ask the right questions. Is the deal too good to be true? Are the sellers saying anything concrete or just hyping a stone? Strangely, many business people cannot tell when they are being conned, or they choose to ignore the little voice in their heads.

Most of what a consumer needs to know to beat the con-artists has already been said in this book. Knowledge is the key. If the actions (not the promises) of the firm being dealt with fall short of total honesty, they could be running a scam or they could be just plain ignorant. In either case, you do not want to do business with them. There are, however, a few things you can do to protect yourself further.

Figure 43 shows what is known as a memorandum (memo). It is a legally binding document that allows a person or firm to "borrow" a stone or jewelry from an owner for a specified period of time either to show to a client or to consider for purchase. The memo transfers the responsibility, but not the title of the piece, to the borrowing party. The borrowers place their signatures either on the memo itself or on a return receipt from the post office. A copy is kept by the owner. Owners can recall items on a memo *on demand. Never* send stones or jewelry to a company without using this document—even for appraisal or repair. *If a company does not want to use a memorandum, forget them.* In cases where consumers do not know the company well, they should also send a copy to their lawyer to keep on file until the goods are sold and payment rendered or until the goods are returned. If something fishy starts to happen, the lawyer has a legal document from which to start working.

Always send stones in registered, insured packages with a return receipt. This proves the company received the goods under the conditions of the memo. The memo should have the registered mail number and return receipt attached.

Figure 43

MEMORANDUM

ISSUED BY	ISSUED TO
John Q. Public 000 Doe Street Anywhere, Any Country Zip Phone Number	Agent The Gem Company The Address The City, The State, The Country Phone Number
Date Issued _________	Due Date For Return ____________

THIS MEMO IS ISSUED TO THE ABOVE COMPANY (BROKER, ETC.) AND THE COMPANY (BROKER, ETC.) WILL CONTACT ME EACH MONTH (WEEK, DAY, ETC.) AND GIVE ME A SATISFACTORY UPDATE ON THE STATUS OF MY MERCHANDISE.

When the stone(s) is/are sold, John Q. Public is to be paid $_________ in the form of _____________________. UPON SALE OF MY MERCHANDISE, PAYMENT WILL BE IMMEDIATE (NET). LATE PAYMENTS WILL BE SUBJECT TO A 1.5% PENALTY ON THE NET AMOUNT PER MONTH. The Gem Company will receive its payment for selling the stones in the following manner:

____

____

Description Of Goods Consigned on Memorandum

EXAMPLE: 2.37 Carat Oval Sapphire @ $1,000 per carat.
Stone Net Price = $2,370.00
Please Note: Copy of AGL certificate #00000 accompanies this stone and identifies its qualities and characteristics.

THE MERCHANDISE DESCRIBED AND VALUED AS ABOVE IS DELIVERED TO YOU FOR EXAMINATION AND INSPECTION ONLY AND REMAINS MY PROPERTY SUBJECT TO MY ORDER AND SHALL BE RETURNED TO ME UPON DEMAND. SUCH MERCHANDISE, UNTIL RETURNED TO ME AND ACTUALLY RECEIVED, ARE AT YOUR RISK FROM ALL HAZARDS. NO RIGHT OR POWER IS GIVEN TO YOU TO SELL, HYPOTHECATE OR OTHERWISE DISPOSE OF THIS MERCHANDISE REGARDLESS OF PRIOR TRANSACTIONS. A SALE OF THIS MERCHANDISE CAN ONLY BE EFFECTED AND TITLE WILL PASS ONLY IF, AS AND WHEN WE THE SAID OWNER SHALL AGREE TO SUCH SALE AND A BILL OF SALE RENDERED THEREFORE. ALL THE ABOVE IN BINDING ON US, REGARDLESS OF PRIOR TRANSACTIONS.

SIGNATURE ____________________________________

Before sending for any purchase obtain, in writing, the return and refund policy of the company. This is particularly important when you are dealing with a company through the mail. Most reputable companies will either personally hold payment or have their bank hold it so that a full refund can be made if the gems are returned by the customer in good condition within 10 to 14 days.

Most of all, use common sense. Does the firm have a high profile so that they are vulnerable to public and trade opinion? Do members of the trade respect and know them? Are they known for consumer advocacy? Do they have any marks against them with the Better Business Bureau or Federal Trade Commission? If these questions cannot be answered to your satisfaction, delaying business transactions cannot hurt. Stand aside until the status of the company is known.

Sealed Stones

During the gemstone bull market of 1976 to 1981, it became common practice for investment companies to sell diamonds and colored stones in sealed containers. Most of these containers were made of plexiglas or plastic. Ostensibly to protect the public from stone switching by the selling company, laboratories sealed the stones when the gemological certificate was created. Sometimes a microfilm of the certificate was encased with the sealed container. Both the sealed stone and the certificate were then sent to the buyer or the gem company. Other companies sealed stones themselves, after laboratory certification.

Sealing, in and of itself, is not disreputable. For limited partnerships and long-term storage, for example, the concept is admirable. For the average buyer, however, sealed stones can create problems. Many investment companies have, or had, a policy that runs something like this: "If the stone remains sealed, the certificate of quality is guaranteed. Once the stone is removed from the sealed container, the guarantee of quality is null and void." However, the only way to know if the stone matches the certificate, or to verify the value, is to break the seal. In addition, nobody in the gem trade will buy a sealed stone from you. The problem is evident: If you break the seal to examine the stone, and the stone is of poor quality (or a synthetic) and does not match the certificate, the company revokes the sales guarantee. If you do not break the seal, you are really buying the paper certificate and cannot know what quality of stone you actually possess.

Some companies who issued sealed stones tried to beat this problem by providing an insurance policy that guaranteed that the stone matched the certificate. First of all, the insurance policy is a sham because if the seal is broken to see if the stone and certificate match, the insurance is automatically voided under the previously mentioned policy of the investment company. Second, our earlier study of the nature of laboratory certificates indicated that tolerance in grading is always present; insurance cannot guarantee grading accuracy. Third, most of these insurance policies ran out after three years. The insurance policy concept was simply a marketing gimmick that served absolutely no purpose. *Sealed stones were not invented to protect the buyer.* They were invented to protect the selling company from stone switching by the customer! Any other statement to the contrary is so much hogwash.

It is acceptable to buy a laboratory sealed stone, but don't ever purchase a stone sealed by a company, particularly if the quality guarantee becomes void if the seal is broken. Most reputable companies will arrange for you to break a laboratory seal to inspect the stone under certain conditions. If the company will not allow seal breakage under any circumstances, forget the purchase. When purchasing, it is *necessary* to examine the stone or have an independent appraiser/consultant verify the value and quality before the payment is released to the selling company. Thus, sealed stones are usually not in the best interest of the investor, you are strongly urged to avoid them.

14 A Personal View

A Personal View

In this chapter, the term *jeweler* refers to anybody who sells to the public including retailers, investment firms, cutters, consultants, or specialty and department stores.

The gem industry is one of the last of the world's free markets. It enjoys virtually no government intervention. The best people in the industry are competent and are known for their rugged individualism. Unfortunately, many customers view jewelers on approximately the same level as they view the archetypal used car salesman. Although this attitude is held indiscriminately and is unfair to the true professional, customers do have many good reasons for holding it. The jewelry industry in general is notorious for stretching the truth in order to make a sale. Thus, although the public has not always given the professional jeweler due respect, without a doubt the bulk of these attitude problems have been caused by the industry itself.

For years, a conspiracy of silence concerning the products jewelers sell has led to mistrust and suspicion by the consumer. The more information that leaks out concerning proper grading of stones, treatments, appraisal incompetence, and phony sales gimmicks, the more mistrust develops. For the gem industry to redeem itself in the eyes of the public, it should come clean concerning these issues and train its sales staff to a higher level. Many "training programs" are a joke. Many of the "old timers" in the business would like to throw away laboratory certificates, detailed appraisals, grading systems, disclosures of treatments, and price charts. The gem industry is very conservative, paranoid, and hates change. To defeat these attitudes, consumer information is the key, not your blind trust. The days are gone when a young man will walk into a jewelry store, plop down $2,000 for an engagement ring, and say "My dad bought from you and that is good enough for me. Pick out a good stone."

Over the last 10 years, the traditional gem trade has been hurt by the disenchantment consumers have felt due to this conspiracy of silence. Retail jewelers, in particular, did not cater to the needs of consumers during the inflationary years of 1978 to 1980. So-called investment firms and alternative gem companies have taken more than one billion dollars' worth of business away from the traditional jeweler since 1978. Some of these companies have given excellent service and value while others have cheated the public terribly. Many intelligent customers do not trust the industry because of obnoxious sales tactics, deceitful grading practices, overpriced goods, inflated appraisals, and general incompetence. They are, therefore, going to seek out jewelers who, at least, give the impression of knowing what they are doing.

The successful alternative and investment companies that have been formed in the last few years have kept overhead low, specialized in consumer education, and offered superb quality stones. Since the late 1970s, there has been a definite shift in the public's shopping attitudes toward this type of firm. High-overhead retail stores will continue to sell volume "bread and butter" jewelry, but the really big sales are slipping away from these venders. Some of the new firms realize as many as 10 or more sales a year of over $100,000. The number of traditional jewelers who accomplish this can probably be counted on two hands. Consumers realize that there is a big difference between paying, for example, $20,000 for a piece of jewelry from an uninformed, underpaid sales clerk and paying $15,000 for the same piece from a knowledgeable specialist.

In the interest of fairness, it must be pointed out that the whole gem industry is not ignorant or incompetent. There are a number of jewelers and gemologists who take their careers seriously. They are experts in their field. These are the people who are hurt by the unprofessional attitudes that are so prevalent and these are the people who should be sought out by consumers.

Common Myths about Jewelers

Despite the fact that many jewelers do not have expert knowledge concerning gems, cannot grade stones accurately, and cannot do a proper appraisal, the public holds certain myths that are patently false. These include:

1. *Jewelers are all dishonest.* Most peoplc believe that jewelers have some amount of dishonesty in their hearts. This attitude is partially due to the fact that consumers have been kept in the dark about jewelry and do not understand it. Most jewelers have to be scrupulously honest. They are handling expensive, luxury items, and most service what is known as a "bedroom community." If a jeweler is enjoying a comfortable living, the last thing he or she is going to do is cheat a neighbor, a member of the church congregation, or the lady he or she sees at the supermarket every Friday night. It is simply not worth it. For many jewelers, one hint of a major scandal involving dishonesty will destroy their business.
2. *A jeweler is liable to switch my stone when I take jewelry in for repair.* In 12 years of being associated with the gem business, I have worked with people with whom I would trust my life and with people who would steal a quarter from a blind beggar. From one end of that spectrum to the other, stone switching does not occur. It is a risky and dangerous form of dishonesty. Why would any jeweler substitute a synthetic or a diamond of lower quality for one of higher quality to make a few hundred dollars when his or her reputable business brings a comfortable income of $30,000 to $60,000 plus per year? It just doesn't make sense. Most consumers think their jewelry is more valuable than it is. Compared to a jeweler's inventory, however, their best piece is often a drop in the bucket. The logistics of finding a stone in an average inventory that can be readily substituted for the better one are amazingly difficult.

   Certainly, there have been instances of stone switching, but the public has the same overblown fear of this as children have of monsters hiding in the bedroom closet. Jewelers take great pains to ensure the integrity of their repair service. In many stores, the paperwork that checks and crosschecks repair work is so voluminous that one employee may spend most of his or her time monitoring it. The liability is too great for any jeweler to be capricious.

When people take their jewelry in for repair, it is often so dirty, old, and worn that upon returning the beautiful, new-looking piece to the customer, the jeweler may be accused of switching stones. In the minds of many consumers, if it looks different it is different. The public has to understand that rebuilt mountings, new heads, and clean stones will make an item look different than it did when it was originally brought in.

The majority of employees in the gem business have to pass polygraph tests before being hired. Any taint of dishonesty will prevent hiring. Whether this process is fair and constitutional is open to debate, but the public is the true benefactor. The switching of stones is as rare as the repeal of an increase in taxes.

3. *Jewelers make excessive profits.* Nobody who runs a successful gem business will argue with the fact that a comfortable living can be had. On a percentage basis, however, jewelers are in the middle net income level. The markups in a typical jewelry store, as we have discussed previously, are average compared to those of other retailers. Most jewelers do not make excessive profits. Those who overcharge do so because they don't know how to buy from suppliers or think they can pull the wool over customers' eyes. These problems are rectified by the comparative shopper.

   Jewelers could be more profitable. There is, however, virtually no way for them to hedge gemstone inventories as farmers do with agricultural products. The industry has not had the unity or foresight to help commodity exchanges develop index futures or physical option contracts in gemstones, particularly diamonds. Currently, jewelers could protect virtually the entire value of their precious metal inventory and keep prices down for the consumer through the use of metal options, but they lack the imagination to do so.

Real Concerns for Consumers

It is important for customers to realize something about the industry. There are essentially two types of jewelers: (1) those that work to make a living and look at their positions in the same way as they would if they were selling refrigerators, and (2) those that work to make a living and love the beauty of fine gems. The latter are a cut above the former because they transcend the term *businessperson*. They are professionals. The difference between the two is tremendous.

Professionals in the gem business always know more about jewelry and gems than the layperson, just as cardiovascular surgeons know more about bypass surgery than their patients. Unfortunately, these minority representatives of the gem business have a difficult time being recognized as professionals by the public. Since the only thing you need to go into the gem business is money, and because the public has been fed so much informational garbage over the years, it is difficult to know who is competent and who isn't. The standards for being recognized as an expert in this field have never been as well defined as they have been in medicine or law.

Since the definition of a gem expert has never been explained to the public, many jewelers, at least subconsciously, realize that customers will buy from the most persuasive salesperson rather than from one who is completely honest and straightforward. Indeed, the public continually purchases items, based on a salesperson's personality, that have about as much quality as a 1950s' Japanese horror movie.

Consumers will hardly ever find that a jeweler lies about his or her product or service. Rather, most problems fall into the area of selective omission. The customer, therefore, has to be astute and asked detailed questions pertaining to the jewelry in question. For example, a well-informed engagement ring customer may ask if the one-carat diamond he is considering is the finest quality in his price range. The answer from the jeweler will be, "Yes, it is an H color and VS_2 clarity, a very high grade." This may be true; however, the stone may be so poorly cut that it would be valued as a three-quarter carat in the diamond trade. That truth is quietly omitted and the jeweler makes extra profit because he bought the stone for less than the same one carat that was well cut.

The omissions that some jewelers use are so varied that a whole book of examples could be cited. They cover a gamut of topics from not telling the customer that topaz and tanzanite should be worn carefully because they have perfect cleavage, to not revealing that a diamond is very poorly cut, to ignoring the fact that some stones are treated, to not revealing that some karat gold jewelry is inexpensive because it is full of microscopic air pockets and is vulnerable to cracking and breakage.

Some jewelers will argue that these examples do not constitute convenient omission. They will claim the public is not interested in facts concerning their purchases. There is undoubtedly some legitimacy to this, particularly with inexpensive items. In my experience, whether somebody was paying $200, $2,000, or $200,000, they were plenty interested!

The professional omits nothing and the conflict this can cause with management is sometimes beyond the scope of logical discourse. It is one thing for salespeople not to know about gems; it is another when they tell the customer the truth and get a lecture about it afterward. This happens more frequently than customers would guess.

For example, many years ago, a salesman delivered a smoky quartz pendant that had been on layaway for a customer. The store owner was gone and the salesman said, "This is a lovely smoky quartz, I am sure your wife will love it." The customer was startled and said, "The owner told me it was a smoky topaz, not a smoky quartz." The salesman was truthful. "Some people call these smoky topaz, but it is a misnomer. It is quartz and isn't related to topaz. The price you are paying is for quartz, not topaz. Topaz is more costly." The fact that the Federal Trade Commission had ruled against representing quartz as topaz in 1967 was carefully sidestepped by the salesman. He didn't want to get his boss in trouble. While he was giving this answer, the owner came in and shoved the salesman to the side. Claiming the salesman was new to the business, he convinced the customer that the pendant was, indeed, a smoky topaz. The client was satisfied, but the salesman was told, "Don't ever tell our customers things like that." The salesman retorted, "Was I wrong?" "No, but customers don't know anything about gems and can never understand them. The public is stupid and we cannot afford to lose a single sale, so cool it with that arrogant gemology junk."

Professionals behind the jewelry counter hear all kinds of misconceptions. They know customers do not obtain their misinformation from watching "Sesame Street." They get them from jewelers who do not know what they are talking about or are omitting key information for some "sales oriented reason." Statements such as, "Rubies that are more purple and pale are the most valuable"; "Light yellow diamonds are rarer than most others"; and "The darker the sapphire, the better," tell the professional that the jeweler is trying to sell, not help or advise the customer.

Another thing that is common in the gem business is the

"knocking" of other jewelers. Knocking is used to place distrust in the minds of customers toward some competing jeweler. It takes the form of demeaning the information or jewelry that came from a competitor. A number of jewelers have made strict rules, fortunately, against knocking, but it does continue. The outcome is that the customer doesn't know who is right. If one jeweler knocks another, that jeweler is probably desperate for the sale and will tell you anything to make it. As soon as this type of conversation is started, simply walk out the door. You don't need the aggravation.

Apart from knocking and omitting facts, there is another area about which consumers should be aware. Many jewelers who sell to the public cannot accurately grade gemstones. Probably 50 percent of all jewelers could not *accurately* grade a diamond if their lives depended on it. At least 80 percent cannot grade colored stones. Only the serious jeweler, usually one with gemological training, can do what most consumers would think is basic to the profession. Many who sell to the public totally rely on their suppliers to grade the stones they buy, a very precarious dependency.

The concerns that have been outlined do not apply to *all* jewelers. This must be emphasized *again and again*. Some are amazingly knowledgeable and competent; they are the ones you should seek out. Hopefully, what you have learned in this book will create a handy reference structure so that you can evaluate the expertise of the jeweler. You will find that fine jewelers welcome a knowledgeable consumer because it makes their job easier. Less competent jewelers will be intimidated by your knowledge and demands for professional service.

The Jeweler-Customer Relationship

The least discussed aspect of the gem business is that of the jeweler-customer relationship. This is unfortunate because it is the most important and most misunderstood topic. In many industries, the relationship between those who provide services and those who receive them are well defined. Few would dare tell a physician how to diagnose an illness, yet many customers automatically assume a superior knowledge to all jewelers and gemologists. Likewise, a CPA can usually be relied upon to complete an accounting task with expertise and integrity. Yet a substantial number of jewelers are neglectful in learning about the products they sell. On both sides of the fence—what to expect from jewelers and what is expected of customers—there is an abysmal fog.

How To Be a Good Customer

In addition to burglary or stealing, a competent jeweler cannot tolerate the public doing the following three things: (1) Wasting the jeweler's time; (2) Asking for something the jeweler does not have in stock, then not showing up to look at the piece when it is available; and (3) Demanding services from trained professionals and not expecting to pay for them.

Wasting a Jeweler's Time A jeweler is in business to make money. He or she will take the time to answer questions concerning an item being purchased. For valued customers, jewelers have been known to work long into the night to complete holiday gifts and deliver them to people's houses, even in snowstorms.

Do not, however, waste their time. Jewelers are not psychologists or marriage counselors. They do not appreciate shoppers who stroll in simply because they have nothing else to do. Jewelers are not in business for people to "show off" to companions by demanding to see the most expensive rings with no intention and/or ability to buy. If a spouse's permission is needed to purchase an item, this should be discussed before going into a jewelry store. If there is anything that aggravates salespeople, it is spending hours showing $5,000 necklaces only to have the customer say, "Well, I'll have to discuss this with my husband (or wife)," and then walk out. Chances are, other customers walked in, couldn't get service, left, and bought somewhere else.

Many jewelers just bite their lip when this occurs. Some of the new companies, however, who specialize in world-class/top-quality stones and have superior consumer knowledge are moving away from this attitude. Some of the world's best consultants charge a nonrefundable fee for locating important pieces. This fee can be applied to their brokerage or consulting fee. There is great justification to this approach. Consultants' markups are lower than the average jeweler's, the items in which they specialize are hard to locate, and much time is often involved in getting the customer the best price. Just to obtain an important piece to show may cost hundreds of dollars in time, insurance, and freight charges. Consultants deserve to be paid for their service, especially if it saves the customer significant percentages. If the customer is playing games and just wants to "look," the consultant will not waste his or her time.

Not Following up on Special Requests Customers will sometimes request certain items and then never show up to look at them. This is the rudest thing a customer can do to a jeweler. Jewelers have spent their time and money to obtain what is desired. Actually, this kind of nonsense happens so frequently that many jewelers act very cautiously or skeptically about such requests. In the trade, these are called "LSD deals" or "You have to be on LSD to believe the customer will even show up to see, or buy, the piece!"

Expecting Service without Paying The public sometimes expects services believing that they shouldn't have to pay for them. If a customer takes up a lawyer's, accountant's, or carpenter's time, a bill will be sent. Why not with a jeweler or gemologist? These people have studied hard and deserve to be paid for their efforts.

Customers often believe that appraisals should be free despite the fact that appraising is the most professionally demanding area in the gem industry. While I was in the retail jewelry business, at least two or three times a week somebody would walk into the store, shove a ring in my face, and demand an appraisal. The ensuing conversation would invariably follow:

Author: I am sorry, but to do a proper appraisal I will need about a half an hour to measure and grade the stone, test the metal, and type the appraisal. There is a minimum charge of $25.

Customer: I don't need a written appraisal.

Author: A verbal appraisal will still involve the same process and there will still be a minimum charge.

Customer: I don't need that kind of accuracy. What is its approximate worth?

Author: I cannot tell without grading the stones and testing the gold.

Customer: Well, the salesman at 'Joe Blow Jewelers' on the other side of the mall looked at it and said it was worth $2,000.

Author: Then you have already received a verbal appraisal?

Customer: Yes, but I want another opinion.

Author: I am sorry. My company's reputation for accurate appraisal work demands a thorough examination of the ring.

Customer: I want to see the manager.

Author: I am the manager.

Customer: Well, as a manager, if you can't tell what it is worth, you don't know much about stones. I am going where I can get the service I want!

This customer's attitude is, however, not entirely unjustified. For decades, jewelers have cavalierly "appraised" jewelry across the counter in this fashion. The industry has demeaned the high professional standards to which it pays lip service. The public should be aware that a proper appraisal *cannot* be done by just looking at the stone across the jewelry counter. Any jeweler who does an appraisal in this fashion is simply telling you that he or she is incompetent. Becoming a good appraiser requires years of academic and practical experience. Therefore, appraisers should be paid just like any other professional.

What to Expect from a Reputable Jeweler

Not only do customers have to behave with respect to receive proper service but the jeweler has to continually earn that respect. It is not necessary for a jeweler to be a walking encyclopedia of gemological trivia, but he or she should know quite a bit. Being a jeweler is actually much more difficult than most people realize. The diverse areas that demand at least a modicum of expertise are mind boggling. Just for openers, there is diamond grading, evaluation, and pricing. There are 20 commonly traded colored stones that have to be graded, priced, and evaluated. Mountings, which come in a myriad of styles and qualities and have various gold contents, have to be considered and selected. There are the watches: quartz, jeweled, pin lever, LCDs, LEDs, stainless steel, anodized steel, solid gold, gold-filled, and so on. There are cultured pearls, natural pearls, and imitation pearls. Porcelains, clocks, flatware, sterling silver jewelry, and china patterns also must be mastered. Repair work, ordering new stock, personnel problems, synthetics being sold as genuine stones, treatments that may not be permanent, new styles that must be anticipated, creative displays, and never-ending questions are just a few of the daily concerns.

There are some key things that a customer should expect and receive from jewelers.

Honesty in Representation Disclosure of all things that impact on the value of the stone(s), whether loose or mounted. Disclosure should include a complete grading analysis for all *major* or *center* stones in a piece of jewelry. In diamonds, description of color and clarity is important, along with particular attention to cut proportions. In colored stones, primary color, secondary color, tone, brilliancy, and clarity should be stated. If the stone has been treated or is likely to have been treated, this should be disclosed. As we explained in the chapter on treatment, this should be no problem for the customer or jeweler so long as the jeweler knows how to present the information.

Other important areas include the availability of an independent laboratory certificate on *major* stones (usually paid for by the customer), the ability for the customer to have an independent appraiser look at the merchandise before the sale is finalized, an explanation of the relative durability of the stone(s), accurate information on care and maintenance, return policies and warranties in writing, and a proper appraisal. The appraisal should represent the true replacement cost (what was paid), not a fictitious higher amount.

Integrity in Salesmanship High-pressure tactics will be avoided at all costs by fine jewelers. Reputable phone solicitation companies never *demand* that a check be sent by an overnight express company. Knocking of other jewelers is never done. No phony sales: Anything over 20 percent to 25 percent off is likely a contrived gimmick. Reputable jewelers answer every question without evading or glossing over the answer. If they do not know an answer, they find out what it is. Information on the nature of stone pricing cycles will be available for major purchases. Outrageous claims about future price appreciation and false gemological or origin information of any type will not be presented as part of the sales presentation.

Resale Capabilities The finest jewelers sometimes have a program to help resell stones and jewelry you have inherited or purchased. This is not a common service, but anybody who can successfully do this is knowledgeable and proficient. Brokerage fees above 20 percent of the realized amount are excessive. The most successful consultants generally charge from 5 percent to 15 percent, depending on the value of the stone or jewelry. Some companies that specialize in top-quality gems also give speeches, lectures, and/or seminars concerning gems. Take advantage of them.

Appraisal Services Knowledgeable jewelers will always offer appraisals for a fee for any item you have not purchased in the store. The best have an in-house gemologist. Jewelers who will not do appraisals on items not purchased in their store are merchants, not professionals. Avoid them! Appraisals that are paid for should have all the essentials listed in Chapter 12. The most reputable charge by the piece or hour, and *not* a percentage of the value.

Courtesy and Respect Perhaps the most intangible, courtesy and respect, go beyond a friendly "hello." In this day of consumer awareness, the reputable jeweler will assume that you can understand, comprehend, and not be fooled by slick talk and vague generalities.

Epilogue

Knowledgeable consumers have a distinct advantage. They obtain better value and beauty for their money and are less susceptible to fraud. Perhaps the biggest difference between customers is in their emotions. Those in the dark often feel apprehension, fear, and paranoia concerning gem and jewelry purchases. Those in the know realize that fine gemstones are a pleasure to shop for and own!

Appendix A How to Judge Metal Work and Mounting Quality

Stones are to be worn. Their value depends on beauty. If they are kept out of sight, the pleasure of ownership is lost. The only possible exception to this rule is diamonds of *flawless* clarity, finish, and cut proportions that are to be used strictly as investments. A flawless stone can eventually become internally flawless due to surface wear.

There are many ways to wear stones. Rings, necklaces, earrings, and bracelets are the most common and are available in thousands of styles. Style is very personal. A jeweler can make suggestions, show a variety of pieces, or create a design, but the decision rests with the client. There are basic concepts concerning mountings and setting work that are applicable to all jewelry. Many people buy expensive gems only to purchase very poor quality mountings. The result of this oversight can be disastrous. Stones may be lost or constant breakage can cause continual disgust.

Barring accidents or maintenance neglect, well-made jewelry should last for years without any need for significant repair or reconstruction. Eventually, precious metals wear down, but this should not occur often. There are three main questions that consumers should consider before buying jewelry:

1. What type, color, and quality of metal are to be used?
2. What type and quality of construction are desired?
3. Is the setting work of high enough quality to enhance the beauty of a stone and still protect it adequately?

Precious Metals: Types, Colors, and Qualities

Two types of metals are used primarily in fine jewelry: gold and platinum. Sometimes, silver and palladium are used in conjunction with gold, but seldom are they used alone. Silver is considered too soft for most fine jewelry. Palladium is a member of the platinum family of metals, but platinum wears better and is more commonly used.

Pure, 24-Karat gold is too soft. It is very ductile and malleable and can easily bend or break. Thus, it is mixed with other, harder metals called alloys. The color of alloyed gold is dependent on which alloys are used. White and yellow gold are most commonly used in jewelry, although rose and green are sometimes available through special order. The art of lavishly using multicolor gold is almost lost. Peter Carl Fabergé, jeweler to the court of Czar Nicholas II, made some of the most exquisite items using multicolor gold. Current labor costs prevent this kind of artistic fantasy from being available on a wide scale.

Gold is normally sold in either 14K or 18K. The former is 58.3 percent pure gold, the latter is 75 percent pure gold. Platinum is not pure. It contains a 10 percent alloy of iridium, another platinum group metal. 14K gold is stiffer and stronger than 18K, but many like the 18K yellow gold look; it can be made to closely resemble pure 24K. Platinum is more durable than any gold alloy, but is more expensive. It is not necessarily the price of platinum that makes it expensive; it is the labor. Platinum melts at a high temperature and requires special equipment and expertise.

White gold is stiffer than yellow gold. Yellow is more malleable and tends to bend rather than crack. White gold can crack more easily than yellow if struck hard enough.

All of these forms of gold and platinum are strong enough for daily and special occasion wearing. Since this is the case, many people wonder why some pieces break or crack frequently, while others wear well. There are two possible explanations for this beyond abuse and neglect.

1. Karat gold or platinum are not necessarily solid metal. Small air holes (porosity) may permeate the mounting. This is caused by fast and sloppy manufacturing processes. For example, in a carefully made ring the gold alloy is formed into the item slowly. The temperature of the metal is uniform. In fast manufacturing processes, the temperature is not uniform and

pieces are made with less care. Porosity is one of the leading reasons why some jewelry tends to wear and break faster than others. A thin chain bracelet can be relatively strong, but it will be more expensive than those that are full of air and are mass produced. It is not always possible to tell if there is significant porosity in a piece, but possible indications are:

A dull polish.

Under 10 power magnification, tiny pits and hairline cracks are evident on the surface.

Where the metal is not polished on the underside of the piece, it looks honeycombed.

Always look at the metal under magnification. Any of the above indications should make you hesitate to buy.

2. Another reason why jewelry may break easily is poor soldering. While some pieces are cast or die struck as one unit, fine jewelry is often made of various components. Where the various, separate components of the ring touch, there will be solder. If the solder appears honeycombed, uneven, or discolored, the piece may be weak in those areas.

The Type and Quality of Construction

There are three basic types of construction in jewelry: castings, die struck, and wire mountings. Some are combinations of these.

Cast jewelry is as old as the ancient Egyptians. The actual physical process is quite involved, and if done well, is painstaking. Making a casting amounts to creating a wax model by hand, creating a mold around it, melting the wax out of the mold, pouring molten metal into the mold, letting it cool, taking the mold apart, and extracting the mounting. The mounting has to be finished and polished to remove any extra gold or unevenness. Cast gold often appears as a dull yellow-brown. Castings may be mass produced by using a large centrifuge or individually produced with a single mold. The quality of castings varies considerably. The speed, temperature of the metal, and quality of the mold all contribute to the final product.

Die struck jewelry is made by taking various shapes of metal and cutting out designs by use of a die. The process is almost like making cookies. Again, the quality varies and some of the important factors include the porosity of the metal, the quality and sharpness of the die (they get less sharp with use), plus finishing, polishing, and soldering.

Wire mounts are often the most expensive and well constructed of all mountings. Many years ago, they were all made by hand. Now, the components of a wire mount may be cast or die struck and assembled. The visual difference in quality between the hand process and the more mechanical one is great. In a handmade piece, each wire is cut to size, formed, finished, polished, and soldered. The wire structure conforms perfectly to the stones.

Bill Bates and James Swenton of Zimmelman & Sons Manufacturing, both knowledgeable and quality conscious in this area, urge discerning consumers to look at the underside of the jewelry. On a finely made piece, the underside should look as good as the outside. The symmetry of the piece should be perfect. In cast or die struck component-made wire mounts, the inside of the ring may be unpolished because each wire is already in place and polishing tools cannot get inside. Also, the wires may be of different widths and wavy. According to Bates, many of the finer jewelers and carriage trade chains are moving to this component-made wire mount, even for the finest goods. Certainly, one of the reasons for this is cost, but if consumers were aware of mounting quality, a few dollars more probably wouldn't matter.

All three processes may produce exquisite to very poor mountings. There are several things to look for other than porosity. The following should be checked:

1. Symmetry. Are the stones in good alignment? Is the shank straight?
2. Polish. Is the metal polished all over? Inside the shank? Inside the mounting?
3. Finish quality. In a piece that has different textures in the metal, are the lines that differentiate, for example, brushed and high-polish distinct? Is the textured design sharp and clear or haphazardly put on? Are soldering points smooth and the same color as the gold they hold together? Slight differences in solder placement and thickness are expected, however, in totally handmade pieces.
4. Gauge of metal. When looking at a piece from the side, is the thickness of the metal the same throughout? In a ring shank, is it thin to thick? If it is, it will not wear well. Are the wires all the same width? Is the gold thick enough in general to wear well over the years?

Setting Work

There are numerous ways to set stones. To name just a few, there are four prong, six prong, bead set, hammer set, bezel set, channel, and pavé. Whatever the type of setting, it does two things: secures the stone from loss and helps bring out its natural beauty. Many contemporary setting styles involve the use of prongs. Prongs require a "seat" to be cut into the prong where the girdle of the stone is to sit. The seat cannot be too shallow or the stone could slip out. It cannot be too deep or the metal holding the stone may crack or break under slight pressure. Once a stone is in a seat, the top of the prong is cut and bent over the stone.

The tips of prongs that go over the top of the stone must be large enough to hold the stone securely, yet not so large as to look unsightly. The metal cannot be too thin or the prong will snag and lift up. Too thick a prong in relation to the size of the stone will look ugly. Prongs must also be placed symmetrically on the stone. If they are not, the piece will give the appearance of being crooked.

Pavé diamond jewelry is very popular. In this type of setting, it appears that diamonds cover the entire surface of an area. Usually, the pavé area is a white gold plate in which holes are bored. A stone is set in each hole with small, beadlike prongs so that the girdle of each stone is almost flush with the metal plate. In the finest pavé the back of the plate is polished, and even the hole shapes where the pavilions of the stones poke through may be beautiful designs such as stars, squares, or diamond shapes. Pavés that have rough and unfinished undersides are the result of cheap craftsmanship. Consumers should watch for uneven prong work, areas of the plate not uniformly covered by stones, and shoddy soldering of the plate in comparison to the rest of the ring.

Bezel setting is sometimes used to hold stones that are vulnerable to cleaving or breakage. A bezel is a setting without prongs. A ridge of gold encases the stone. Bezels should be uniform in gauge and height and should hug the stone evenly. Hammer setting is a difficult, but a beautiful and safe form of setting. Like the bezel, the stone's girdle is totally encased in gold except there is no ridge. The gem is set directly into a plate of metal and the table is almost flush with the top of the plate. The hole in the plate must be cut to fit the stone exactly. The metal is "pulled" up to the sides of the stone.

Channels are expensive and popular, particularly in bracelets and rings. Channel setting involves embedding gems, one after the other, between two "rails" of gold. Good channel setting is secure. There are no prongs to break. The stones should be touching one another. Channels with gaps between stones are offered either to cut cost through use of less stones or because of poor workmanship.

Other Tips on Selecting Jewelry Mountings

1. Avoid eternity rings with stones all the way around. Stones are more apt to be broken or to come out. Sizing is very difficult if the finger size changes.
2. When choosing a necklace, don't just look in a mirror. Walk around. Find out if it feels comfortable and does not turn or twist.
3. Large earrings should have a clip *and* post for security.
4. Ring guards are terrible. They chew up the shank of the ring over time. Always have a ring sized if it fits incorrectly. Ring guards can also be uncomfortable.
5. Colored stones are not often cut with the precision of diamonds. With expensive colored stones, it is worth buying a handmade mounting for extra security and eye appeal.
6. Stones that are bought primarily for investment should be mounted simply. No matter where people buy a mounting, much of the cost will be in labor. It will be difficult to recoup that cost. Investment stones that are mounted cleanly and elegantly may appeal to a future buyer.
7. Accent or side stones should compliment the center stone, not detract from or compete with it. The same holds true for mounting styles. The finer the center stone, the less accent stones or metal "gingerbread" is used. Even in quality pieces that are ornate, accent gems are in pavé, a simple geometric pattern, or they frame the center stone.

Appendix B The Care and Maintenance of Gemstones

One of the most surprising things to jewelers, particularly beginners in the field, is the brutal and neglectful way some people treat their jewelry. It is not unusual for a woman to receive an engagement ring and immediately torture the metal and stone by doing dishes and cleaning the bathroom while wearing it. Other indignities include coating it with cosmetics and creams and wearing it while gardening and moving furniture. Bracelets are ripped apart during a playful wrestle with a partner. Opals crack because they lose moisture, pearls become dull with coatings of perfume, and men's rings suffer countless percussions in factories and offices. Large diamonds are cleaved as swinging arms hit furniture at parties. Prongs are smashed while the wearer types. Tanzanite and topaz split apart when caught in slamming doors. The miniature world of jewelry can be a daily demolition derby.

By definition, gemstones are durable. Often their durability is excellent, but the range of punishment stones will take varies. If people treated their cars and furniture the way they treat their jewelry, these possessions would be useless wrecks in a short period of time. Other than specific recommendations for cleaning and maintenance, there are some commonsense things that can be done to extend the life and beauty of jewelry.

Many women never take off their jewelry while cleaning or gardening. They are afraid of losing it. A simple solution to the problem is to build a small shelf in the kitchen (away from drains and sinks) and place all jewelry on it before cleaning. Make this a habit and your jewelry will not be misplaced. This is particularly important while you are doing dishes. A prong may break and the stone will slip out and go down the drain with the dirty water. This type of incident probably accounts for 25 percent of all diamond losses.

In restaurants, leave rings with a spouse or partner or put them into a pocket or purse before washing your hands. Soap scum is bad for jewelry, and destroys the beauty of stones. Accidental smashing of the ring on a basin is also possible.

For those who cannot take their rings off because they are too snug, they must be resized. A jeweler can cut them off. Rings that will not come off are *dangerous;* they could cut off all circulation in the finger.

Some people get so wrapped up in what they are doing, they forget they are wearing jewelry and end up constantly breaking it. Always be conscious of jewelry, particularly its monetary value. How many weeks' pay would it take to replace the item? People's awareness of their actions increases quickly if this is kept in mind.

Jewelry that is worn regularly should be cleaned at least once a week. Items worn for special occasions should be stored safely. If jewelry is allowed to get dirty, a beautiful stone will look like an ugly blob. Stones are prisms that reflect light. When properly cut, they are dazzling to the eye. Even the slightest coating of grease or dirt, particularly on the bottom of the stone, will destroy its optical qualities.

It is imperative to have jewelry checked every six months by a jeweler for worn or broken prongs, loose stones, and wear in the shanks of rings or in necklace and bracelet clasps—even if nothing is apparently wrong. Professional cleaning by steam or an ultrasonic unit may be warranted, but let the jeweler determine this.

Guidelines for proper cleaning and maintenance follow. These guidelines will help ensure the beauty of the piece every time it is worn.

Precious Metals

Never use toothpaste or any strong abrasive. Precious metals are soft enough to be worn away by these. Too much wear will weaken prongs, resulting in the subsequent loss of the stone. Use jewelry cleaner that is a solution of water and ammonia. Use a soft, lintfree or jeweler's cloth to dry. When removing finger prints use a chamois or other soft, nonabrasive cloth. Do not store gold, silver, or platinum on top of one another. The metals will scratch each other.

Beryl

Emerald Clean in *mild* soap and a warm water solution to prevent stripping of the oil that is present in most stones. Do not soak them, use commercial jewelry cleaners, or water that is too hot. Use a chamois for wiping. Do not use abrasives or strong detergents. *Do not* steam clean or put in ultrasonic cleaner. Breakage may occur. Store away from other jewelry, preferably in its own box.

Aquamarine May be cleaned with commercial jewelry cleaner. Do not soak for more than a few minutes. Use a soft toothbrush to get dirt out of inaccessible regions. Use chamois for drying. Steam cleaning and ultrasonic cleaning may be permissible depending on the stone, but have this done professionally. Do not stack with diamonds or corundum in a jewelry box. These will scratch the stone.

Other Beryl Follow the same procedure as for aquamarine. Be particularly careful with morganite.

Chrysoberyl

Chrysoberyl is a very hard and durable stone. Jewelry cleaner is fine. All types may be steam cleaned or put in ultrasonic units unless severely included or fractured.

Corundum

Same as chrysoberyl.

Diamond

Same as chrysoberyl. However, diamonds have perfect cleavage. If a stone is highly included, it should be checked carefully before steam or ultrasonic cleaning is used. Diamonds, in particular, have to be cleaned regularly as a thin coating of oil from the skin or air will make the stone lifeless.

Garnet

May be cleaned like chrysoberyl, corundum, and diamond. The same restrictions apply to steam and ultrasonic cleaning.

Jade

Unless severely cracked, jade may be cleaned in any of the previously mentioned ways.

Opal

Opal is very porous and somewhat softer than many other gems. *Never* steam clean or put in ultrasonic cleaner. *Do not* use commercial jewelry cleaners or ammonia. If the stone gets dirty, soak it in distilled water and remove the dirt carefully. *Do not* store in glycerin or petroleum products as they leech water out of the stone which will lead to crazing and cracking. Store away from other jewelry. For storage, wrap carefully and keep in a moist environment.

Pearls

Pearls are highly sensitive, organic gems. Very dirty pearls must be left with a jeweler for professional cleaning. If slightly dirty, use *only* mild soap and water. Do not soak. Wipe pearls very lightly. A pearl's nacre can be damaged when subjected to perfumes and cosmetic powders. Do not apply these while wearing pearls. All genuine pearls should be French knotted (a knot between each pearl). This will prevent all from falling to the floor should the strand break. Percussion from the fall can cause serious damage. Always store separately from other jewelry and wrap in soft cloth to prevent damage.

Spinel

May be cleaned by steam, ultrasonic, or commercial jewelry cleaner when devoid of serious fractures or inclusions.

Topaz

Never steam clean or put in an ultrasonic unit. Jewelry cleaner is fine, but do not soak. Use a soft cloth for drying.

Tourmaline

May be steam or ultrasonically cleaned. Jewelry cleaner is fine. On highly included rubellite or pink tourmaline, avoid steam and ultrasonic.

Zoisite (Tanzanite)

Never steam clean or put in an ultrasonic unit. Use warm water and mild soap only. Avoid commercial jewelry cleaners. Dry carefully and avoid extremes in temperature.

A Final Note

For jewelry that has combinations of stones, the cleaning procedure that is used must be the one recommended for the most vulnerable stone of the group. For example, pearl and diamond jewelry is popular. Since pearl is the most vulnerable, clean and store as if it were only pearl. If the piece gets very dirty, take it to a jeweler for professional cleaning. When purchasing jewelry, have the jeweler write down all cleaning, maintenance, and storage particulars pertaining to the item and follow them!

Appendix C Recommended Reading

Books

The following books are available through the Gemological Institute of America's Bookstore. Some are available through popular bookstores, but not all. The GIA bookstore is located at 1660 Stewart St., Santa Monica, CA 90406.

Technical Gemology

Beginner's Guide to Gemmology, by Peter G. Read, 234 pages, 1980, paperback (for the novice). $9.95

Dictionary of Gems & Gemology, by Robert M. Shipley, 6th ed., 230 pages, 1974, (4,000 definitions). $7.50

Gems Made by Man, by Kurt Nassau, 382 pages, 1980, (major synthetic gem reference). $28.50

Gemstone Enhancement, by Kurt Nassau, 216 pages, 1984, (the definitive guide on gem treatments). $34.95

Handbook of Gem Identification, by Richard T. Liddicoat, Jr., 11th ed., 450 pages, 1981, (technical reference). $22.75

Internal World of Gemstones, by Eduard J. Gubelin, 236 pages, 1983, (360 microphotographs of gemstone inclusions). $125

Jewelry

Antique & 20th-Century Jewelry, by Vivienne Becker, 301 pages, 1980, (excellent photographs). $24.95

Art Deco, A Guide for Collectors, by Katharine Morrison, McClinton, 278 pages, 1972. $17.95

Art Nouveau and Art Deco Jewelry, by Lillian Baker, 176 pages, 1981. $9.95

Crown Jewels of Europe, by Prince Michael of Greece, 144 pages, 1983, (fine quality photographs). $19.95

Gems

The Book of Opals, by Wilfred Charles Eyles, 229 pages, 1964, (fine photos and good reference). $11.50

Brazil, Paradise of Gemstones, by Jules Roger Sauer, 136 pages, 1982, (magnificent full color photography). $22.95

Chinese Jade throughout the Ages, by Stanley C. Nott, 372 pages, 1962, (a major, comprehensive reference). $47.50

Color Encyclopedia of Gemstones, by Joel E. Arem, 174 pages, 1977, (well illustrated including rare gemstones). $40.00

Emerald & other Beryls, by John Sinkankas, 688 pages, 1981, (everything you would ever want to know about beryl). $37.50

Gemstones of the World, by Walter Schumann, 256 pages, 1977, (photos of more than 1,400 specimens). $17.95

Jade, Stone of Heaven, by Richard Gump, 260 pages, 1962, (best lay guide to jade). $14.95

History of Gems

Curious Lore of Precious Stones, by George Frederick Kunz, 406 pages, 1971, paperback, (study of mystical powers ascribed to gemstones). $6.95

Diamonds, by Eric Burton, 2d ed., 532 pages, 1978, (excellent overview of history and structure of diamond market for novice). $25

Available from American Gemological Laboratories

Gemstone Training Manual, by Caspar Beesley, (approximately 200 pages on every aspect of colored stone grading and evaluation. Forty color slides. Superb for an in-depth study of colored stones). $185. Also available for the gem enthusiast is *Color Scan*, a portable colored stone grading system that will fit into a pocket. For more information write, AGL, 580 Fifth Ave., Suite 1211, New York, NY 10036.

Available from California Gemological Laboratories

Gem Color Guide & Colored Gemstone Grading Manual. (Approximately 40-page manual. *Gem Color Guide* contains chromatic lacquer squares of graded colors for use in Munsell color grading system. Excellent for learning Munsell color theory as applied to gemstones). $295. For more information write, CGL, 3698 A South Bristol, Santa Ana, CA 92704.

Gemological Institute of America Gemological Courses

For those who wish to enter the gem business or learn as much as possible, the GIA offers home study courses in diamond grading, colored stones, gem identification, pearls, and other topics. They also offer a gemologist degree through correspondence courses or a graduate gemologist in residence in Santa Monica, California. For more information, write the GIA at 1660 Stewart Street, Santa Monica, CA 90406.

Index